# *The Best C/C++ Tips Ever*

# *The Best C/C++ Tips Ever*

*Anthony Porter*

Osborne **McGraw-Hill**

Berkeley New York St. Louis San Francisco
Auckland Bogotá Hamburg London Madrid
Mexico City Milan Montreal New Delhi Panama City
Paris São Paulo Singapore Sydney
Tokyo Toronto

Osborne **McGraw-Hill**
2600 Tenth Street
Berkeley, California 94710
U.S.A.

For information on translations or book distributors outside of the U.S.A., please write to Osborne **McGraw-Hill** at the above address.

**The Best C/C++ Tips Ever**



1234567890 DOC 99876543

ISBN 0-07-881820-6

**Acquisitions Editor**
William Pollock

**Associate Editor**
Emily Rader

**Technical Editor**
Werner Feibel

**Project Editor**
Mark Karmendy

**Copy Editor**
Joseph Ferrie

**Proofreader**
Mick Arellano

**Indexer**
Richard Shrout

**Computer Designer**
J.E. Christgau

**Cover Designers**
Communications Design
Mason Fong

# Table of Contents

## C/C++ The C and C++ Languages

## 3 Functions and Operators

## 4 C++ Declarations

## 5 Creating and Destroying C++ Instances

## 6 Type Conversions and Overloading

## 7 Inheritance and Member Access Control

# The Libraries

Tip #

## 11 The Standard C Library

## 12 The C++ iostream Library

## MS-DOS Specifics

Tip #

### 13 Segmented Architecture



### 14 Directory Services

## 15 Debugging

# Acknowledgments

I believe that many of the tips here are original, I cannot be sure one or the other has not been published before, and I apologize if I have failed to acknowledge a tip's inventor. On the other hand many tips, especially in the early chapters on the C language, are quite well known and have certainly been written about by many authors.

While it is impossible to acknowledge each tip's original author, I can at least acknowledge authors who have inspired me or jogged my memory about a tip. Herbert Schildt has written a number of excellent books about C and C++ programming; you should consider one of his books if you need a tutorial or a reference for the language. Try *C: The Complete Reference* or *C++: The Complete Reference* (Schildt, Osborne/McGraw-Hill).

The official reference for the C++ language is *The Annotated C++ Reference Manual* (Ellis & Stroustrup, Addison-Wesley). This book, commonly called the ARM, might not be an easy read but it is the means by which C++ lawyers settle disputes. The annotations are an interesting facet of this reference manual; they help to explain obscure features of the C++ language and give reasons why potentially useful features were not implemented. A number of tips in Chapters 4, 5, and 6 were inspired by these annotations.

Another useful source of inspiration was *Effective C++* (Meyers, Addison-Wesley). Meyers book carefully explains 50 specific ways to improve the effectiveness of your C++ programs. *Advanced C++ Programming Styles and Idioms* (Coplien, Addison-Wesley) inspired a couple of tips in Chapter 8. This is a book for the competent C++ programmer and it explains a number of interesting advanced C++ techniques.

If Chapter 10 interests you then you might take a look at *C Style: Standards and Guidelines* (Straker, Prentice-Hall). Although this book does not cover C++, it suggests many possible standards for C programming.

# Introduction

This is the book that I would have liked to have had when I was learning C and C++. This book is not a tutorial—it assumes that you understand at least the basic syntax and semantics of C or C++. What this book tries to do is lead you past the traps and pitfalls of the language and show you how you might improve your programs. If you have ever spent a day or two finding an obscure bug in your program only to have someone say, "Ah yes, a common mistake—I did that once too," then you will realize the benefits of being forewarned.

Once you have written a number of programs, you know how to avoid the most common bugs and you become more concerned with writing programs that are elegant, efficient, and easy to maintain—especially if you are likely to have to maintain them yourself. With that in mind, the majority of the tips in this book are concerned with general programming solutions.

While this book covers both C and C++, many of the C tips apply to C++ as well. Most professional programmers still use C although many are now moving over to C++. If you are still using C, I shall give you a tip now. Move to C++. Remember that you do not have to learn object-oriented programming to use C++. You can use C++ for procedural programming and take advantage of C++'s better type checking and its numerous improvements over C. Do not listen to people who tell you that C++ and object-oriented programming are inefficient—that might have been true with the early experimental C++ translators, but modern C++ compilers are just as efficient as C compilers.

Notice that this book covers ANSI C. Quite a large number of programmers are still using the pre-ANSI C especially in the UNIX world where a pre-ANSI C compiler is bundled with the UNIX system. If you are still using a pre-ANSI C compiler then you must absolutely move to an ANSI C compiler, if not C++. Pre-ANSI C programmers spend an inordinate amount of time finding obscure run-time bugs that an ANSI C or C++ compiler would report during compilation.

## About this Book

The book is divided into three parts. The first part covers features of the C and C++ languages and the second part covers the standard libraries that are delivered with the compiler. The third part is devoted to MS-DOS specifics. That may seem unfair to the UNIX programmers, but most programmers use MS-DOS and even a few UNIX programmers also program for MS-DOS.

This is of course not a book that you read from cover to cover; it is a book to dip into while you wait for your program to build. Even so, you will find that the tips often lead from one to the other, and that a tip builds on one or more of the preceding tips. If you open the book and find that you do not understand a tip, try backing up a couple of tips and read on from there.

I have tested the code examples on two C++ compilers but I cannot guarantee that all C++ compilers will compile all the code examples correctly. Some compilers do not support all the features of the language and you might find a compiler bug. It is also possible that I have let an error slip in somewhere—if so, I apologize in advance.

## How this Book is Organized

### Part 1: The C and C++ Languages

The first three chapters of Part 1 concentrate on C programming but they will also interest C++ programmers. Chapter 1 covers the ten most common C programming bugs and will be especially interesting to beginners. The tips in Chapters 2 and 3 cover different facets of the C language and will, I hope, improve your understanding of the C language.

Chapters 4 to 8 cover C++ and depending on your experience, get either more interesting or more complicated as the chapters progress. If you are a pure C programmer, dip into these chapters to see what you are missing.

Chapter 9 covers the C preprocessor. Some but not all of these tips will also be useful for C++ programmers. C++ provides features that replace preprocessor macros for many common programming tasks.

Chapter 10 covers some elements of programming style. Program layout and style is a very emotive issue. Many of you will have developed a style which is not the same as mine, and you may work for an employer who enforces a certain style or standard. The tips in Chapter 10 try to be non-intrusive and suggest ways in which you might consider refining your own or your employer's coding standards. Often the tips propose a number of alternative styles. With coding style or layout it does not matter so much which style you choose, so long as it is consistent.

## Part 2: The Libraries

There are two chapters in Part 2—Chapter 11 covering the ANSI C functions and Chapter 12 covering the C++ iostream library. Many of the tips in Chapter 11 will be useful to C++ programmers. There is not yet a standard for the iostream library but the tips in Chapter 12 cover what appears to be the *de facto* standard. You should find the tips useful for whatever compiler you are using, but you might find that the iostream library for your compiler uses different function or identifier names from those in the code examples. Some iostream packages also provide additional facilities that are not covered in Chapter 12.

Some compiler packages include additional libraries of general C++ classes. These libraries often include general storage classes such as strings, lists, and arrays. Unfortunately, there is not yet a standard for these classes and each compiler writer implements them in a different way. Since I have avoided compiler-specific tips, I have also avoided specific tips on using these general classes.

## Part 3: MS-DOS Specifics

Chapter 13 covers the Intel segmented architecture. This chapter will interest those of you writing 16-bit applications for DOS or Windows since it will help you to avoid many of the common segmentation programming problems. Even if you only write 32-bit applications for Windows or OS/2, you might find that this chapter helps you understand the Intel architecture.

The MS-DOS file and directory services are probably the most complex part of MS-DOS that an applications programmer still has to face; this is covered in Chapter 14. Interfacing with the PC hardware or the communication ports is even more complex, but only a few specialist programmers do this directly. The rest of us use a device driver or a library of routines to control the hardware and communication ports.

The final Chapter 15 covers some debugging techniques that are specific to the Intel hardware. Even if you are not an assembler programmer you will find that debugging a C programming is much easier if you have at least some idea of how the machine executes the compiled code.

# The C and C++ Languages

# Ten Ways to Avoid Common C Programming Bugs

TIP 1

## Initialize All Data Before Using It

Although the compiler will initialize static data to zero, functions variables will contain garbage before your program explicitly initializes them. You should always initialize your data before using it, and you must initialize function-local variables every time the function is called.

In particular, if you declare a pointer, the compiler does not initialize the pointer to reference something valid. You must initialize the pointer to point to something that you have declared or allocated elsewhere in your program.

## Do Not Return Pointers to Items on the Stack

A mistake that all C programmers make at least once is to return a pointer to an item declared in a function like this:

```
char* HexToAscii(unsigned nHex)
{
   char AsciiValue[10];

   /* fill AsciiValue with hex digits */

   return AsciiValue;    /* wrong !! */
}
```

This is wrong because the compiler will allocate temporary space for local items such as **AsciiValue** on the stack. When the item is no longer in scope, in this case when **HexToAscii** returns, the compiler can reuse the space for something else.

The traditional solution for C programmers is to declare the referenced item as static:

```
char* HexToAscii(unsigned nHex)
{
   static char AsciiValue[10];
```

```
    /* fill AsciiValue with hex digits */

    return AsciiValue;    /* OK */
}
```

When a local item is static, the compiler will allocate permanent storage for it. The name will still have a restricted scope, so other functions will not be able to access **AsciiValue** directly. Although a pointer to a static item is always valid, the function will overwrite the item every time it is called, so that pointers returned by previous calls are left pointing to a valid address, but with invalid contents. A better solution is to require that the caller of the function supply the buffer, like this:

```
char* HexToAscii(unsigned nHex, char* pBuffer, int nBufferSize)
{

    /* fill pBuffer with hex digits */
    /* check that nSizeBuffer is large enough */

    return pBuffer;    /* for convenience */
}
```

Good practice requires that the caller specify the size of the buffer so that the function can check that it is large enough.

## Do Not Forget the Null Terminator When Allocating Space for Strings

The C programming language does not provide array bound checking, and so there is nothing to stop a program from declaring an array of, say, ten elements and then trying to access element 15. If you write beyond the bounds of an array, the program will fail, sometimes in a strange and unpredictable way.

Of course, programmers are careful not to trespass beyond an array's boundary, but many forget the null terminator when allocating space for strings. Consider the following code, which is attempting to concatenate two strings:

```
char* pString1 = "Hello ";
char* pString2 = "World";
```

```
/* wrong, forgot the terminator */
char* pString3
  = (char*)malloc(strlen(pString1) + strlen(pString2));

strcpy(pString3, pString1);
strcat(pString3, pString2);    /* will write beyond the array */
```

The call to **malloc** should have allocated an extra byte for the null terminator of the final string:

```
char* pString3
  = (char*)malloc(strlen(pString1) + strlen(pString2) + 1);
```

As it is, the code will corrupt information that **malloc** uses to administer the heap, so that **malloc** or **free** will subsequently fail.

## Remember That the Index of the Last Element of an Array Is One Less Than Its Size

In C, arrays are zero-based, and although few programmers forget to index the first element of an array as [**0**], many forget that the last element has an index one less than the array size:

```
char Buffer[30];
int i;
/* initialize an array to zero */
for (i=0; i<=30; i++) Buffer[i] = 0;    /* wrong! */
```

The last element of **Buffer** is **Buffer**[29], but the loop tries to initialize **Buffer**[30].

Notice that if you do run off the end of the array **Buffer**, you will not necessarily be overwriting the item declared afterwards, **i** in this case. On the Intel architecture, for example, you will overwrite the item declared before the array, or the stack function return frame, if there is nothing declared before the array.

## Use Function Prototypes

TIP 5

The original version of C, which I shall call classic C, did not allow function prototypes with argument definitions. A function that converted hexadecimal numbers to text might have been written like this:

```
char* HexToAscii(Number, pBuffer, nBufferSize)
long Number;
char* pBuffer;
int nBufferSize;
{
   /* code of function */
}
```

In classic C the type of the function arguments had to be declared at the head of the function. The function would have been declared at the top of the module or in a header file like this:

```
char* HexToAscii();
```

Since there is no argument list, the compiler would be unable to check that the arguments passed to the function were of the correct type, and it would be unable to convert arguments when this was necessary. The compiler would accept the following two incorrect function calls:

```
   char Buffer[10];
   long HexNumber = 0x13ef;
   HexToAscii(Buffer, 10, HexNumber); /* wrong! */
   HexToAscii(0x2ed, Buffer, 10);  /* wrong! */
```

The first call is incorrect because the argument order is wrong. The second call looks correct to most people, but it is incorrect because the first argument is short when it should be long. To force it long, the programmer would add the suffix L after the constant:

```
   HexToAscii(0x2edL, Buffer, 10);  /* correct */
```

ANSI C allows function prototypes with argument definitions, so that the same function would be written:

```
char* HexToAscii(long Number, char* pBuffer, int nBufferSize)
{
```

```
    /* code of function */
}
```

The function prototype now defines the arguments:

```
/* prototype for HexToAscii */
char* HexToAscii(long Number, char* pBuffer, int nBufferSize);
```

Notice that the argument names are optional in the prototype, but it is a good idea to leave them in, because they help readers understand how the function will be called. With this prototype the compiler is able to reject invalid argument types. Furthermore, if the compiler is able to convert an argument to a valid type, it will do so. If a caller supplies a short hexadecimal number to this function, the compiler will silently convert it to a long number.

Many programmers who first learned classic C continue to use function definitions with no arguments (or no definitions at all), even though they are using an ANSI C compiler.

## Be Careful When Using the char Type in Expressions

If you declare an item of type **char**, without explicitly declaring it to be **signed** or **unsigned**, the sign will depend on the implementation. On most Intel compilers a plain **char** item is signed by default.

Because the ASCII or ANSI character set runs from 0 to 255, many programmers assume that a **char** type is unsigned by default. If you simply use the **char** type for storing characters, there is no problem: you can store extended characters in the range 128 to 255 in a **signed char** type and they will be printed or displayed correctly.

The problems arise when you do comparisons of **char** types with integers, or when you use them to index an array. The following code sample contains two examples of signed character bugs:

```
char c = getchar();     /* c is signed by default */

if (c>135 && c<155 ) {  /* this is never true */
}

char converted = LookupTable[c]; /* wrong! */
```

If **c** contains a character in the range 128 to 255, the machine will treat it as a negative number, because the most significant bit will be treated as a sign bit. Since the maximum value of **c** is 127, it will never be greater than 135. Even worse, when the code uses the negative number to index the array **LookupTable**, it will access whatever happens to be in memory before the array.

The solution is to declare **c** to be of type **unsigned char**. There is no need to declare all character items as unsigned, you only need to make the distinction when you want to use the character value in an expression.

```
unsigned char c = getchar();     /* c has range 0 - 255 */

if (c>135 && c<155 ) {  /* OK*/
}

char converted = LookupTable[c]; /* OK */
```

## Do Not Confuse the Logical and Bitwise Operators

A common mistake is to confuse the logical operators && (logical AND) and || (logical OR) with the bitwise operators & (bitwise AND) and | (bitwise OR). The logical operators combine Boolean results, so the expression:

```
if ( a>b && c<d || IsValid(e) )
```

means "if **a** is greater than **b** *and* **c** is greater than **d** *or* the function **IsValid** returns a non-zero value..." In C, Boolean results and integers are interchangeable, so any non-zero integer is equivalent to TRUE, and zero is equivalent to FALSE.

The bitwise operators combine bit patterns, so that the expression:

```
0x55 & 0x16 | 0x22
```

would take the bits common to 0x55 ( 01010101 ) and 0x16 ( 00010110 ) to give 00010100, and then combine that with 0x22 ( 00100010 ) to give ( 00110110 ), which is 0x36. Although bit operations are useful in certain types of algorithms, in most expressions you will want to use the logical operations.

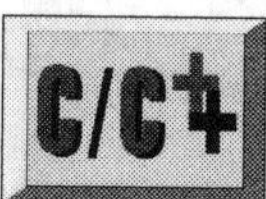

These operations are confusing, because in many cases you can use the bitwise operators in place of the logical operators and the result will still be correct. The expression:

```
// used bitwise operators by mistake
if ( a>b & c<d & IsValid(e) )
```

is a Boolean expression, but it incorrectly uses bitwise operators instead of logical operators. The expression is intended to mean "if a is less than b *and* c is less than d *and* e is valid..." Even though the expression is wrong, it will work as expected in this case, provided that **IsValid** returns the value 1 for TRUE and 0 for FALSE. The subexpressions a>b and c<d also evaluate to 1 if they are TRUE, and the bitwise combination of these subexpressions is equivalent to the Boolean result. If all the subexpressions are true, the expression is equivalent to:

```
if (1 & 1 & 1)
```

which evaluates to 1, and so the expression is TRUE.

Now imagine that the item **e** is valid if it contains a non-zero value. The expression would be written with logical operators as:

```
if ( a>b && c<d && e ) /* true if a>b, c<d */
                       /* and e is non-zero */
```

because the logical operators consider any non-zero value as true. If this expression were written using bitwise operators, the result would depend on the least significant bit of **e**, and this bit could be zero even if **e** contained a valid value.

```
if ( a>b & c<d & e ) /* true if a>b, c<d */
                     /* and e is odd!!! */
```

You see that although the bitwise operators can act as a substitute for the logical operators in some types of Boolean expressions, they do not work for all Boolean expressions. Note also that the logical operators are more efficient than the bitwise operators, since logical subexpressions are only evaluated when necessary. In the expression:

```
if (a>b && c<d && e ) /* true if a>b, c<d */
                  /* and e is non-zero */
```

the compiler will not evaluate the last two subexpressions if **a** is less than **b**, because there is no point: it has already determined that the expression is FALSE. Bitwise expressions are usually evaluated completely, unless the compiler is especially good at optimizing expressions.

# Do Not Rely on the Order of Evaluation in Expressions

With the exception of the &&, the ||, the ?:, and the comma operators, expressions can be evaluated in any order. Indeed, many compilers rearrange the order of evaluation in order to optimize the code. In general a compiler will try to call functions first and then evaluate complex subexpressions before dealing with simple terms. For example, given the expression:

```
a + b/c + GetNumber()
```

a simple compiler might do the following:

1. Get **a** in register 1.
2. Get **b** in register 2.
3. Divide register 2 by **c**.
4. Add register 2 to register 1.
5. Push register 1 to the stack.
6. Call **GetNumber**, which leaves the result in register 1.
7. Add the contents of the stack to register 1.

By rearranging the expression, the compiler can generate more efficient code, like this:

1. Call **GetNumber** which leaves the result in register 1.
2. Get **b** in register 2.
3. Divide register 2 by **c**.
4. Add register 2 to register 1.
5. Add **a** to register 1.

By calling the function first, the compiler generates 5 instructions instead of 7.

In this example there is no harm in rearranging the expression, provided that **GetNumber** does not change **a**, **b** or **c**. Beware of expressions containing ++ or – – operators or assignments. Expressions such as:

```
array[i] + i++

b + (b=b*b)
```

depend on the order of evaluation.

## The Order of Evaluation of Function Arguments Is Not Defined

Like expressions, optimizing compilers may rearrange the order of evaluation of function arguments. Beware of function arguments that read values from a file or use the autoincrement operator. Function calls such as these:

```
MyFunction(getchar(), getchar());
int i = 5;
MyFunction(i, i++);
```

are incorrect.

Assuming that **getchar** returns successive characters `'O'` and `'K'` from a file, **MyFunction** could be called as **MyFunction(**`'O', 'K'`**)** or **MyFunction(**`'K', 'O'`**)** depending on the evaluation order. In the second case, **MyFunction** could be called as **MyFunction(5, 5)** or **MyFunction(6, 5)**, depending on the evaluation order.

## Do Not Confuse the = and the == Operators

A very common mistake is to use the assignment operator = in place of the relational operator ==.

```
while ( a = 0 ) {  /* should be a == 0 */
}
```

This code assigns 0 to **a** and then tests whether **a** is non-zero. As a result, the loop is never executed. This error is so easy to make that most compilers will generate a warning when they see this code. Always take such warnings seriously!

# Identifiers and Data

## Do Not Use C++ Keywords as Names in C Programs

C++ introduces a number of additional keywords such as **new** and **delete**. You should avoid using these keywords for identifier or function names in your C programs, because you will need to change the names if ever you want to port the code to C++.

```
struct DataRecord;
int delete(DataRecord* pRecord); /* OK in C, but not C++ */
```

The keywords to avoid are:

| | | | |
|---|---|---|---|
| **asm** | **friend** | **private** | **this** |
| **catch** | **inline** | **protected** | **throw** |
| **class** | **new** | **public** | **try** |
| **delete** | **operator** | **template** | **virtual** |

In addition, if you are still using classic C, you should avoid the keywords **signed**, **const** and **volatile**, which were introduced in ANSI C.

## Avoid Identifiers Containing Double Underscores or Starting with an Underscore

The C language reserves identifiers starting with a single underscore **_LikeThis** for the implementation. Similarly, C++ reserves identifiers containing double underscores, **Like__This**, for the implementation, and for the standard libraries.

You may use single underscores within an identifier name to separate words: **account_monthly_rate**.

## Avoid Tentative Definitions

TIP 13

In C you can define an item tentatively, without an initializer. If there is another definition later in the module, the tentative definition will be ignored, otherwise it will be used with a default initializer of zero:

```
int Item;   /* tentative definition */
  . . .
   /* can use Item here */
  . . .
int Item = 123;   /* final definition */
```

Tentative definitions are not allowed in C++, so you should avoid using them if you want your code to be portable to C++. Instead of a tentative definition, declare the item as external.

```
extern int Item;   /* declaration */
  . . .
   /* can use Item here */
  . . .
int Item = 123;   /* final definition */
```

## How to Lay Out Long Strings

The compiler will concatenate strings if they are separated by white space and comments. This is useful when you are laying long strings out over several lines.

```
char* pEpitaph = "Goodbye, "
                 "cruel world."
```

The compiler will concatenate these two strings into one:

Goodbye, cruel world.

Notice that if you split the string between words, you will need to keep the space character at the end of the first line.

## Remember to Double the Backslashes in File Paths

Although UNIX file paths use forward slashes (for example, **/usr/bin**), many systems, including DOS, use backslashes (for example, \WINDOWS\SYSTEM\GDI.EXE). If you put a path specification in a string, the compiler will consider the backslash an escape and will combine it with the character that follows it to form an escape sequence, such as **\n**, the escape for a new-line character. To indicate that you really mean a backslash, you must insert an extra backslash:

```
char* pFileSpec = "C:\\DOS\\SYSTEM\\GDI.EXE";
```

## Take Care When Inserting Hexadecimal Constants in Strings

You can insert special characters, such as those from the extended character set, into strings using the **\x** escape and the hexadecimal value of the character. Be aware that in ANSI C, the hexadecimal escape may be followed by any number of hexadecimal constants. This may cause problems if the text that should follow the escape also contains hexadecimal numbers. The string "\xa9Alpha Industries" is intended to be a copyright sign © (hex a9 in the ANSI character set used by Windows), followed by the words "Alpha Industries". However, an ANSI C compiler will take the first A of "Alpha" as part of the hexadecimal string. What the result will be is not defined: some compilers will issue an error message.

The solution here is to cut the string in two:

```
"\xa9""Alpha Industries"
```

The compiler will then concatenate the strings to produce the desired result.

## Escapes Are Lower Case

TIP 17

It is easy to forget that the escape character in strings must be lower case. Other syntactic characters in the C language may be either lower or upper case, for example, 0xa9, 0Xa9, .23e4, .23E4, 6000L, and 6000l are all correct. An upper case escape character in a string, by contrast, will be represented as itself. Thus the string "\Xa9""Alpha Industries" will become "Xa9Alpha Industries", whereas the string "\xa9""Alpha Industries" will produce the intended "©Alpha Industries".

## When You Need to Escape the Question Mark

There is an escape for the question mark, so the string "Quit now\?" will be compiled as "Quit now?" The escape is only necessary when the string contains a sequence of two question marks and a character that happen to match a trigraph. The string "Quit now??!" contains the trigraph ??!, so the compiler will replace it with the | character to give "Quit now|". To specify that you really mean the three characters and not the trigraph, you must escape the second question mark like this: "Quit now ?\?!". Note that it is not sufficient to escape the first question mark, because that would leave the trigraph intact, and the compiler replaces trigraphs before doing anything else.

## When to Use a Trigraph

TIP 19

You can write a C program using the characters in the seven-bit ASCII character set (characters from 0 to 127,) but this is a superset of the ISO 646-1983 Invariant Code Set. In order to allow programs to be written using the ISO character set, ANSI C defines a set of three-character trigraphs that act as replacements for the missing characters. The compiler will replace the trigraphs before doing any other processing. The trigraph sequences are:

| Trigraph sequence | Replacement character |
|---|---|
| ??= | # |
| ??( | [ |
| ??< | { |
| ??/ | \ |
| ??) | ] |
| ??> | } |
| ??' | ^ |
| ??! | \| |
| ??- | ~ |

European users with seven-bit character sets would have to use the trigraphs instead of the standard ASCII punctuation marks, since on European systems these characters would be replaced by national characters.

US programmers are unlikely to need trigraphs, and these days most European users have systems with 8-bit characters sets, and so they are less likely to need trigraphs than in the past.

## You Can Use Extended Characters in Strings If Your Editor Uses the Same Character Set As Your Program

Strings may contain extended characters in the range 128 to 255, so you can put European characters and symbols in strings and comments.

```
/* insert a coin */
char* pMessage = "Insérez une pièce.";
```

However, this will only work if your editor uses the same character set as the target system. Usually this is the case, but the Microsoft Windows system uses the ANSI character set, which is different from the IBM PC character set that DOS applications use. If your target system is Microsoft Windows you must use a Windows editor. If you use a DOS editor, you must convert the file to the ANSI character set, otherwise the extended characters will be displayed incorrectly.

## There is Rarely Any Advantage in Using the char Type for Small Integers

The **char** type is intended for characters in text strings. An item of type **char** occupies an eight-bit byte on most computer architectures and can contain values from 0 to 255 if it is unsigned, or –128 to 127 if it is signed.

You might be tempted to use an item of type **char** for a small integer, such as a person's age, which is unlikely to exceed these limits. Most machines handle items of the natural word length more efficiently, so on a 16- or 32-bit machine integers are more efficient than bytes. To handle a byte, the compiler may have to add additional instructions that mask off the high order bits of the word containing the byte. In addition, most machines operate most efficiently when items are aligned on a natural word boundary, and so the compiler will pad out solitary bytes so that they occupy a word.

The **char** type is efficient when there is an array of **char** values, so they are appropriate for text strings or arrays of small numbers.

## Enumeration Constants Are More Convenient Than #define Statements

C programs often contain **#define** statements that give names to integer constants, perhaps something like this:

```
#define EVENT_MOUSE_MOVE      100
#define EVENT_MOUSE_LBUTTON   101
#define EVENT_MOUSE_RBUTTON   102
#define EVENT_MOUSE_LDCLICK   103
#define EVENT_MOUSE_RDCLICK   104
```

These **#define** statements are very useful in documenting the program, but they are awkward should you ever wish to insert extra items among them. If you wanted to add events for a middle mouse button, for example, you would either have to add them at the end of the list, or else renumber all the items in the list.

If you define these constants as enumeration constants, the compiler will number them for you. You can specify a starting value in the **enum** statement, for example:

```
enum Event {
  EVENT_MOUSE_MOVE = 100,
  EVENT_MOUSE_LBUTTON,
  EVENT_MOUSE_RBUTTON,
  EVENT_MOUSE_LDCLICK,
  EVENT_MOUSE_RDCLICK};
```

If you wish, you may still give each item in the **enum** statement a value, as with the **#define** statement.

Using enumeration statements also offers the possibility of some extra type checking, although not all compilers check **enum** types rigorously. Some compilers will give a warning on this example where the program uses an **Error** type in place of an **Event** type:

```
enum Event {
  EVENT_MOUSE_MOVE = 100,
  EVENT_MOUSE_LBUTTON,
  EVENT_MOUSE_RBUTTON,
  EVENT_MOUSE_LDCLICK,
  EVENT_MOUSE_RDCLICK};

enum Error {
  ERROR_NO_SPACE,   /* 0 by default */
  ERROR_DISK_FULL,
  ERROR_CAT_HAS_MOUSE};

void test(Event theEvent);

void func()
{
  /* incorrect, using an Error as an Event */
  test(ERROR_CAT_HAS_MOUSE);
}
```

## There Is No Need to Use the enum Keyword When Declaring Instances of an enum

Although you need to declare an **enum** type with the **enum** keyword, you do not need to state **enum** when declaring instances of that **enum**. You may if you wish, however, because the compiler accepts both forms:

```
enum Color {Red, Green, Blue, White};

/* Once enum Color is defined, the enum is optional */

Color Foreground = Red;
enum Color Background = Green;
```

Once this program has declared **enum Color**, it may declare instances of **Color** omitting the **enum** keyword.

## Arrays Are Passed by Reference

TIP 24

When you pass arguments to a function, they are passed by value so that the function receives a copy of the argument. This is useful, because the function can modify the argument without modifying the original. If you want the function to be able to modify the original, you can pass a pointer to it instead.

Arrays are an exception to this rule. If you pass an array as an argument the compiler will actually pass a pointer to the array, and if the function modifies the array, it will modify the original array.

For function arguments, it makes no difference whether you declare the argument as an array or as a pointer, and inside the function, you may subscript the pointer or dereference the array, as in the following example:

```
void func (char* pBuf, int IArray[])
{
  char c = pBuf[2];
```

```
  int i = *(IArray+3);
}

void test()
{
  char Buf[20];
  int Array[20];

  func(Buf, Array);
}
```

Even so, if the argument is actually an array or a buffer, it is better to declare it as such, and reserve pointer arguments for pointers to single items. Doing so underlines the fact that the function expects an array argument, but does not make the program any more efficient.

## The Equivalence Between Arrays and Pointers to Arrays Is Only Valid for Function Arguments

It is important to realize that arrays and pointers to arrays are two different things and are generally not equivalent. The only exception is for function arguments, as explained in the last tip, but this is only because function arguments can never be arrays—they are always converted to pointers.

An easy mistake to make is to declare an array as:

```
char SomeData[100];
```

in one module, and as:

```
extern char* SomeData;
```

in another module. This will not work: you must declare it as:

```
extern char SomeData[];
```

or as:

```
extern char SomeData[100];
```

## If an Argument Is a Multidimensional Array, You Must Specify Its Size

When a function argument is an array of more than one dimension, you must declare the size of the dimensions. The compiler needs the size of the dimensions to calculate the position of the element within the area occupied by the array:

```
void func (char Matrix[6][8])
{
  Matrix[2][3] = Matrix[4][5];
}

void test(){
  char Matrix[6][8];
  func(Matrix);
}
```

The address of **Matrix[2][3]** will be:

Address of **Matrix** + 2*8 + 3

## The Size of the First Dimension Is Optional on Multidimensional Array Arguments

The previous tip explained that you must specify dimension sizes if an argument is a multidimensional array. In fact, the size of the first dimension is optional, because the compiler does not need the size of the first dimension to calculate the address of elements, only the size of subsequent dimensions.

A side effect of this is that even if you do specify the size of the first dimension, the compiler will not check its size. For example:

```
void func (char Matrix1[6][8], char Matrix2[][8])
{
```

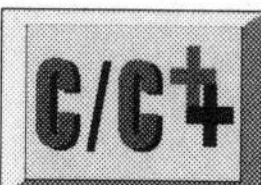

```
  Matrix1[2][3] = Matrix2[4][5];
}

void test(){
  char Matrix[10][8];  /* array is larger than 6 */
  func(Matrix, Matrix); /* OK */
}
```

Here the function **func** declares the arguments with and without the first dimension: both are acceptable. Furthermore, the function **test** supplies an array where the first dimension is greater than six. This is also acceptable, but the compiler would not have issued an error if the size of **Matrix** had been less than six, and that could be a potential error.

If there had been any mismatch in the size of the other dimensions, for example, if **Matrix** had been declared **char Matrix[6][10]**, the compiler would have issued an error.

## Incorrect Handling of Large Multidimensional Arrays Can Cause Page Thrashing

*Page thrashing* is not what happens to disobedient servants; it is a phenomenon that occurs on virtual memory systems when an application accesses memory in a scattered manner. Most operating systems do not keep an entire application in memory: they load it in as pages from secondary storage when it is needed. If part of an application is not used for some time, the operating system will discard it, or if it has been modified, write it back to secondary storage to make room for something else.

Most applications spend a relatively long time in one area before moving to another, so virtual memory works well. If the application accesses a large address space in a scattered fashion, the operating system will be obliged to load in a page of memory for almost every access. If in addition the application is writing to memory, the system will need to write out the modified pages. The result is known as page thrashing: the system spends all its time swapping memory pages and the application proceeds at a snail's pace.

In a multidimensional array, the elements of the last dimension are next to each other in memory, so in any loop, accessing the last dimension in the innermost loop will minimize the chances of page thrashing. Here are two ways to initialize a multidimensional array:

```
int ai[60][250][1000];
int i,j,k;

/* wrong! will cause page thrashing */
for (k=0; i<1000; k++)
  for (j=0; j<250; j++)
    for (i=0; i<60; i++)
       ai[i][j][k] = 0;

/* correct--innermost loop for last dimension */
for (i=0; i<60; i++)
  for (j=0; j<250; j++)
    for (k=0; k<1000; k++)
       ai[i][j][k] = 0;
```

The first way accesses memory in a scattered fashion, while the second way goes through the array sequentially.

## You Are Allowed to Refer to One Element Beyond the End of an Array, But No Further

When scanning through an array with a pointer, a common trick is to check that the pointer is less than the address of the hypothetical element just beyond the end of the array.

```
int Array[30];
int* pElement;
for (pElement=Array; pElement<Array[30]; pElement++){
}
```

The problem here is that in a system with a segmented architecture, the hypothetical element might be out of the range of the current segment, and since the code would normally only compare offsets within a segment, the result would be undefined.

To guard against this, ANSI C states that pointer comparison within an array and for one element beyond is legal, and the compiler will ensure that this address is valid.

Note that this hypothetical element is not a safety element, and will usually be occupied by some other data. If you read or write to the element beyond the end of an array, you are in trouble.

## The Subscript Operator Is Commutative

This is not so much a tip as a curiosity, although you can use it to amaze your friends at C/C++ parties.

The array subscript operator [ ] is commutative, so you can put the subscript outside the brackets and the array inside! The code:

```
char* pChar = &15["The Wonders of C/C++"];
printf("%s party tricks\n",pChar);
```

will print out "C/C++ party tricks" followed by a new line. The pointer **pChar** points to the 16th character of the string "The Wonders of C/C++" (not the 15th, since the array is zero-based.)

I am not suggesting that you use this trick for normal programming, but you might come across the construction if you have to maintain or modify some other joker's code.

## C Does Not Define a Way of Determining the Bounds of an Array

The C language does not provide a way of determining the number of elements in an array:

```
int func (int ai[])
{
  return sizeof ai;
}

void test()
{
  int ai[5];
```

```
  int x = sizeof ai;
  int y = func(ai);
}
```

In the code above, **x** will be initialized to the size of **ai** in bytes, which might be 10 or 20, depending on the compiler and the machine. **func** will return the size of a pointer, which is typically two or four bytes.

Programs quite often need to know the size of an array that is defined elsewhere in the application. One way of making the size available is to put the size in a **#define** statement:

```
#define AISIZE 5

void test()
{
  int ai[AISIZE];
   . . .
  int x = AISIZE;
}
```

An additional advantage here is that if ever you wish to change the size of the array, you only need to modify the code in one place.

If you pass arrays as arguments to functions, you should specify an extra argument for the array size:

```
void func (int ai[], int aiSize)
{
  int i;
  for (i=0; i < aiSize-1; i++) pai[i]=0;
}

  . . .

#define AISIZE 5

void test()
{
  int ai[AISIZE];
  func(ai, AISIZE);
}
```

The C language omitted the array size for the sake of efficiency on the computers of the 70's. These days machines are powerful enough for this small overhead not to be a concern, but it is impossible to add an array size feature without breaking most existing C programs.

Note that C++ programmers can define array classes that have the size feature.

## If Variables or Functions Are Private to a Module, Declare Them Static

If you declare an item in a file module, it has external linkage by default. This means that other modules will be able to access the items when they are linked together. You will need some external linkage between modules, but it is inconvenient to have everything external. If you use an identifier name in another module for another purpose, the linker will issue an error message. If many items are external, the linker will slow down trying to cope with them all.

If an item is intended to be used only within a module, declare it static. You can declare functions static as well as data:

```
#define TEMPARRAYSIZE 100

static char TempArray[TEMPARRAYSIZE];

static void HelperFunc(char Array[], int ArraySize);
```

## Static Items Local to a Function Are Preserved Across Function Calls

If you declare an item within a function it will have the **auto** storage class by default. The compiler will allocate space for it on the program stack, and the space will be reclaimed before the function returns. Sometimes you would prefer to have the item keep its value across functions calls.

If you give the item the **static** storage class, the compiler will allocate permanent storage for it. In that sense, the item will be similar to an item declared at the module level, outside of the function. The

advantage of a local static item is that the scope of its name is still limited to the function or block in which it is declared, and so another function may use the same name for some other purpose:

```
void test1()
{
  static int nCalled;
  nCalled++;
}

void test2()
{
  static int nCalled;
  nCalled++;
}
```

In this example both **test1** and **test2** keep track of the number of times they are called. Because they declare **nCalled** as **static**, the value is preserved across calls, but the two functions still have their own private copy of **nCalled**.

## Static Arrays Are Useful for Local Initialized Arrays

Sometimes you need an initialized array in a function, perhaps as a look-up table. You can declare it in this form:

```
unsigned long DaysToDoomsDay(int Year, int Month, int Day)
{
  char DaysInMonth[13]=
    {0, 31, 28, 31, 30, 31, 30, 31, 31, 30, 31, 30, 31};
  /* algorithm left as exercise for reader */
}
```

but then the compiled code will initialize the array every time the function is called. The compiler would have stored the initial values in static storage ready for copying into the array.

If you are planning to change the contents of the array within the function then this is fine, but if the array is read only, as it is here, you can declare the array as **static const**.

```
unsigned long DaysToDoomsDay(int Year, int Month, int Day)
{
  static const char DaysInMonth[13]=
    {0, 31, 28, 31, 30, 31, 30, 31, 31, 30, 31, 30, 31};
  /* algorithm left as exercise for reader */
}
```

Now the array is only initialized once at load time. The **const** storage class is optional, but if you specify it, the compiler will make sure that you do not accidentally overwrite the array.

## If a Function Does Not Change an Array Argument, Declare It with the const Qualifier

Because arrays arguments are always passed as pointers, if a function modifies the array it will modify the original array that it received, and not a private copy. If the function does not modify the array, it should declare the argument with the **const** qualifier to indicate that the array will not be modified.

The reason for doing this is that the compiler will object if you try to pass a constant array to a function that has not declared the argument as constant. This example will fail:

```
int MyFunc(char* pString);

void test()
{
   const char* pMessage = "Oops!";
   MyFunc(pMessage);    /* wrong! */
}
```

If the argument is declared **const**, then the function will accept any array, whether it is constant or not:

```
int MyFunc(const char* pString);

void test()
{
   const char* pMessage = "Aaah!";
```

```
    MyFunc(pMessage);   /* OK */
}
```

When you decide to use the **const** qualifier, you have to start from the bottom and work up. All your low level routines and libraries must use the qualifier where appropriate before you can start using it at the application level.

## The const Modifier on its Own Is Equivalent to const int

If you see an item declared as **const** without a specific type, the item is a **const int**:

```
const int FreezingH2O = -32;
const BoilingH2O = 212;   /* const int */
```

## How to Declare Constant Pointers

Given an integer **i**, the declarations:

```
const int* pInt = &i;
int const* pInt = &i;
```

are equivalent and both declare a non-constant pointer to a constant integer. This means that you can modify **pInt** to point at any integer, but that you cannot modify the integer through the pointer.

The declaration:

```
int* const pInt = &i;
```

declares a constant pointer to an integer. Here you may modify the integer through the pointer, but you cannot modify the pointer to point to something else. In the code:

```
int i;
int *const pi = &i;
const int* pci = &i;
*pi = 2;        /* OK */
*pci = 3;       /* illegal */
pi = pci;       /* illegal */
```

the last two statements are illegal: one tries to modify the constant integer pointed to by **pci**, and the other tries to modify the constant pointer **pi**.

Notice that you can assign the address of a non-constant item to a pointer to a constant item, as in **pci = &i**. When you do this you can still modify the item directly or through another ordinary pointer, but not through **pci**.

## There Is Rarely Any Need to Use the register Modifier with Modern Compilers

The **register** keyword was intended to be a hint to the compiler that a certain variable in a function is going to be used heavily, and that the compiler should keep it in a machine register rather than on the program stack. A machine can access registers much faster than it can access RAM memory where the stack is kept. The snag is that there are only a limited number of registers available. Some machines have a dozen spare registers, while others, such as the Intel 80x86 series, have just two or three available for storing variables.

If you omit the **register** keyword, most compilers are able to decide for themselves which variables are best kept in registers. Since priorities change as a function proceeds, the optimal policy is often to keep one variable in a register for a few statements while it is being used heavily, and then to push it out and let another variable in. If you specify register variables yourself, you run the risk of forcing the compiler to adopt a suboptimal register allocation strategy.

## When to Use the volatile Modifier

TIP 39

The **volatile** modifier is intended for items that might be modified asynchronously by an external process. The other process may be an interrupt routine, or more likely for a C program, a process thread using the same address space.

By declaring an item volatile, you are instructing the compiler not to keep the item in a register, or to make any optimizations that rely on the item being temporarily constant.

In fact, these optimizations rarely make any difference to the logic of the program. Although the compiled code might be using an out-of-date value in a register for a few statements while the original item has changed, this will not matter, because the item changes asynchronously, and might well have changed a few statements later in any case.

The exception is code that relies on the other process changing the item:

```
volatile int Item;
  . . .
int WaitForChange()
{
  Item =0;
  while (!Item) continue;    /* loop until another */
  return Item;               /* process changes Item */
}
```

Without the **volatile** modifier, the compiler might have optimized out the **while** loop and returned zero. You are unlikely to see this sort of code in an ordinary application, since it is far more efficient to wait on an operating system event.

## An Item Can Have Both the const and the volatile Modifiers

You can declare an item to be both **const** and **volatile**:

```
const volatile Item;
```

This apparent contradiction means that the item cannot be modified by the program, but might be modified by an external process.

Although this is allowed in C, it will not work in C++. A C++ compiler will allow the declaration, but will treat the item as constant anyway.

## Be Careful when Declaring Several Pointers in One Statement

You are probably aware that in C, you can declare several items in one statement:

```
int a, b, c; /* declare three integers */
float f, g, h; /* declare three floats */
```

So it would be logical to write:

```
int* pA, pB, pC;  /* !!! */
```

when you want to declare three pointers.

Every C programmer makes this mistake at least once. In C, the indirection operator * only applies to the item that follows it, so the statement above will declare **pA** as a pointer to an integer, and **pC** and **pB** as ordinary integers. The correct way to declare three pointers would be:

```
int *pA, *pB, *pC;  /* declare three pointers */
```

You should note that this style is considered unfashionable and that it is even better to declare each item in a separate statement, and to initialize it at the same time:

```
int* pA = &a;
int* pB = &b;
int* pC = &c;
```

# Functions and Operators

## If a Function Takes No Arguments, You Should Specify void in its Prototype

If you have a function that takes no arguments, you might declare a prototype like this:

```
void func();
```

This is equivalent to a classic C function declaration, and so an ANSI C compiler will not check the function's arguments when you call it. ANSI C compilers will accept classic C function declarations without arguments so that the old code will not need modifying. If you accidentally supply an argument, the compiler will not generate an error (although some compilers will generate a warning.)

To enable argument checking, specify **void** as the argument list:

```
void func(void);
```

This is not necessary in C++. Because C++ insists on full function prototypes with arguments, there can be no confusion with a classic C prototype without arguments.

## Old Style Function Definitions Treat the float Type as double

Old style function definitions, as used in classic C, promote the float type to a double, while the new style definition does not. This can lead to problems if you mix old and new style function definitions, and if one of the arguments is a float, or a pointer to a float.

You would not normally mix function definition styles, of course, but you might need to do so when interfacing new code with an old library. The following example will cause a compiler error:

```
/* new style declaration */
extern void Example(float x);

void Example(x)
float x;
```

```
{
  /* old style function */
}
```

The old style function will promote `x` to a double, and expect a double as an argument. Any code using the new style function prototype will call the function with a float. Even if the code calls the function with a double argument, the compiler will convert the argument to a float. On most machines, a float is 32 bits long and a double is 64 bits long, so calling a function with a float argument instead of a double will cause an error.

If you do not want to modify the source of your trusty old library, you should change the type of the argument to double in the new style function prototype:

```
extern void Example(double x);
```

If you really want to use floats instead of doubles, you will need to change the definition of the function to the new style. Be careful: because the old function promoted the float arguments to doubles, it might not work correctly with floats. There might not be enough precision for intermediate results within the function. The safest course, when converting old style functions to new, is simply to replace the float arguments with doubles. If you do that, the function will work just as it did before conversion.

## The main Function Should Return a Result

The **main** function should return a result code. A zero code indicates success while a non-zero code indicates abnormal termination. You may also use the macros EXIT_SUCCESS and EXIT_FAILURE defined in **stdlib.h**.

```
int main()
{
  /* if something goes wrong ... */
  if (!InitializeApp()) return EXIT_FAILURE;

  RunApp();

  /* Everything was OK */
  return EXIT_SUCCESS;
}
```

When you run your program from the command line interface, the result code might not serve any purpose, but if another application runs your application, perhaps as part of a batch sequence, the application may use the result code and take some action if the code is non-zero, perhaps aborting the batch sequence.

If you do not return a code, then the controlling system or application will probably take the contents of a machine accumulator register as the result code, and this arbitrary value is very likely to be non-zero. Declaring **main** as void in your program will prevent the compiler from issuing a warning, but the controlling application will still expect a result code.

Note that returning a value from **main** is equivalent to calling the **exit** function with a result code.

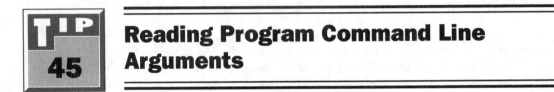

## Reading Program Command Line Arguments

You may define the function **main** in two different ways, either as:

```
int main(){}
```

without any arguments, or as:

```
int main(int argc, char* argv[]){}
```

If you use the second form, you will be able to access the program command line arguments which the user supplied when calling the program. The first argument, **argc**, specifies the number of arguments, while the second argument, **argv**, is an array of pointers to the actual arguments.

The list of pointers in **argv** are always terminated by a null pointer, so **argv[argc]** is null. That means you do not need **argc** at all if you just want to examine each argument. The **argc** argument is useful if your program expects a certain number of arguments, in which case you can check the value of **argc** before doing anything else. Here is a program that displays each argument on a new line:

```
int main(int argc, char* argv[])
{
  printf("There are %d arguments\n", argc);
  while (*argv) printf("%s\n",*argv++);
  return EXIT_SUCCESS;
}
```

The first argument is the full path specification of the application, and the second argument is the first user-supplied item. If you are not interested in the file path, you should skip the first argument.

```
int main(int argc, char* argv[])
{
  /*  report number of user-supplied arguments */
  printf("There are %d arguments\n", argc-1);

  /* skip the first argument */
  argv++;

  while (*argv) printf("%s\n",*argv++);
  return EXIT_SUCCESS;
}
```

The operating system will consider anything separated by white space (not commas) to be an argument. A string containing white space but enclosed in quotes, however, will be a single argument. If the user calls the program like this:

```
test Arg1,Arg2 "Hello World"
```

then **argv** will contain three strings. The first will be path of test, perhaps "/usr/bin/joesoap/test". The second will be "Arg1,Arg2" and the third will be "Hello World". You will not find the quotes in the string, of course, not even for the third argument.

## Avoid Recursive Functions Where Possible

Recursive functions are a clever way of writing loops. Here is a recursive function that calculates n!, the factorial of a number. Recall that n! = n * (n–1) * (n–2) * . . . * 2 * 1.

```
long double factorial(int n)
{
  if (!n) return 1.0;
  return n * factorial(n-1);
}
```

This function calls itself recursively until **n** is 0. There are two practical problems with recursive functions. The first is that calling a function is a time consuming operation, at least when compared with the execution time of other statements. The second problem is that whenever a program calls a function, it requires a small amount of stack space. The function relinquishes this stack space when it returns, but recursive functions keep on allocating stack until the recursion finishes. Since the stack is a limited resource, sooner or later a recursive function is likely to exhaust it. When the stack overflows in this manner, most systems will abort the program.

While recursive functions are an interesting novelty, it is best to avoid them in production programs, unless you are sure that the recursion is limited to a few levels. Recursion may be appropriate for handling trees, or for functions that converge rapidly, limiting the recursion depth.

The factorial routine is faster written as a loop like this:

```
long double factorial(int n)
{
  long double result=n;
  while ( --n > 1) result *= n;
  return result;
}
```

Note that the factorial function can return large numbers. A long double can hold the value of 1754! which is approximately 2.0e4930. A 16-bit integer can only hold the value of 7!, which is 5040.

## If a Function Does Not Return a Result, Declare the Result Type as void

In classic C, it was customary to omit a result type for a function when the function did not return a result:

```
BeepSound()
{
   /* Code to make a beep sound */
   /* No result returned */
}
```

ANSI C introduced the **void** type, and so functions such as these could be declared:

```
void BeepSound()
{
   /* Code to make a beep sound */
   /* No result returned */
}
```

In both classic and ANSI C, if you omit the result type, the compiler will assume the **int** result type by default. This is to maintain compatibility between the two versions of C.

If you declare functions as **void**, the compiler is able to check that you do not accidentally use the result when it is not defined:

```
void BeepSound();

if (BeepSound() != 0) Error(); /* compiler error */
```

Another reason for using the **void** type is that when you move the code to C++, you will find that the compiler will issue an error if a function does not return a result, unless the function is declared **void**.

## Avoid Using Floating-Point Arithmetic for Fixed-Point Numbers

C provides the **float** and **double** types for handling floating-point numbers, but arithmetic operations on floating-point numbers are much slower than integer operations. Exactly how much slower depends on the floating-point support provided by the hardware running the program, but floating-point operations are typically one or two orders of magnitude slower than equivalent integer operations.

If you really need floating-point numbers, then you will just have to accept the performance that your hardware provides, but many programmers use floating-point numbers for fixed-point arithmetic.

As an example, consider an application for arranging floor space in an office. The programmer might decide that all measurements will be metric and use the meter as a unit. The application might then use the **float** type to store all the measurements. A desk might be 1.80 meters wide and 0.95 meters deep.

This is actually a fixed-point application, because all the measurements are to two places of decimals. The programmer should have chosen the centimeter as the unit and used an integer or a long integer to store the measurements.

Although you may find it convenient to use the floating-point types for a fixed-point application, if you are interested in performance, reserve the **float** type for numbers that span a large range. The trigonometric functions are examples of functions that return values that are really floating-point.

## Avoid Equality Comparisons on Floating-Point Numbers

Floating-point arithmetic lacks the precision of integer arithmetic, and after any calculation involving floating-point numbers there may be a small residue error. Because of this error, you should avoid the equality and inequality comparisons on floating point numbers. Code like this:

```
float f;
/* do some operation of f */
if (f==0.0) {
  /* do something */
}
```

is likely to fail. Even though you expect **f** to be zero, as a result of rounding errors it may actually be a very small value such as 0.00000019. Instead, you should check whether the number lies in some range, like this:

```
#define DELTA 0.0001

  . . .

if (f < 0.0+DELTA && f > 0.0-DELTA){
}
```

## Be Careful That Your Integer Expressions Do Not Temporarily Overflow

The following function converts degrees Celsius into degrees Fahrenheit:

```
int CelsiusToFahrenheit( int Celsius)
{
  return Celsius*9/5 +32;
}
```

If the computer uses signed 16-bit integers, the maximum value for a degree Fahrenheit is 32,767, which corresponds to 18,186 degrees Celsius. The application is only interested in temperatures up to 10,000 degrees Celsius, so it would be reasonable to use 16-bit integers for these temperatures.

This program will fail when it tries to convert a large Celsius value, say 5000, to Fahrenheit, because 5000 * 9 is 45,000, which is too large for a signed 16-bit integer: the operation overflows and the result is incorrect.

To avoid this overflow, use the **long** type during the calculation:

```
int CelsiusToFahrenheit( int Celsius)
{
  return ((long)Celsius*9L/5L) +32;
}
```

This expression keeps the result long until the division brings it safely into the range of a signed short integer again.

## Avoid Mixing Signed with Unsigned in a Division Operation

Mixing signed and unsigned integers is never a good idea, but you should take special care to avoid the mix in a division or modulus operation. If you mix a signed integer with an unsigned integer in a division or modulus operation, you will get some unexpected results should the signed integer be negative.

```
int n = -6;
unsigned m = 3;
int result = n / m; /* result is 21,843 ! */
```

Here the compiler will convert **n** to an unsigned integer. The bit pattern for –6 is Hex FFFA, which is equivalent to 65,530 in an unsigned integer. Dividing that by 3 will yield 21,843 instead of –2 as expected.

If you cannot change the types of either operand, you should cast one of them so that the types are the same. In the case above, you would cast **m** to a signed integer if you knew that it would never exceed the maximum for a signed integer (32,767):

```
int n = -6;
unsigned m = 3;
int result = n / (int)m; /* result is -2 */
```

## If Either Operand of a Division Is Negative Then Rounding Is Implementation-Dependent

If either operand of a division is negative (but not both) the result may be rounded either towards or away from zero, depending on the implementation. An expression such as –8/3 may give either –2 when it is rounded towards zero, or –3 when it is rounded away from zero.

The compiler will just do whatever is fastest on the target machine. The Intel 80x86 processors, for example, round towards zero, so all Intel compilers will produce code that rounds towards zero as well.

If there is any chance that your code might be ported to another architecture, you should take care with divisions when one operand is negative.

## Avoid Comparing Signed and Unsigned Values

If you compare a signed value with an unsigned value, the compiler will treat the signed value as unsigned. If the signed value is negative, it will be treated as an unsigned integer having the same bit pattern as the signed value, and the result of the comparison will be arbitrary.

You should cast one of the two values so that they are both signed or both unsigned. You can only cast an unsigned value to signed if it is less than or equal to 32,767. If you think the unsigned value may be larger than that, you should cast both values to signed long integers for the comparison.

```
int n = -6;
unsigned m = 35000;
if ((long)n < (long)m) {  /* a valid comparison */
   /* do something */
}
```

# Logical Operations Are Evaluated Left to Right Until the Result of the Expression Is Known

Given the expression **a && b || c**, the compiler will first evaluate **a**. If **a** is FALSE, the complete expression is FALSE and the compiler will not evaluate either **b** or **c**. If **a** is TRUE, the compiler will evaluate **b**, and if **b** is TRUE the complete expression is TRUE and the compiler will not evaluate **c**.

You can make use of this property to first check on some preconditions before doing something that might otherwise fail, for example:

```
                                /* do not get record */
if ( IsOpen(DataFile)           /* if file is not open */
     && FreeMemory() > 500      /* or not enough memory */
     && GetRecord(DataFile))
{
  /* process record */
}

/* do not call strlen if pMessage is null */
if (pMessage && strlen(pMessage) < 80 ){
  Display(pMessage);
}
```

The first statement checks that a file is open and that there is adequate memory before attempting an operation. In the second statement, **strlen** would fail if the argument was null, but because the expression first checks that **pMessage** is non-zero, the compiler will not call **strlen** if **pMessage** is zero.

# TIP 55 The Unary Negation Operator ! Is Useful as a Test for Zero

The unary negation operator ! returns TRUE if its operand is zero and FALSE if it is non-zero. The operator is useful when testing whether an item is zero. For example:

```
int Handle = GetHandle();   /* valid handles are non-zero */
if (!Handle) Error();       /* error if Handle is zero */
```

This reads as "If Handle is not valid then call Error." A test of this sort is often used to check the value returned by a function that allocates memory or some other resource. Such functions typically return zero to indicate that they were unable to allocate the resource.

There are those who argue that such use is bad style and that the alternative

```
if (Handle == 0) Error();
```

is more readable. Even if you choose not to use the ! operator yourself, you will certainly see it quite often in other people's code, so you should understand what it does.

# TIP 56 Assignments Can Be Chained Together

The assignment operator = returns the value of the assignment as well as actually assigning the value to the left-hand operand. Because of that, assignments can be chained together. This can be useful when assigning the same value to a number of items, for example:

```
a = b = c = 0;
```

This statement assigns the value zero to **a**, **b** and **c**.

# Understand the Difference Between Prefix and Postfix Increment and Decrement Operators

The increment operator ++ adds 1 to an item, while the decrement operator – – subtracts 1 from an item. For example:

```
n++;                /* add 1 to n */
array[index]--;     /* subtract 1 from array[index] */
```

These operators can be prefix (++n) or postfix (n++). When the operators are used on their own to increment an item, there is no difference between the prefix and the postfix forms, for example:

```
++n;                /* add 1 to n */
--array[index];     /* subtract 1 from array[index] */
```

If you use the incremented (or decremented) item in an expression, however, there is a difference: the prefix operator will first change the item and then give its changed value, while the postfix operator will first give the value of the item and then change it, for example:

```
int n = 7;

int b = n++;
/* b = 7, n = 8 */

int c = ++n;
/* c = 9, n = 9 */
```

The prefix operator only applies to the immediate use of the item. If you use the item later on in the same expression, you will get the changed value, for example:

```
int n = 7;
if ( n++ == 7 && n == 8 )    /* this is true */
```

# The Bitwise Operators Are Useful for Storing Flags

Often you will need to store a number of associated flags, perhaps to indicate optional properties that an item might have. If you keep these flags as bits in a word, the bitwise operators will store and extract them. Use the OR operator | to set the bits, and the AND operator & to test them. The following example uses bits to represent hotel facilities:

```
enum HotelFacilities {
 AIR_COND    = 0x1,
 LIFT        = 0x2,
 PARKING     = 0x4,
 POOL        = 0x8,
 RESTAURANT = 0x10,
 CONFERENCE = 0x20};

void AddHotel(char* pName, int Facilities)
{
  if (Facilities & PARKING) {
    /* do something if there is an automobile park */
  }
}

void test(){
  AddHotel("Tether's End", LIFT|PARKING|POOL);
}
```

The **AddHotel** class uses the bitwise AND & operator to test whether a facility is available. The test function combines a number of facilities using the OR | operator.

Note that the values are all powers of two to ensure that they are single bits.

The Microsoft Windows API is an example of a set of functions that use this technique quite extensively.

## To Clear Certain Bits in a Word, Use the "and not" Operation

To clear the last two bits in a 16-bit integer, you could do a bitwise AND operation with the other 14 bits:

```
flags &= 0xfffd;
```

but that would not work on a 32-bit word, since it would clear the 16 highest bits as well. It is far simpler to use the "and not" construction:

```
flags &= ~0x3;
```

Not only is this independent of the word length, but the constant specifies the actual bits to clear.

## To Toggle a Bit, Use the XOR Operator

The XOR operator ^ will set a bit if it is clear, and clear a bit if it is set. Use the assignment XOR operator ^= to toggle a bit in a word:

```
flags ^= 0x4;   /* toggles third bit from right */
```

## How to Pack Small Values Using Bitwise Operators

As Tip 86 will explain, C provides bit fields for dividing words into fields that are each capable of holding small values. The problem with bit fields is that they are implementation-dependent, so if you want to pack small values into a word in a portable manner, you should use the bitwise operators.

You should realize that unpacking values from words is slow: a typical machine will be able to load several natural integers in the time it needs to unpack one value. Packing values is usually only worth doing for very large arrays or structures that would otherwise consume too much memory.

To pack a value into a word, you must first shift the left into the correct position, and then place it into the word using the bitwise OR operator. To unpack the value, you must use a bit mask to extract the bits of the value from the word, and then shift it right to the end of the word. As an example, you might want to store some details about a person for a marketing database. The details might be the person's age, the number of children that person has, and the number of rooms in the person's household. If the number of children is 15 or less, and the number of rooms 31 or less, the values can be packed into a 16-bit word:

| 15 — 11 | 10 — 7 | 6 — 0 |
|---|---|---|
| Rooms | Children | Age |

The age occupies bits 0 to 6, the number of children bits 7 to 10, and the number of rooms bits 11 to 15. Here is some code that stores values into a word:

```
unsigned int aPerson;

aPerson = 54 ;           /* age is 54 */
aPerson |= 3 << 7;       /* 3 children */
aPerson |= 8 << 11;      /* 8 rooms */
```

This is the quick way to store values. It assumes that all the values are stored in one go. Notice that the first value is stored as a straightforward assignment, which has the effect of clearing the other fields. The second and subsequent values are combined using the OR assignment |= operator.

If you want to change one value, you must first clear the bits for that value and then add the new value, like this:

```
aPerson &= ~0x0780;   /* clear children bits */
aPerson |=  4 << 7; /* store new value of 4 children*/
```

The first line clears all the bits occupied by the children field. An alternative way of clearing these bits is to write:

```
aPerson &= ~(0xf << 7);   /* clear children bits */
```

To extract the values, you shift the value to the right of the word and then mask off the high-order bits:

```
unsigned int Age =
      aPerson & 0x7f;
  unsigned int nChildren =
      (aPerson >> 7) & 0xf;
  unsigned int nRooms =
      (aPerson >> 11) & 0x1f;
}
```

## Beware of the Difference Between an Arithmetic and a Logical Shift

When you shift an unsigned value to the right, the leftmost bits are set to zero. That is a logical shift. If you shift a signed value to the right, then on most machines, including Intel's, the sign bit is propagated into the left bits. That is an arithmetic shift. For example:

```
unsigned int i = 0xfe16; /* 1111 1110 0001 0110 */
i >>= 3;
/* i is now 0x3f85 = 0011 1111 1000 0101 */

signed int j = 0xfe16;
j >>= 3;
/* j is now ff85 = 1111 1111 1000 0101 */
```

## Understand the Assignment Operators

Programmers who learn C after having used another programming language are often puzzled by the assignment operators. As an alternative to writing this:

```
n = n + p;   /* add p to n */
```

you can write:

```
n += p; /* add p to n */
```

This applies to the binary operators + – * / % & ^ | << and >>. For example:

```
n *= 3;         /* multiply n by 3 */
n |= FLAGBIT;   /* set the flag bit in n */
n >>= 2;        /* shift n right 2 bits */
```

The assignment operators are concise, and once you understand what they do, they are easier to read than the long form of the expression. This is especially true when the operand is itself an expression. This, for example:

```
Array[x + y] += 4; /* add 4 to the array element */
```

is simpler than:

```
/* add 4 to the array element */
Array[x + y] = Array[x + y] + 4;
```

## The Conditional Expression Is Especially Useful as a Function Argument

The conditional expression is an expression of the form:

*expression* ? *choice1* : *choice2*

If *expression* is true, *choice1* is taken, otherwise *choice2*. The following code assigns the greater of two values:

```
int a = 25;
int b = 49;
int c = a>b ? a : b;
/* c is now 49 */

a = 67;
b = 32;
c = a>b ? a : b;
/* c is now 67 */
```

For ordinary assignments, the conditional expression does not offer much advantage over a traditional **if** statement, and many programmers find the **if** statement easier to read.

```
if ( a > b) c = a;
else c = b;
```

The conditional expression is useful, however, for calling functions. A piece of code like this:

```
if (bUrgent)
  WriteReport(pRecord, pTemplate, HIGH_PRIORITY);
else
  WriteReport(pRecord, pTemplate, LOW_PRIORITY);
```

could be written as:

```
WriteReport(pRecord, pTemplate,
            bUrgent?HIGH_PRIORITY:LOW_PRIORITY);
```

The advantage of the second form is that there is no duplicated code, so if you find that you need to change **pRecord** to **pLastRecord**, you will only need to modify one line of code.

## Beware That the Conditional Expression Has a Low Precedence

The conditional expression ?: has a lower precedence than most other operators, which surprises some programmers. The code:

```
int n;
int Total = n + pInt?*pInt:0;    /* wrong! */
```

is trying to add **n** and the contents of whatever **pInt** is pointing to. If **pInt** is a null pointer, the code should add 0. This code will not work, because the conditional expression will take the expression **n + pInt** and if that is non-zero, it will return just the contents of **pInt**. The code should be written:

```
int n;
int Total = n + (pInt?*pInt:0);    /* right */
```

## Bitwise Operations Have a Lower Precedence Than the Comparison Operators

The arithmetic operators have a higher precedence than comparison operators, so you can write expressions such as:

```
if ( a + b > 0 )
```

without parentheses. If you use a bitwise operator and test the result, you will need parentheses:

```
if ( (a & BIT_MASK) == 0 )
```

## In C, Blocks Are Useful for Localizing Variables Within a Function

One minor annoyance with C, which was removed in C++, is that you must declare local variables at the top of a function. This is a pity, because declaring variables just before they are used makes for a more readable program.

In C, you can also declare variables at the top of inner blocks bounded by parentheses, so you can declare items in the body of **for** loops or **if** statements like this:

```
void test()
{
  int a = 0;
  int b = 0;
  . . .
  while (a--) {
    int d = a;
    . . .
  }
}
```

If you do not have a loop or an **if** statement, you can just start a block and declare a variable in it:

```
void test()
{
  int a = 0;
  int b = 0;
  . . .
  {
    int d = a;
    . . .  /* use d here
  }
  . . .
}
```

# In Nested if Statements, a Dangling else Statement Goes with the Preceding if Statements

In an expression such as this:

```
if (bCatAbsent)
  if (bSmellCheese) FetchCheese();
  else NibbleWainscot();
```

the last **else** statement goes with the immediately preceding **if** statement that does not already have an **else** statement. Here **NibbleWainscot** is executed when **bSmellCheese** is FALSE, not when **bCatAbsent** is FALSE. If you add an extra **else** statement to the code, like this:

```
if (bCatAbsent)
  if (bSmellCheese) FetchCheese();
  else NibbleWainscot();
else Sleep();
```

the only **if** statement that does not already have an **else** is the first one, so the **Sleep** statement is executed when **bCatAbsent** is false.

Many programmers prefer always to use braces to make the code unambiguous, at the cost of spreading the code over twice as many lines.

```
if (bCatAbsent){
  if (bSmellCheese){
    FetchCheese();
  }
  else {
    NibbleWainscot();
  }
}
else {
  Sleep();
}
```

## A switch Statement Is More Efficient Than Nested if - else Statements

A statement that tests a value against different constants like this:

```
if (Condition == RED) {
  . . .
}
else if (Condition == YELLOW) {
  . . .
}
else if (Condition == GREEN) {
  . . .
}
else {
  . . .
}
```

is better written as a **switch** statement:

```
switch (Condition) {
case RED:
  . . .
```

```
  break;
case YELLOW:
  . . .
  break;
case GREEN:
  . . .
  break;
default:
  . . .
  break;
}
```

A **switch** statement only evaluates the expression once, while the **if** statement will evaluate it repeatedly until it finds a match.

## Always Put a break Statement After the Last case Statement in a switch

You do not need a **break** after the last statement in a switch, since control will leave the statement anyway. The reason for putting a **break** after the last statement is to avoid forgetting the **break** when you add another **case** statement at the end of the **switch**.

All but the most simple compilers will optimize out the extra break statement, so there will generally be no overhead associated with it.

## You Can Initialize and Test Variables in a while Loop

You will often see algorithms that look something like this:

```
int Value = GetNextValue();
while (Value != -1 ) {
```

```
  /* body of loop */

  Value = GetNextValue();
}
```

The algorithm sets the first value outside the loop, and gets the next value at the end of the loop. It is always better to avoid duplicating statements, because then if you ever need to change the code you will need to make the change in only one place.

The code will be simpler if it initialized the variable and tested it in the **while** statement, like this:

```
int Value;
while ( (Value = GetNextValue()) != -1 ) {

  /* body of loop */

}
```

Now the code needs call **GetNextValue** only once. As an alternative, you could use the comma operator:

```
int Value;
while ( Value = GetNextValue(), Value != -1 ) {

  /* body of loop */

}
```

Recall that the comma operator executes both expressions, but only returns the result of the right-hand expression.

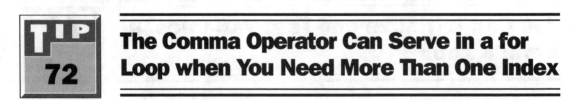

## The Comma Operator Can Serve in a for Loop when You Need More Than One Index

Sometimes you need a **for** loop that can handle more than one loop variable. Here is a loop that processes the first ten elements of a linked list:

```
Element* pElement;
```

```
int i;
for (i=0, pElement=pList;
     i<10 && pElement;
     i++, pElement=pElement->Next)
{
  /* process pElement */
}
```

The loop runs until either ten elements have been processed, or until **pElement** becomes NULL, perhaps because there are no more elements available.

## Do Not Confuse the break and continue Statements

Sometimes you need to abandon a loop prematurely. A **break** statement inside a loop will abort the loop and transfer control to the statement following the loop. A **continue** statement will just abandon the current iteration and let the loop start the next iteration:

```
while ( i < nValue ) {

  /* . . . */

  if (/* condition */ ) continue;

  /* . . . */

  if ( /* condition */ ) break;

  /* continue jumps to here */
  /* ready for next iteration */
}
/* break jumps to here */
```

## You Can Tell Whether a Loop Has Executed a break Statement by Examining the Loop Variable

When a loop ends, prematurely or not, the loop variable is still in scope and you can examine it to see whether a loop containing a **break** statement has ended prematurely:

```
int i:
for (i=0; i<100; i++) {
  . . .
  if ( array[i] == -1 ) break;
  . . .
}
if (i<100) /* ended prematurely */
```

Here the loop may end prematurely if the array contains a certain value. If that happens, the loop variable **i** would not have reached 100.

## The Expressions in a for Loop Initialization Statement Are Optional

You may omit one or all of the three for loop initialization expressions, but you must keep the two semicolons. There are a number of cases where you might wish to omit one of the expressions.

You might have already initialized the loop variable:

```
int i= GetLowerBound();
for (; i<100; i++){  /* i already initialized */

  /* body of loop */

}
```

You might calculate the new value of the counter inside the body, using items declared within the body:

```
for (i=0; i<100; ){
  int a;
  . . .
  /* calculate new i here using a */
  i = a + 1;
}
```

You might want to terminate the loop only when some internal condition arises:

```
for (i=0; ; i++){

  if (/*condition*/) break;
}
```

Finally, you might want to declare an infinite loop, or at least a loop that executes until a statement breaks out of it:

```
for (; ; ){  // infinite loop

  if (/*condition*/) break; // breaks out of loop
}
```

## The Autoincrement Operator ++ Increments the Pointer, Not the Contents of the Pointer

In the code:

```
int array[10];
  . . .
int* pInt = array;
*pInt++;  /* increments pInt, not array[0] */
```

the last statement increments **pInt** to point at **array**[1]. The dereference operator * fetches the contents of **array**[0] but discards them. To increment the contents of the address, put parentheses around the dereference:

```
(*pInt)++;   /* increments array[0], pInt unchanged */
```

A better alternative is to use the prefix autoincrement when incrementing the contents:

```
++*pInt; /* increments array[0], pInt unchanged */
```

The difference arises because unary operators associate right to left.

## It Is Faster to Use an Element Pointer Rather Than a Subscript when Scanning Arrays

You often need to carry out an operation on successive elements of an array, perhaps to search for something. Here is a loop that initializes an array to zero:

```
#define ARRAY_LEN 10

int array[ARRAY_LEN];
int i;

for (i=0; i<ARRAY_LEN; i++) array[i]=0;
```

To find the address of **array**[**i**], the compiler generates code that multiplies the subscript **i** by the size of an array element. A faster alternative would be to use a pointer:

```
#define ARRAY_LEN 10

int array[ARRAY_LEN];
int* pInt;

for (pInt=array; pInt < &array[ARRAY_LEN]; pInt++) *pInt=0;
```

Now the compiler only needs to evaluate a subscript once, when setting up the loop, and so saves nine multiplication operations.

# When Nested Array Pointers Are More Efficient Than Multidimensional Arrays

C provides multidimensional arrays. The compiler implements these as a single block of storage and uses the subscripts to calculate the position of an element within the block. For example:

```
int ChessBoard[8][8];
  . . .
ChessBoard[2][5] = WHITE_BISHOP;
```

The compiler will allocate 64 integers for **ChessBoard**. The program will store the value **WHITE_BISHOP** at the 21st element (2*8+5).

A multidimensional array may be appropriate for a chess board, but for most applications of multidimensional structures, the data space is not rectangular. A typical structure would be an array of names. Since a name is also an array of characters, you could declare a two dimensional array:

```
char Names[500][32]   /*  500 names of up to 31 chars*/
```

but that would limit names to 31 characters. In addition, if most names were less than 32 characters long, the structure would be wasteful of space. An array of pointers would be better:

```
const char* Names[500];  /* 500 names */
Names[0] = "Washington";  /* assign a name */
if (Names[0][3] == 'h');  /* syntax same as for 2-dim array*/
```

Although there is an overhead due to the extra pointer, the structure uses less space overall. When you have initialized the space, you can access it using the same syntax as for multidimensional arrays.

The major drawback with arrays of pointers is that the pointers have to point to things that either exist already, or that you have allocated using **malloc** or **new**. If you allocate something, you will need to deallocate it when you no longer need the structure. If the array is relatively small, you might find it easier to just use a multidimensional array and forget the wasted space, but for large arrays you should consider using pointers.

# TIP 79 Use Function Pointers as Callbacks

A common programming problem is to have an algorithm that is difficult to place in a function because it must perform a slightly different action each time the program uses it. You might, for example, have to traverse a complex structure, such as a tree or a list. Although the algorithm for traversing the structure is fixed, each time that you traverse the structure, you do something different. The first time you may be searching for something, the second time you may be changing items that fit a certain pattern, another time you may want to increment a field in all the items.

The naive solution is to copy the algorithm and change the action, but that will give you a lot of work when you find a bug in the algorithm, or find a more efficient version.

It is better to put the algorithm in a function and have it call back another function that you supply as a parameter. Here is a function that scans a linked list:

```
typedef struct Element{
  Element* pNext;  /* pointer to next in list */
  int Data;
} Element;

/* a function to scan through a linked list */
void ScanList(Element* pElement, BOOL(*pFunction)(Element*))
{
  /* Scan until there are no more elements */
  /* or pFunction returns FALSE */
  while (pElement && pFunction(pElement))
    pElement = pElement->pNext;
}

/* A typical action */
BOOL Increment(Element* pElement)
{
  pElement->Data++;
  return TRUE;
}

void test()
{
  Element List;
  . . . /* Build list here */
```

```
  ScanList(&List, &Increment);  /* increment data in list */
}
```

**ScanList** takes an extra argument **pFunction**, which is a pointer to a callback function. **ScanList** calls this function back for every element in the list until either there are no more elements, or the callback returns FALSE.

The **Increment** function is a typical callback that simply increments the data in an element. This function always returns TRUE, since it has no reason to stop the scan. A callback that searched for an element would return FALSE when it had found the element.

## Use typedefs to Define Function Pointers

One problem with function pointers is that a function pointer definition is not easy to read. For example:

```
BOOL(*pFunction)(Element*)
```

means that **pFunction** is a pointer to a function that takes as an argument a pointer to an **Element** structure, and which returns a Boolean value. To avoid repeating complex declarations such as these, declare a **typedef**, for example:

```
typedef BOOL (*LISTCALLBACK)(Element*);
```

Now you can declare function pointers using the **typedef**, like this:

```
void ScanList(Element* pElement, LISTCALLBACK pFunction)
{
  /* Scan until there are no more elements */
  /* or pFunction returns FALSE */
  while (pElement && pFunction(pElement))
    pElement = pElement->pNext;
}
```

TIP 81

# Understand Complex Declarations

Complex declarations in C, especially if function pointers are involved, can be difficult to read. What does this mean?

```
int (*(*Function(int))[])()
```

or this?

```
long (*(*Array[4])())[7]
```

These declarations are difficult to read because they must be read from the inside out, starting from the identifier name. One way to understand them is to analyze them step by step, replacing parts of the declaration by a word description. To analyze the first declaration proceed as follows:

```
int (*(*Function(int))[])()
```

is a pointer to a function that takes an **int** argument and returns:

```
int (*(*returns)[])()
```

a pointer to:

```
int (*pointerTo[])()
```

an array of pointers:

```
int pArray()
```

to a function returning an **int**.

So the complete specification is a pointer to a function that takes an integer argument and returns a pointer to an array of pointers to functions returning an integer.

The second example:

```
long (*(*Array[4])())[7]
```

is an array of 4 pointers to:

```
long (*ArrayOf())[7]
```

a function returning a pointer to

```
long pointerTo[7]
```

an array of 7 longs.

The complete expression is an array of 4 pointers to functions that return a pointer to an array of 7 items of type long. Try analyzing these declarations:

```
int(*Puzzle1(char[],void(*)(int)))();

int (*(*Puzzle2(int(*)(int)))[])(int[]);
```

## Use a typedef to Declare Structures in C

In ANSI C, if you declare a structure you will have to use the keyword **struct** whenever you use the structure:

```
struct Thing {
   . . .
};

void Function (struct Thing* pThing)
{
  struct Thing MyThing;
   . . .
}
```

To avoid this, declare the structure as a **typedef**, then you do not need to use the **struct** keyword.

```
typedef struct Thing {
   . . .
} THING;

void Function (THING* pThing)
{
  THING MyThing;
```

```
    . . .
}
```

Note that there is no need for this trick in C++. There you can declare the structure without the **typedef** and use it without the **struct** keyword.

## ANSI C Allows Structure Assignment

In ANSI C you can assign structures, pass them as arguments, and return them as function results. In classic C you were only allowed to assign pointers to structures: if you wanted to assign a complete structure, you needed to use a function like **memcpy** that copied blocks of memory.

Many C programmers are unaware of the change, and continue to use **memcpy** even though they have an ANSI compiler.

## Do Not Inadvertently Pass a Structure Argument when You Mean to Pass a Pointer

If you pass an array to a function the compiler will convert it into a pointer to an array. If you pass a structure, the compiled code will copy the entire structure, so that the function works on a copy. This may not be what you want. Copying takes some time, so if you are not going to change the structure in the function, or if you want the function to modify the original structure, you should pass a pointer. Here is a summary of the different forms.

```
typedef struct Enormous {
/* lots of data */
} Enormous;

void AFunc( int Array[200]);
void BFunc( Enormous Data);
void CFunc( Enormous* pData);
```

```
void test()
{
int Array[200];
Enormous Thing;
AFunc(Array);  /* Passes pointer to array */
BFunc(Thing);  /* Copies Thing */
CFunc(&Thing); /* Passes pointer to Thing */
}
```

## If You Want to Assign an Array, Wrap It Up in a Structure

Array arguments to a function are always passed as a pointer whether you declare them as pointers or not. There are times when you would like the function to have a copy of the array, so that it can modify the contents without disturbing the original. At other times you might want to return an array from a function, or assign an array.

In ANSI C, you can do this by wrapping the array in a structure and then assigning or passing the structure containing the array.

```
typedef struct Element{
 int Data[10];   /* structure containing array */
} Element;


void Func(Element anElement)
{
  anElement.Data[0]++;
  . . .
}
```

The function **func** will now receive a copy of the structure containing the array.

## Bit Fields Offer an Alternative to Masks when Storing Flags

As Tip 61 explained, you can store flags in an integer using bit masks and the bitwise operators. An alternative is to use bit fields in a structure. The declaration:

```
typedef struct Facilities {
  unsigned int bHasPool : 1;
  unsigned int bAirCond : 1;
  unsigned int bLift     : 1;
  unsigned int bParking : 1;
} Facilities;
```

declares a structure containing four bit flags. The number 1 indicates the size of the field in bits. The compiler will try to pack the bits into a word, but the C language does not define exactly how it should do so. Indeed, the compiler is not obliged to pack the fields at all, and it could allocate a byte or a word to each field. Most compilers do pack the fields, but you cannot be sure how they will be packed. The fields above might be packed into the least significant bits of a word, or into the most significant bits.

Once you have declared the structure, you can access the bits as if they were ordinary integers, except that they are limited to values of 0 and 1. For example:

```
Facilities aFacility;
  . . .
aFacility.bLift = TRUE;

if (aFacility.bParking || aFacility.bHasPool)
```

## You Can Use Bit Fields for Storing Small Values

If you assign a bit field more than one bit, it can hold small values, for example:

```
typedef struct Facilities {
  unsigned int bHasPool : 1;
  unsigned int bAirCond : 1;
  unsigned int bLift    : 1;
  unsigned int bParking : 1;
  unsigned int nFloors  : 5;
} Facilities;
```

Since **nFloors** is five bits wide, it can hold values up to 31.

You should only consider tricks like this if you are really desperate for space and you have a large array or data structure containing thousands of such values. Accessing bit fields is much slower than accessing natural integers.

## Bit Fields Are Implementation-Dependent

If you define a bit field structure, you have no control over where the compiler places the bits. It could place them in the left half of a word, or in the right half. If there are eight bits or less, the compiler might store them in one byte.

This need not matter if you use the fields for temporary storage while an application is executing, but you should be careful about reading and writing bit field data to external files, and you should avoid unions of bit fields and integers. If you need portability, use bit masks.

## Look Out for Uninitialized Pointers

If your program crashes or causes some sort of system error, you have probably tried to store an item in the address contained in an uninitialized pointer:

```
int* pInt;

*pInt = 13;      /* unlucky for some */
```

This code has not initialized the pointer **pInt** to point at anything valid, so **pInt** could be pointing anywhere in the computer system's memory. The code will overwrite a random memory address with the value 13. This type of error can be difficult to find, because the program may fail quite a long time after it has corrupted the memory.

If your program behaves in an inexplicable way after you have made a modification, first check that you have not inadvertently used an uninitialized pointer.

To avoid this problem, you should always initialize pointers when you declare them:

```
int i;
int* pInt = &i;
```

Notice that this is easier to do in C++ than in C, because in C++ you can declare items in functions just before you use them, while in C you are obliged to declare all items at the head of a function.

If the pointer is not going to be local to a function, and you cannot initialize it to a valid item when you declare it, you should initialize it to the zero value NULL, defined in the standard header file **stddef.h**, then whenever you use the pointer, first check that it is non-zero:

```
/* declare a pointer and initialize it to NULL */
int* pInt = NULL;

 . . .

/* somewhere else in the program, initialize it. */
int UnluckyNumber;
pInt = &UnluckyNumber;

 . . .

/* check that the pointer is valid before using it */
if (pInt) *pInt = 13;
```

# C Does Not Allow You to Add Pointers, but You Can Subtract Them

Adding two pointers together would not normally make sense, but you sometimes would like to do it in an expression. In many search algorithms you need to create a pointer midway between two other pointers:

```
pMiddle = (pFirst + pLast)/2;   /* wrong */
```

Although this might make sense on a machine with a linear address space, in many cases the compiler is unable to add two pointers (for instance, on a segmented architecture), and so the C language forbids it.

To work around this, rearrange the expression so that it performs a subtraction rather than an addition:

```
pMiddle = pFirst + (pLast - pFirst)/2;
```

Now the expression subtracts the pointers to give an integer, and then adds an integer to the pointer **pFirst**, so there is no longer a direct addition of two pointers.

# Understand What Happens When You Add 1 to a Pointer

Pointer arithmetic is a source of many obscure bugs. The important thing to remember is that when you add 1 to a pointer you are actually adding the size of whatever the pointer is pointing at. Consider this code:

```
Record * pCurRecord = &RecordArray[0];
while ( /* some condition */ ) {
   /* process record */
   pCurRecord += sizeof (Record); /* wrong! */
}
```

Here the programmer is attempting to advance the pointer to the next record in the array, but all that is necessary is to increment the pointer:

```
pCurRecord++;
```

The compiler will then add the size of **Record** to the pointer.

A similar problem can arise if you use a pointer of one type to point to data of another type using a cast:

```
int* pGeneralPurpose;
  . . .
pGeneralPurpose = (Record*)&RecordArray[0];
while ( /* some condition */ ) {
   /* process record */
   pGeneralPurpose++; /* wrong! */
}
```

Here the compiler will add the size of an integer to the pointer, so unless **Record** just contains an integer, the pointer will not point to the next record in the array.

## TIP 92 The Null Pointer

C does not ordinarily allow assignment of integers to pointers, but makes an exception for the constant zero. Assigning zero to a pointer initializes it to a value which cannot be a legal pointer. A program can later test a pointer against zero to see whether it contains a legal pointer or not, for example:

```
int* pInt = 0;  // does not point to a legal address

/* . . . */

if (pInt != 0) {
  int i = *pInt;
   // use the pointer if it points to a legal address
}
```

The include file **stdlib.h** defines the macro NULL as 0, so you may use NULL to initialize pointers to a defined non-legal value. NULL is simply a stylistic convention, used because it might not look completely right to assign the constant zero to a pointer. The code above may be rewritten:

```
int* pInt = NULL;  // does not point to a legal address
```

```
/* . . . */

if (pInt != NULL) {
  int i = *pInt;
   // use the pointer if it points to a legal address
}
```

Note that rather than writing:

```
if (pInt != NULL) {
```

you may use the equivalent:

```
if (pInt) {
```

## The Null Pointer Need Not Contain Zeroed Bits

The null pointer will always be declared as the constant 0, but a compiler is not obliged to implement the null pointer as a value with all the bits set to zero. For some machines or compilers the machine address with a value 0x0 may be a valid address, and the compiler would use another value, perhaps 0xffffffff, to indicate a null pointer.

Even if the compiler does this, you still use NULL or 0 to set and test null pointers: the compiler will convert to the actual internal value for a null pointer. There is no need to redefine NULL to be 0xffffffff or whatever, and it would be an error if you did.

You may also continue to use the form:

```
if (pInt) {
```

because this is equivalent to:

```
if (pInt != 0) {
```

## In ANSI C, Use Casts on Void Pointers

ANSI C allows you to assign void pointers directly to pointers of another type, for example:

```
void func(void* pVoid)
{
  int* pInt = pVoid;
  char* pBuf = malloc(60);
}
```

are both legal under ANSI C.

C++ and classic C both require that you cast void pointers explicitly to pointers of other types, and for portability you should do so under ANSI C as well, for example:

```
void func(void* pVoid)
{
  int* pInt = (int*)pVoid;
  char* pBuf = (char*)malloc(60);
}
```

Remember that the **new** operator in C++, which replaces **malloc**, does not need a cast, since it allocates space for a specified type, rather than just a certain number of bytes.

TIP 95

## When to Use Pointers to Pointers

When you pass a pointer to a function, the pointer is passed by value. The function may modify the local pointer to reference something else, but that will not affect the original pointer. If you want to pass the pointer by reference, so that the function modifies the original pointer, you will need to declare the argument as a pointer to a pointer. Use the double asterisk "**" syntax, like this:

```
void NextSpace(char** ppString)
{
  /* skip leading spaces */
  while (**ppString == ' ') ++*ppString;
  /* find next space */
```

```
  while (**ppString != ' ') ++*ppString;
}

void test()
{
  char* pString ="One Two Three";
  NextSpace(&pString);
  printf("%s", pString);
  /* prints " Two Three" */
}
```

As you see, one inconvenience with pointers to pointers is that you need to use double indirection to dereference the pointer, and single indirection to modify the original pointer. Notice also that the expression **++*ppString** increments the contents of **ppString**, the original pointer, while ***ppString++** increments **ppString** itself. This distinction was explained in Tip 76.

You might find things easier if you keep a local pointer inside the function, which you wrote back to the argument before returning, like this:

```
void NextSpace(char** ppString)
{
  /* dereference pointer */
  char* pString = *ppString;

  /* skip leading spaces */
  while (*pString == ' ') pString++;
  /* find next space */
  while (*pString != ' ') pString++;

  /* write back result */
  *ppString = pString;
}
```

# C++ Declarations

# In C++ There Is No Reason for Not Initializing Items While Declaring Them

In C, function-local items had to declared at the top of a block, before the statements. For that reason, they were often difficult to initialize. In C++, items may be declared anywhere within the block. You should declare them just before using them. At that point you will be able to initialize them.

```
void test(int Array[])
{
  int nMax = 0;
  // find largest element
  int* pMax = Array + nMax; // declare and initialize
}
```

# How to Use Default Arguments

In C++ you can give function arguments default values when you declare the function.

```
void ExampleFunc(int a, int b=2, int c=0);
```

When you subsequently call the function, you may omit one or more of the default arguments. The following statements are all legal ways of calling **ExampleFunc**:

```
ExampleFunc(7, 8, 6);
ExampleFunc(7, 8);   // Equivalent to (7, 8, 0)
ExampleFunc(7);      // Equivalent to (7, 2, 0)
```

In this example there is no default for the first argument, so you must always specify it, but the definition could have specified a default for the first argument as well.

Notice that you can only specify defaults for function arguments starting from the rightmost argument and working towards the left. You cannot provide a default for the first argument only, or for an argument in the middle. You do not repeat the defaults when you define the function, you just write the function in the normal way.

Defaults are useful when you are sure that an argument is usually going to have the same value.

## Use Default Arguments to Extend a Function That Is Already Widely Used

Sometimes you will have a function in a library and you will want to add an argument to provide a new facility. If you give the new argument a suitable default value, you will not have to rewrite all the code that uses the function. Here is an old function:

```
// draw a black line;
void DrawLine(POINT& From, POINT& To);
```

and here is the new function, with an extra facility:

```
enum Color{BLACK, RED, GREEN, BLUE};
// draw a colored line;
void DrawLine(POINT& From, POINT& To, Color aColor=BLACK);
```

Since the new argument has the default color black, there is no need to change the old code that calls the function with just two arguments.

## You Can Declare a Loop Variable in a for or while Condition Statement

C++ does not restrict you to declaring items as a statement, so you can declare them within a **for** or **while** loop condition statement.

```
for(int i=0; i<Limit; i++){
  . . .
}

while ((char c = nextchar())!=0){
  . . .
}
```

Doing so means that you can initialize the item when you declare it.

## If You Declare an Item in a for or while Condition Statement, It Will Stay in Scope After the Statement

Because you have not declared the item within the braces of the loop block, the item will still be in scope when the loop terminates. That means that you cannot then use the same item name for another loop in the same scope.

```
for(int i=0; i<Limit; i++){
  // . . .
}

if (i<Limit){  // i still in scope here
  // terminated early
}

for (int i=Bound; i; i--) { // Wrong!
  // . . .
}
```

The second loop is in error here because it redefines **i**. Change the variable name or leave out the **int** definition.

## An Item Declared in a Conditional Statement Cannot Be Accessed Outside That Statement

This has particular relevance to loop initializers. If you write the following conditional statement:

```
if (/*condition*/)
  for (int i=0; i<100; i++){
    if (Array[i] == -1) break;
```

```
  }

if (i<100){ // Error! i not in scope
}
```

you will not be able to access **i** in the next statement, because it was declared within a conditional statement, which might have been false. The code would be correct if both the loop and the next statement were in a block associated with the condition, like this:

```
if (/*condition*/){
  for (int i=0; i<100; i++){
    if (/*Error*/) break;
  }
  if (i<100){ // OK
  }
}
```

## If You Declare Initialized Variables in a Case Statement, You Will Need to Enclose the Case in a Block

C++ does not allow a jump past initialized variables, which means that a **switch** statement like this is in error:

```
switch (ErrorCode){
case DISKFULL:
  int a = 5;   // Error
  . . .
  break;

case NOMEMORY:
  . . .
  break;
}
```

The error occurs because there is a jump past the initialization to the **NOMEMORY** case. Obviously this could be an error if the program used **a** in the **NOMEMORY** case, but C++ forbids it even if the initialized item is just used locally. For the code to be correct, enclose the **case** code in a block.

```
switch (ErrorCode){
case DISKFULL:
  {
    int a = 5;    // OK
    . . .
  }
  break;
case NOMEMORY:
  . . .
  break;
}
```

Note that some compilers allow the jump even though it is incorrect C++, but you should still use the block, otherwise the code will not be portable to other compilers.

## You May Take the Address of a Register Variable in C++

C does not allow you to take the address of a register variable. The reason was that if a variable is stored in a register, it is impossible to take the address. C++ does allow pointers to register variables, and leaves it to the compiler to sort things out. The compiler might keep the item in both a register and a memory location, copying the register to memory whenever the code might use the pointer.

```
register int Item;
int* pItem = &Item;  // allowed in C++ but not in C
```

## The :: Operator Will Uncover a Hidden File Scope Item

File scope items are normally hidden when you use the same name for an item within a function, but you can uncover them with the :: operator.

```
int Item;

void func(int Item)
{
  ::Item=Item;   // Copies argument to file scope
}
```

## The Conditional Operator is Allowed on the Left Side of an Expression

In C++ the result of the conditional operator ?: is an lvalue, provided that the two alternatives are themselves lvalues of the same type. An *lvalue* is an expression to which you can assign a value. The expression to the left of an assignment operator must be an lvalue. Constant values and identifiers are not lvalues and can only appear to the right side of an assignment operator.

This means that you can assign a value to a conditional expression, something that C did not allow.

```
void test(BOOL bChoice)
{
  int a;
  int b;
  . . .
  bChoice?a:b = 1; // assign to either a or b
}
```

Notice that the Boolean part of the expression does not need to be an lvalue, so the following expression is correct:

```
// bDebug is not an lvalue
const BOOL bDebug = TRUE;

int a;
int b;

bDebug?a:b = 1;
```

The following example is incorrect, because **b** is not an lvalue.

```
// bDebug is not an lvalue
const BOOL bDebug = TRUE;

int a;
const int b=0;   // b is not an lvalue

// incorrect
bDebug?a:b = 1;
```

Note that the expression is incorrect even though it would always assign to **a**, which is an lvalue. If either of the two choices in not an lvalue, the conditional expression is not an lvalue either.

## You May Derive Classes from Ordinary C Structures

An ordinary C structure counts as a simple C++ class where all the member items are public. As such you can derive classes from it.

This is a useful way of enhancing C structures that you use in existing C libraries. In the derived class you can add constructors and member functions to simplify usage of the structure in your C++ programs. If you pass an instance of the derived class to a C library, the compiler will pass the original base structure. Here is an example of a typical C structure and library routine:

```
typedef struct tagPoint {
  int x;
  int y;
} POINT;

extern void DrawLine(POINT* pA, POINT* pB);
```

In order to call the routine, a C programmer would write something like this:

```
    POINT aPoint, bPoint;
    aPoint.x = 0;
    aPoint.y = 0;
    bPoint.x = 5;
    bPoint.y = 8;
    DrawLine(&aPoint, &bPoint);
```

A C++ programmer might not want to rewrite the library containing **DrawLine**, but could derive a class from **tagPoint** like this:

```
class Point : public tagPoint {
public:
  Point(){x=0;y=0;}
  Point(int x, int y){Point::x=x; Point::y=y;}
};
```

The class **Point** adds two constructors to the structure. That enables the C++ programmer to call the **DrawLine** routine like this:

```
  extern "C" void DrawLine(POINT* pA, POINT* pB);
  . . .
  Point theOrigin;  // Initialized to zero

  // draw line from origin to (5,8)
  DrawLine(&theOrigin, &Point(5, 8));
```

## Using References as Function Arguments

C++ introduces the reference type. A reference differs from a pointer in that it is an alias for an object rather than a pointer to it.

```
int Item;              // an integer
int& RefItem = Item;   // a reference
int* pItem = &Item;    // a pointer

Item = 3;
Item++;         // both Item and RefItem now 4
RefItem++;      // both Item and RefItem now 5
++*pItem;       // both Item and RefItem now 6
```

Although a reference is syntactically equivalent to an alias, internally the compiler will implement it as a pointer, so that the code generated for the last two statements in the listing above will be quite similar.

The main use for references is for function arguments and return types. If you declare a function argument to be a reference, the compiler will call by reference instead of by value. You can accomplish the same result with a pointer, but then you would need to dereference the pointer every time that you wanted the value.

```
void func ( int& a)
{
  if ( a>0) a++;
}

void test()
{
  int Item = 4;
  func(Item);   /* Item is now 5 */
}
```

This is neater than using pointers the way one does in a C program:

```
void func (int* pa)
{
  if (*pa > 0) (*pa)++;
}

void test()
{
  int Item = 4;
  func(&Item);   /* Item is now 5 */
}
```

The reference is also useful for large structures. If a function declares a structure argument as call-by-value, the compiler will generate code to copy the entire structure. With a reference, the compiler will just pass the address of the structure.

TIP 108

## Using References as Return Types

Declaring a function return type as a reference gives you all the advantages of reference arguments, but in addition, it allows you to use the function on the left side of expressions. Here is some code that sets the largest element of an array back to zero:

C/C+

```
// FindMax returns reference to largest element
int& FindMax (int Array[], int ArraySize)
{
  int nMax=0;

  for (int i=0; i<ArraySize; i++){
    if (Array[i] > Array[nMax]) nMax = i;
  }

  return Array[nMax];
}

void test()
{
  int Item[10] ;
  . . .
  FindMax(Item,10) = 0; // set largest to 0
}
```

# Dealing with Error Conditions in Functions That Return References

A function that returns a reference may encounter an error condition that prevents it from returning a valid reference. For example, in the last tip, there is an error condition if the size of the array is zero. A function that returns a pointer would return a null pointer and expect the caller to check that the result is not null. If the caller omits the check and uses the null pointer, this will cause a system error.

A function that returns a reference can return a reference to a dummy value. The caller can then check that the result is not the dummy value; however, if the caller omits the check and uses the reference anyway, there is little harm done, because the reference is a valid item.

```
static int ErrorInt;

int& FindMax (int Array[], int ArraySize)
{
  if (!ArraySize){
     ErrorInt = 0;
     return ErrorInt;     // error
```

```
  }

  int nMax=0;
  for (int i=0; i<ArraySize; i++){
    if (Array[i] > Array[nMax]) nMax = i;
  }

  return Array[nMax];
}

void test()
{
  // Declare an empty array
  int Item[0];
  int ItemSize = 0;
  . . .
  FindMax(Item,ItemSize) = 0; // no check, but no harm done

  // check that the return value is valid
  int& MaxInt = FindMax(Item,ItemSize);
  if (&MaxInt != &ErrorInt){  // Check result
     MaxInt = 0;
  }
}
```

The function test calls **FindMax** with an empty array, and so **FindMax** will treat that as an error. The first call to **FindMax** does not check the result, but simply stores a value to it. Since the result is **ErrorInt**, there is no harm in writing to it. The second call checks that the address of the reference returned is not that of **ErrorInt**, and uses the result only in the case that it is not.

## TIP 110 When to Use Inline Functions

If a function is declared inline, the compiled code will not actually call the function. Instead, the compiler will insert the code for the body of the function inline at the place where it is called. An inline function avoids the overhead of a function call, and may allow the compiler to better optimize the code that calls the function, and to make better use of the machine registers.

Even so, you should only consider using inlining for very small functions consisting of one or two statements. If you use inlining for larger functions, the compiler will generate a lot of code whenever

the function is called. On virtual memory operating systems the extra time spent swapping the larger code sections in and out of memory could exceed the time saved on the function calls.

## Functions Defined in a Class Specification Are Automatically Inline

If you define a function member in a class specification instead of merely declaring it, that is, you add the function body to the definition, then the body is automatically inline. For example:

```
class Example {
  int a;
  int GetA(){return a;}   // inline
};
```

Remember that the inline property is only a hint to the compiler. While it will be rare to find a compiler that does not inline simple functions, many will refuse to inline large complex functions, especially if they contain loops. The overhead of calling a function containing a loop is likely to be minuscule in comparison to the time spent executing the loop.

## Use Inline Functions to Give Access to Private Members

In general, when designing a new class, you should make member objects private, and provide public functions to access the data.

```
class Window {
public:      // functions to access attributes
  unsigned GetWidth(){return Width;}
  unsigned GetHeight(){return Height;}
  BOOL IsOpen(){return bIsOpen;}

private:  // attributes
  unsigned Height;
```

```
  unsigned Width;
  BOOL bIsOpen;
};
```

The compiler will optimize these inline functions so that they are just as efficient as accessing the data directly. Protecting the data in this way prevents other classes from accidentally modifying the data. The system will be more robust, and if the items ever contain incorrect values, you can be sure that it is caused by a bug in the class that owns the values.

## Hiding Class Data Gives You the Freedom to Change Your Implementation

The previous tip showed how to use inline functions to give access to internal data. If you do this, you will have more freedom to change the class implementation without having to modify any code that uses the class. For example, you might start with a class like this:

```
class Window {
public:      // functions to access attributes
  unsigned GetWidth(){return Width;}
  void SetWidth(unsigned NewWidth){Width = NewWidth;}

  unsigned GetHeight(){return Height;}
  void SetHeight(unsigned NewHeight){Height = NewHeight;}

  BOOL IsOpen(){return bIsOpen;}

private:  // Attributes
  unsigned Height;  // in cms
  unsigned Width;   // in cms
  BOOL bIsOpen;
};
```

Later on you might decide that measurements in centimeters are too coarse, and that you would like to store the measurements in tenths of a millimeter. In addition, you would like to provide an interface for inches as well as metric measures. You are free to change the implementation:

```
class Window {
public:       // functions to access attributes
  enum Scale{TENMM = 1, MM = 10, CM = 100, INCH = 254};
  unsigned GetWidth(Scale aScale=CM)
    {return Width/aScale;}
  void SetWidth(unsigned NewWidth,Scale aScale=CM)
    {Width = NewWidth*aScale;}

  unsigned GetHeight(Scale aScale=CM)
    {return Height/aScale;}
  void SetHeight(unsigned NewHeight, Scale aScale=CM)
    {Height = NewHeight*aScale;}

  BOOL IsOpen(){return bIsOpen;}

private:  // attributes
  unsigned Height;  // in 1/10 mm
  unsigned Width;   // in 1/10 mm
  BOOL bIsOpen;
};

void test()
{
  Window aWindow;
  // code for centimeters same as before
  aWindow.SetWidth(23);
  aWindow.SetHeight(45);

  // now get a value in inches
  int xInch = aWindow.GetWidth(Window::INCH);
}
```

The class scales all the measurement to and from the internal value, but in spite of that, any existing code that relied on the value being in centimeters will work as before without change, although it will have to be recompiled.

# A Reference Type Member Function Will Give Read and Write Access to an Item

You can give both read and write access to a member by declaring a reference type function that returns it. For example:

```
class Window {
public:     // functions to access attributes
  unsigned& Width(){        // can do a check before
    if (!bIsOpen) Error(); // returning reference
    return nWidth;}

  unsigned& Height(){
    if (!bIsOpen) Error();
    return nHeight;}

  BOOL& IsOpen(){return bIsOpen;}

private:  // attributes
  unsigned nHeight;
  unsigned nWidth;
  BOOL bIsOpen;
};

void test()
{
  Window aWindow;
  // can use the function on both sides of an expression
  aWindow.Width() = 23;
  aWindow.Height() = 45;
  int x = aWindow.Width();
}
```

A reference can be used as an lvalue, and therefore it can appear on the left-hand side of an expression. If necessary, you can add a check in the function to ensure that the value is valid, but you cannot apply any arithmetic operations on the value before returning it.

Notice that giving a reference to private data is practically equivalent to making the data public. This trick is most useful for classes that are used by a large body of existing code. If you are designing new classes, you should avoid providing references or pointers to private data.

## How to Access a Protected Member in a Library Class

Often while using a commercial class library you will find that you need access to a protected member object. Even if you have the source, you will not want to change it, because that will cause all sorts of maintenance problems. The thing to do is to derive a class from the library class and provide a member function to give access to the item. Imagine that you have a library class defined like this:

```
class LibraryClass {
public:
  . . .
protected:
  int Alpha;
  int Beta;
  int Gamma;
};
```

For some special purpose, you need access to **Gamma**, so you derive a class from **LibraryClass** like this:

```
class MyClass: public LibraryClass {
public:
   int& Gamma(){return LibraryClass::Gamma;}
};
```

The public function **Gamma** now gives access to the item. You use the class like this:

```
MyClass aClass;
int x = aClass.Gamma();
```

TIP 116

# When to Use Virtual Functions

If you have a class that contains a member function, you may derive a class that redefines the function. The redefinition must have the same name and argument specifications. Here is an example of a function redefinition:

```
class Shape {
public:
  void Draw(){Error();};   // cannot draw anything
};

class Circle : public Shape {
public:
  void Draw();  // draws the circle
};

class Rectangle : public Shape {
public:
  void Draw();  // draws the square
};
```

The base class **Shape** has a **Draw** member function, but the **Shape** class does not have enough information to draw anything—only derived classes can do that. The two derived classes redefine **Draw** so that it will draw an actual shape. A program can then create instances and draw them.

```
Circle aCircle;
Rectangle aRect;
. . .
aCircle.Draw();   // draw the circle
aRect.Draw();     // draw the rectangle
```

So far so good, but now imagine that the program has an array of shapes, and that it wants to put the shapes into the array and then draw them later in one go. The program could do this:

```
// array of pointers to shapes
Shape* pShapes[10];
int nShape = 0;

// put shapes in the array
Circle aCircle;
```

```
pShapes[nShape++] = &aCircle;
Rectangle aRect;
pShapes[nShape++] = &aRect;
// more shapes

// draw all the shapes
for (int i=0; i<nShape; i++)
  pShapes[i]->Draw();    // Error!
```

When the program tries to draw the shapes, it causes an error. Even though the program has correctly placed drawable circles and rectangles in the array, the final loop only knows about shapes in general. The loop calls the **Draw** function in the **Shape** class, which gives an error.

To avoid this problem, the **Shape** class must declare the **Draw** function as virtual:

```
virtual void Draw(){Error();};  // Cannot draw anything
```

Now when the loop calls the **Draw** function, the code will call the **Draw** function in the derived class, **Circle** or **Rectangle**, and not the **Draw** function in **Shape**.

You should use virtual member functions when you have a number of different classes derived from a base class, and when you need to group instances of these classes together. You can then refer to the objects as being instances of the base class, and let the virtual functions redirect calls to the correct derived class.

## Do Not Declare Functions to be Virtual Unless That Is Really Necessary

Virtual functions may be useful, but you should avoid declaring all class member functions as virtual, just in case a derived class might need to redefine one of them.

To implement virtual functions, the compiler places a pointer to a virtual function look-up table, known as a v-table, which is in every instance derived from the base class. The table contains pointers to the correct function.

If a class declares just one virtual function, then instances of the class and all derived classes will each carry the overhead of the v-table pointer, usually two or four bytes. Moreover, the compiled code must call the virtual functions indirectly, and will need to execute three or four extra instructions. Finally, the compiler cannot put virtual functions inline.

The compiler needs only one v-table for each class, but some compilers insert a copy of the v-table in each module that uses the corresponding class.

## There is No Need to Use the Virtual Specifier for Virtual Functions in Derived Classes

Once you have declared a function to be virtual in a base class, it will remain virtual in derived classes. Some programmers like to add the virtual specifier in the derived classes, to indicate that the function is indeed virtual, but this does not have any other effect:

```
class Shape {
public:
  virtual void Draw(){   // declares Draw as virtual
    Error();
  };
};

class Circle : public Shape {
public:
  virtual void Draw();  // the virtual keyword
                        // is optional here
};
```

Most of the examples in this book omit the virtual specifier in derived classes, which means that the presence of the virtual specifier generally indicates the topmost function in the class hierarchy.

# A Common Error When Using Virtual Functions Is to Change Argument Types in Only Certain Classes

Virtual functions only work if the arguments and the return type match exactly. Most programmers know that, but a common error is to change the type of an argument, or the return type, and then to forget to change the function in all derived classes. This is easy to do when the classes are defined in different modules. You might have a class hierarchy like this:

```
class Base {
  virtual void f(int nIndex, char* pTitle);
  . . .
};

class DerivedA : public Base {
  void f(int nIndex, char* pTitle);
  . . .
};

class DerivedB : public Base {
  void f(int nIndex, char* pTitle);
  . . .
};

class DerivedC : public Base {
  void f(int nIndex, char* pTitle);
  . . .
};
```

where each class is declared in its own header file. Everything works as it should, but later you realize that you should have declared **nIndex** as unsigned. You go back and change classes **Base**, **DerivedA**, and **DerivedB**, but forget to change class **DerivedC**. Most compilers will issue a warning, but this is easy to overlook when you are rebuilding the system.

The result is that function **f** in class **DerivedC** will no longer be virtual.

## Using Abstract Classes with Pure Virtual Functions

The example in Tip 116 had a base class **Shape**, but the application could only create instances of subclasses. If your application tried to call the function declared in **Shape**, it would generate an error message at run time.

An alternative would be to make the virtual function in the base class a pure virtual function. When a program calls a pure virtual function from outside the class, the call will always pass down to a virtual function in a derived class.

If any function in a base class is a pure virtual function, the base class is an abstract class. That means that you may derive classes from the abstract class and create instances of these derived classes, but you may not create an instance of the base class itself. If you accidentally try to create an instance of the base class, you will get a compiler error, which is preferable to the run-time error that you get in the previous example.

To declare a pure virtual function, add the specifier = **0** to the function declaration:

```
class Base {  // base is now abstract
  // pure virtual function
  virtual void f(int nIndex, char * pTitle) = 0;
  . . .
};
```

Remember that the class becomes abstract when it contains at least one pure virtual function. There is no abstract specifier.

## A Pure Virtual Function May be Defined

You may define a body for a pure virtual function:

```
class Base {  // base is abstract
  // pure virtual function
```

```
  virtual void f(int nIndex, char* pTitle) = 0;
  . . .
};

void Base::f(int nIndex, char* pTitle)
{
  // Do something here
}
```

But what use is that? The whole point of having the pure virtual function was to ensure that calls are passed down to derived classes.

Although you may not call a pure virtual function from outside the class, it is often useful to call them from inside the class or from a derived class. In particular, the pure virtual function may contain some general processing that the derived classes can use, for example:

```
class Derived : public Base {
  void f(int nIndex, char* pTitle);
};

void Derived::f(int nIndex, char* pTitle)
{
  // class specific actions
  SetupTable(DerivedValues);
  if (!pTitle) pTitle = "Derived Title");

  // call base function to do general processing
  Base::f(nIndex, pTitle);
}
```

## You Must Redefine All Pure Virtual Functions in a Derived Class, Otherwise the Derived Class Is Also Abstract

Before a derived class becomes non-abstract, it must ensure that none of the pure virtual functions declared in any of its base classes remain undefined.

```
class Base {  // base is abstract
  virtual void a() = 0;
  virtual void b() = 0;
  virtual void c() = 0;
}

class Derived : public Base {
  void a();
  void b();
};
```

The **Derived** class is also abstract, because it inherits the pure virtual function **c** from **Base**.

## The Compiler Will Give an Error If a Pure Virtual Function is Incorrectly Derived

Tip 119 showed how easy it is to incorrectly specify an argument in a derived virtual function. If the base virtual function is pure, you can still make the mistake, but then the derived class will be abstract, since it has not properly redefined the pure virtual function. Since it is abstract, the compiler will give you an error when you try to create an instance of the derived class.

If you see an error saying that you cannot create an instance of an abstract class, and you did not think that the class was abstract, it is probably because you have incorrectly redefined a pure virtual function.

```
class Base {  // base is abstract
  virtual void a() = 0;
  virtual void b() = 0;
  virtual void c(int) = 0;
}

class Derived : public Base {
  void a();
  void b();
  void c();  // c is incorrectly derived
};

Derived aDerived;  // error, Derived is abstract!
```

In this example, **Derived** is still abstract: although it has defined a function **void c( )**, it has not redefined the pure virtual function **void c(int)**.

## How to Avoid Warnings When You Do Not Use All the Arguments in a Virtual Function

If you use virtual functions in a derived class, it often happens that you do not need all of the function arguments. You must still specify them, because the argument types in a virtual function must match the definition in the base class.

The compiler will issue a warning saying that the argument was declared but not used in the virtual function. This is benign, but if there are many such warnings, you are likely to miss a more serious warning hidden among them. The way to avoid the warning is to simply omit the argument name in the function definition. This is not allowed in ANSI C, but it is allowed in C++.

```
class Base {
  virtual void f(int nIndex, char* pTitle);
}

class DerivedC : public Base {
  void f(int nIndex, char* pTitle);
  . . .
};

void DerivedC::f(int, char* pTitle) // don't need nIndex
{
   SetTitle(pTitle);
}
```

You may also do this with ordinary functions when you do not use an argument, perhaps because you have reserved it for future use, or because you have not completely implemented a function.

```
void ReadFile( char* pFileName, unsigned /*OpenMode*/){
  // OpenMode not yet implemented

  // . . .
}
```

The person developing the **ReadFile** routine has commented out the name of the **OpenMode** argument while the function does not use it.

## A Base Class Should Have a Virtual Destructor

The destructor in a base class should be virtual, since otherwise there is a risk that the destructor in a derived class might not be called. That would typically result in the derived class not releasing resources.

You should declare a virtual destructor in the base class even if the base class itself does not need one. In that case, you declare an empty function:

```
class Base {
  . . .
  virtual ~Base(){}; // virtual destructor
  . . .
};
```

## A Base Class Can Omit a Virtual Destructor When None of the Derived Classes Will Have a Destructor

Declaring the destructor virtual will mean that all instances will carry a pointer to the v-table virtual function table. You might omit the virtual destructor when you are sure that none of the derived classes will have a destructor.

If you are creating a public class library, you can never be sure that someone will not derive a class with a destructor. For this reason you should make the base class destructor virtual. When you have a private class hierarchy that you have designed for a certain application, you might well be sure that there will

never be any other derived classes, and in that case you can declare the base class destructor non-virtual. Such class hierarchies will typically be shallow—perhaps only two classes deep.

Notice that you will only save the overhead of the v-table pointer if the classes do not have any other virtual functions.

## Understanding Member Pointers

TIP 127

C++ allows pointers to members in structures and classes. An ordinary pointer can point to a certain member in one instance of a class, but a member pointer points to a certain member in any instance of the class. To dereference a member pointer, you have to specify which instance of the class you want to use, and the pointer will return the member from that instance of the class.

```
class TestClass {
public:
  int a;
  int b;
  int c;
};

void test()
{
  // a pointer to an int member of TestClass
  int TestClass::*pInt = &TestClass::b;

  TestClass aClass;

  // return the int pointed to in aClass
  int x = aClass.*pInt;
}
```

The preceding code assigns the member **b** in **TestClass** to the member pointer **pInt**. The pointer does not point to an actual integer in any particular instance, it just refers to member **b**. The last statement applies the member pointer **pInt** to an instance **aClass** of **TestClass**. The statement will assign **aClass.b** to **x**. The syntax may look strange, but it is logical, because ***pInt** returns **b**.

# How to Use Pointers to Member Functions

The major use of member pointers is to point to member functions. You cannot simply assign the address of a member function in an instance to a function pointer like this:

```
class TestClass {
public:
  int a;
  int b;
  int c;
  void funcA(int);
  void funcB(int);
  void funcC(int);
};

void test()
{
  TestClass aClass;
  void (*pFunc)(int) = &aClass.funcB;   // Wrong!!
}
```

Here, **pFunc** is a pointer to a static function, and you cannot assign the address of a member function to it. When the program calls a static function through **pFunc**, the compiler will generate code to call a function at that address. When the compiler calls a class member function, it passes the function the address of the class instance, and if the function is virtual, the compiled code must also look up the address in a virtual function table.

Because of these differences in calling conventions, the compiler will only let you assign static functions to static function pointers.

You are allowed to assign a member function to a member pointer, because when you call the function through a member pointer, the compiler will know what type of function it is, and generate the correct code to call the function. You assign a member function pointer like this:

```
  void(TestClass::*pFunc)(int) = &TestClass::funcB;
```

**pFunc** is now a pointer to a function **funcB** in **TestClass.** To call it, you need to supply an instance.

```
TestClass aClass;
TestClass* pClass = &aClass;

// two ways of calling a member function
(aClass.*pFunc)(4);
(pClass->*pFunc)(4);
```

Both of these statements will call the function within **aClass** pointed to by **pFunc**, in this case **FuncB**. You need the parenthesis, because the argument operator (4) has a higher precedence than the ., -> and * operators.

## Implementing Callbacks to Non-Static Member Functions

As mentioned in the last tip, C++ does not directly support pointers to non-static member functions. Nevertheless, it is possible to call a non-static member function given pointers to both the function and the instance. The main problem here is type checking.

Imagine that you have a windowing system. There may be a **Button** class, and you would like to have an instance of **Button** call a member function when it is clicked. The function could be a member of any class, perhaps a **Window** class, or a **PopUpBox** class. The **Button** class might look something like this:

```
class Button {
public:

  // constructor and other functions here

  void Initialize(/*pointer to Member function*/);
private:
  // pointer to member function here
  void Click(){/* call member function*/}
};
```

You will have to assume that there is some link between the system and the actual button, so that when the button is clicked, the function **Click** in that instance of the button is called. The **Window** class might look like this:

```
class MyWindow : public Window{
public:
  Button OK;
  Window(){
    B.Initialize(/*pointer to OKClicked*/);
  }
  void OKClicked();
};
```

This class, derived from **Window**, initializes the button with a pointer to the function **OKClicked**, so that later on, when the button is clicked, the button should call back **OKClicked** in the instance of **MyWindow** that initialized the button.

So far so good, but how to implement the function pointers? Since it is possible to call a member function given a pointer to both the instance and the function, you could implement the **Button** class like this:

```
class Button {
public:

  // constructor and other functions here

  void Initialize(Window* pInstance, void (Window::*pFunc){
    // store call back member function and instance
    Button::pInstance = pInstance;
    Button::pFunc = pFunc;
  }

private:
  // instance and function for call back
  Window* pInstance;
  void(Window::*pFunc)();

  void Click(){
     // call the call back member function
    (pInstance->*pFunc)();
  }
};
```

The **Button** class stores pointers to both the instance and the function so that it can call the function back. Now you try to write the **MyWindow** class:

```
class MyWindow : public Window{
```

```
public:
  Button OK;
  MyWindow(){    // Wrong!
    B.Initialize(this, &MyWindow::OKClicked);
  }
  void OKClicked();
};
```

The class tries to initialize the button with a pointer to itself, and its function. The compiler objects (or at least it should, some compilers accept this), saying that it cannot convert type **void**(**MyWindow**::*)( ) to type **void(Window::*)( )**. Although the class **MyWindow** is a type of **Window**, that relation does not apply to the member functions.

One solution is to cast the function pointer to make it of type **void(Window::*)( )**. You could declare a typedef to do this, and place it in the header file for the button class.

```
typedef void(Window::*BUTTONCALLBACK)();
```

With this typedef, the **MyWindow** constructor would look like this:

```
MyWindow(){    // OK
  B.Initialize(this,
      (BUTTONCALLBACK)&MyWindow::OKClicked);
}
```

This will work with all classes derived from the **Window** class, provided that the classes are not virtual classes.

If your compiler supports templates, the next tip shows a cleaner way of implementing member function pointers.

## Using Templates to Implement Member Function Pointers

The last tip showed a way of implementing member function pointers. The implementation relied on a cast, and would only work in a well ordered class hierarchy, such as a windowing system. A more general way of implementing member pointers is to use a member pointer template class. The class is defined like this:

```
class MemberFunction{
public:
  virtual void Call() = 0;
};

template<class Type> class Callback : public MemberFunction {
public:
  Callback(Type* pInstance, void (Type::*pFunc)())
    :pInstance(pInstance),pFunc(pFunc){};
  void Call(){(pInstance->*pFunc)();}

private:
  Type* pInstance;
  void(Type::*pFunc)();
};
```

The callback class stores the two pointers, and the function **Call** will call the member function stored in the pointer. The template is derived from the virtual base class **MemberFunction**, so that classes that provide a callback service can declare pointers to **MemberFunction** like this:

```
class Button {
public:
  void Initialize(MemberFunction& MF){pMF = &MF;};
  void Click(){pMF->Call();}

private:
  MemberFunction* pMF;
};
```

The **Button** class is no longer concerned with the type of the callback function: it lets the virtual **Call** function take care of everything. Another class may declare a callback like this:

```
class MyWindow {
public:
  // constructor sets callback
  MyWindow():cbOK(this,&MyWindow::OKClicked){}

  // initialize button
  Initialize{
    OK.Initialize(cbOK);
  }

private:
```

```
  Callback<MyWindow> cbOK;
  Button OK;
  void OKClicked();
};
```

The class declares instances of both a **Callback** and a **Button**. It initializes the **Callback** instance **cbOK** in the constructor, to point to a member function **OKClicked**, and it passes the **Callback** instance to the button during initialization.

It is important that the callback and the class using it have the same lifetime, and that is the case if the two instances are declared as members of another class, as in the previous example. You must avoid writing the following:

```
  // initialize button
  Initialize{
    OK.Initialize(
       Callback<MyWindow>(this,&MyWindow::OKClicked));
  }
```

because this will create a temporary instance of **Callback** which will be destroyed before the other (**Button**) class has a chance to use it.

## Declaring Static Class Members

When you declare a static class data member, you must also define the static member somewhere:

```
class Example {
int a;    // non static members
int b;
int c;

static int s;  // static members declared here
static Example* pExample;
};


// static member definition
int Example::s;
Example* Example::pExample;
```

When you define the static members, you omit the **static** keyword, but you add the class name just before the member name. As with other static data, static class data is initialized to zero by default.

## Do Not Put the Static Data Definition in the Header File

Static class data should only be defined once in the system. Do not define it in a header file or it will be defined by every module that includes that header file.

You would normally find the definition of static data at the head of the **.cpp** file that implements the class.

## Static Member Functions May Access Only Static Data

When you declare a static class member function, that function may only access the static class data. This is true even if there is an instance of the class. If you call a static function in a class instance, that function still has access only to static data.

Non-static functions have access to both non-static instance data and static data.

## Using a Static Pointer to Identify the Active Instance

Frequently, when a system contains a number of instances of some class, there is one instance that has some special status. In a graphical user interface, for instance, there is usually one window that is the active window, and it receives all the user events.

It is useful to use a static data member to point to this active instance. That enables the application to get a pointer to the instance. Here is an example:

```
class Window {
public:
  // static function to return active instance
  static Window* GetActive(){return pActive;}

  // called by the system when an instance
  // becomes active
  void OnActivate()
  { pActive = this;}

private:
  // static pointer to active instance
  static Window* pActive;
};


Window* Window::pActive;

void Func()
{
  // get a pointer to the active instance
  Window* pActive = Window::GetActive();
}
```

You have to imagine here that the system calls the function **OnActivate** when a certain window becomes active. The **OnActivate** function sets the static data member to point to itself. After that, whenever the application wishes to have a pointer to the active window, it calls the static member function **GetActive**, which returns the static pointer.

Notice that the static function **GetActive** is simply there to provide access to the private static data member **pActive**, since it is considered bad form to make data members public.

## Using an All Static Class to Group Functions

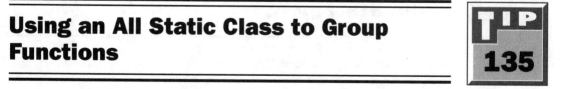

It is possible to have a class where all the members are static. This would usually be a class of which it would not be logical to have more than one instance in a system.

It is also possible to use static member classes to group functions together, as in this error reporting class:

```
class Errors {
public:
  enum ErrorMessages {
    NoMemory,
    NoDiskSpace,
    PrinterNotReady
  };
  static void CriticalStop(int MessageNumber);
  static void Error(int MessageNumber);
  static void Warning(int MessageNumber);
};

void Func()
{
  Errors::Error(Errors::NoMemory);
}
```

Notice, by the way, that it is still possible to create an instance of this static class, although there is little point in doing so.

```
  Errors X;
  X.Error(Errors::NoMemory);
```

If you try this, the compiler may warn that the instance X is not referenced, because accessing a static member does not count as a reference.

## const Items May Replace #define or enum Statements

In C++, **const** items are internal by default, while in C they are external by default. If **const** items have internal linkage, the compiler does not need to allocate any space for them, it can just assign the constant value directly, as it does for ordinary constants. If the item has external linkage, the compiler is obliged to allocate space for the object and initialize it, since another module may refer to it.

As a result, in C++ you can use **const** items instead of **#define** statements. There will be no overhead, and the type of constant will be clear from the declaration. You can write, for instance:

```
const unsigned MaxLimit = 45000;
const char Bell = 7;
```

instead of:

```
#define MAXLIMIT 45000
#define BELL 7
```

You will still find the **enum** statement useful when you need a list of sequentially numbered constants.

## How to Declare the Size of an Array in a Class

If a class contains an array member, it is useful to use an identifier for the size of the array. You could use a **#define** statement as in traditional C programming, but the **#define** statement is in scope for the rest of the compilation, so you could have problems if you used the same name in a another class. You would like to write something like the following:

```
class TestClass {
public:
  int a;
  int b;
  const int ArraySize = 30;   // Wrong !!
  int vector[ArraySize];
  void func(int);
};
```

This would be neat if it worked, since **ArraySize** would have the same scope as the array. Unfortunately, C++ requires that class members be initialized in a constructor, and if you do that, you cannot use the item as the size of the array.

An alternative is to use an anonymous enumerator containing the item, like this:

```
class TestClass {
public:
```

```
    int a;
    int b;
    enum {ArraySize = 30};
    int vector[ArraySize];
    void func(int);
};
```

This is correct, and the scope of **ArraySize** is still limited to that of the class, so you can use the name in another class for a different sized array.

# TIP 138 How to Call C Functions from a C++ Program

All C++ programmers will have libraries of useful C functions that they would like to call from a C++ program. You cannot just declare the function and call it, because the compiled code to call a C function is different from the code to call a C++ function. If you just declare an external function, a C++ compiler will assume that it is a C++ function. The compilation will succeed, but you will see some odd errors when you link the application.

The solution is to specify the linkage as "C" when you declare the function, like this:

```
// C function
extern "C" void DrawLine(POINT* pFrom, POINT* pTo);
```

If you have several external functions, you may declare them all as having "C" linkage in one go by enclosing them in braces, like this:

```
extern "C" {
  void DrawLine(POINT* pFrom, POINT* pTo);
  POINT GetPosition();
  void SetPosition(POINT* pNew);
}
```

Of course, definitions such as these will usually be grouped into a header file, but you can just declare everything within the header file as having "C" linkage, like this:

```
extern "C" {
  // headers for some C libraries
```

```
  #include "draw.h"
  #include "printer.h"
}
```

## How to Make Header Files Portable Between C and C++

The previous tip explained how to use the "C" linkage definition when including C function definitions in a C++ module. An alternative would be to place the **extern "C"** statement in the header file, so that it enclosed all the definitions in the file. That would allow a C++ module to include the file and use the functions defined there without any further concerns about linkage.

The problem is that a plain C compiler will not accept the **extern "C"** statement. To get around this, place the statement in a **#define** statement so that the header file looks like this:

```
#ifdef __cplusplus
  extern "C" {
#endif

/* body of header file */

#ifdef __cplusplus
  }
#endif
```

The C++ language states that a C++ compiler must define the macro **__cplusplus**. If the header file is compiled by a C++ compiler, the function will have "C" linkage, while if it is compiled by a C compiler, the compiler will not see the **extern "C"** statement, and so will not give an error.

When a header file is modified in this way, C++ modules do not need to use the **extern "C"** statement when including them, although it does not matter if they do anyway.

# Creating and Destroying C++ Instances

# TIP 140 How Using new and delete Can Cause Memory Leaks

The **new** and **delete** operators are undoubtedly useful, but have the drawback that it is easy to forget to delete something that was previously allocated with **new**, leaving an *orphaned* memory block—a block that is still allocated but which has nothing referencing it.

The problem of orphaned memory can become quite acute in applications that run for some time, because whenever the user uses a certain function, a small amount of memory may disappear, and eventually the amount of memory consumed has an adverse effect on the system. This situation is known as a *memory* leak.

Finding the causes of these memory leaks can take some time in the later stages of a project. There are many possible causes of memory leaks, but the most common are these:

- Simply forgetting to delete something that has been allocated.
- Failing to notice that code may bypass a **delete** statement under certain circumstances.
- Assigning the result of a **new** statement to a pointer that was already pointing to an allocated object.

The following tips show ways of avoiding these problems.

# TIP 141 C++ Lets You Delete Null Pointers

C++ allows you to delete a null pointer. Nothing will happen, but you are saved the trouble of checking whether the pointer contains something valid. Instead of writing this:

```
class Example {
public:
   Example(){pInFile = NULL;}
   ~Example(){if (pInFile) delete pInFile;}
   // other functions

private:
```

```
  ifstream* pInFile;
};
```

you need only write this:

```
class Example {
public:
  Example(){pInFile = NULL;}

  // delete pInFile unless it is null
  ~Example(){delete pInFile;}
  // other functions that might initialize
  // pInFile

private:
  ifstream* pInFile;
};
```

The **Example** destructor can delete just **pInFile**. If **pInFile** is null nothing will happen, but if another member function in **Example** has assigned **pInFile** to an instance allocated with **new**, the destructor will free that instance.

# When You Use Pointers in a Class, Initialize Them to Null in the Constructor and Delete Them in the Destructor

A common cause of memory leaks is a class that calls **new** to initialize a pointer member and then forgets to delete the memory in its destructor. If you declare a class that contains pointers, you must also initialize the pointers in the class constructor and delete the contents in the destructor.

When you initialize the pointer, you may either initialize it directly using **new**, or if the pointer is optional, then initialize it to null. A typical class containing pointers should look like this:

```
class OtherClass;

class Example {
```

```
public:
  Example(unsigned nArraySize){
    nSize = nArraySize;
    pArray = new char[nArraySize];
    pOther = NULL;
  }
  ~Example(){
    delete [] pArray;
    delete pOther;
  }
  . . . // other functions

private:
  char* pArray;
  unsigned nSize;
  OtherClass* pOther;
};
```

This class has two pointers. It initializes **pArray** to some valid data in the constructor. The other pointer, **pOther**, might be assigned the address of a class instance by another function later on. In the meantime, the constructor sets **pOther** to null so that it is not left pointing to an invalid address.

As the previous tip pointed out, the destructor can legitimately delete null pointers, so it can delete **pOther**, even though **pOther** might still be null.

## When a Class Contains Pointer Members, Declare a Copy Constructor and an Assignment Operator

When a class contains pointers to other resources, and the class itself deallocates the resources, you will run into trouble when you copy an instance of the class. Consider this:

```
class Example {
public:
  Example(){pArray = NULL; nSize=0;}
  virtual ~Example(){delete pArray;};
  void Init(int n){pArray = new int[n]; nSize = n;}
```

```
protected:
   int * pArray;
   int nSize;
};

void test(Example* pEx)
{
   Example anEx;
   anEx.Init(10);
   *pEx = anEx;   // copy anEx
}
```

This code initializes an instance **anEx** of **Example** and copies it into the instance that **pEx** is pointing at. By default, the compiler will just copy the values of the member items, so the other instance will have its member **nSize** set to the value 10, and its member pointer **pArray** set to point the buffer.

The problem occurs when the function test returns and the compiler deletes **anEx**. The class will delete the contents of **pArray**, which will leave the other instance containing a pointer to an invalid address. In addition, if the other instance was already initialized before the copy, its own buffer would be orphaned.

To avoid this problem, define an assignment operator for the class. In the body of this operator you can specify exactly how the members can be copied. For the **Example** class, you will want to create a new buffer and copy the contents into it.

If you declare an instance and assign another instance to it in the same statement, like this:

```
Example anEx;
anEx.Init(10);

Example anOther = anEx;
```

the compiler will use a copy constructor. If the copy constructor is not explicitly defined, the compiler will use a member by member copy again, even if you have defined an assignment operator. The reason C++ does this is for efficiency: it is better to initialize the instance in the constructor than to first call the constructor and then call the assignment operator.

In general then, you will need to define both an assignment operator and a copy constructor. Here is how this might work for the **Example** class:

```
class Example {
public:
```

```
  // Default constructor
  Example(){pArray = NULL; nSize = 0;}

  // copy constructor
  Example(const Example&);

  // assignment operator
  Example& operator = (const Example&);
  virtual ~Example(){delete pArray;};
  void Init(int n){pArray = new int[n]; nSize = n;}

protected:
  int * pArray;
  int nSize;
};

// copy constructor
Example::Example(const Example& RightSide)
{
  nSize = RightSide.nSize;
  pArray = new int[nSize];  // create a new buffer
                            // and copy into it.
  memcpy(pArray, RightSide.pArray, nSize*sizeof(int));
}

// assignment operator
Example& Example::operator = (const Example& RightSide)
{
  nSize = RightSide.nSize;
  // create a new buffer and copy the contents
  int* pTemp =  new int[nSize];
  memcpy(pTemp, RightSide.pArray, nSize*sizeof(int));

  // delete the old buffer
  delete pArray;
  pArray = pTemp;
  return *this;
}
```

Note here that you should declare the arguments as constant, otherwise you will not be able to assign constant instances of **Example** to non-constant instances. Note also that the assignment operator returns the address of the instance being assigned, for the case where assignments are chained together in the form a = b = c.

## When You Write the Assignment Operator, Remember X = X

It is possible to assign an instance to itself. While you are unlikely to do this directly, it may occasionally happen by chance when the right-hand side of the assignment is a pointer or a reference that just happens to be referring to the instance on the left-hand side.

If both the left and right side are the same object, you must take care not to delete the contents of the pointer before you have copied it. The example in the previous tip took care to allocate the buffer and store the address in a temporary pointer, so that it could copy the buffer and delete the old buffer before assigning the address.

You might think that you could first check that the left- and right-hand sides are not the same before continuing:

```
if (*this == RightSide) return *this;
```

Although this will work, the comparison is an expensive operation, because it compares each member of the class. An alternative is to compare addresses:

```
if (this == &RightSide) return *this;
```

This is quicker, but it is not guaranteed to work if you use multiple inheritance. The safest solution is to use a temporary pointer during the copy, as was done in the previous example.

## The Copy Constructor Can Call the Assignment Operator

As you saw in the previous tip, the copy constructor and the assignment operator are quite similar, so it makes sense to have the copy constructor just call the assignment operator. Before it does that, it must set all the pointers to null, so that when the assignment operator deletes them, nothing will happen. The copy constructor for the **Example** class could be rewritten like this:

```
Example::Example(const Example& RightSide)
```

```
{
  pArray = NULL;        // clear the pointers
  *this = RightSide;   // use the assignment operator
}
```

There is a minimal overhead here in the form of the redundant calls of **delete** in the assignment operator, but that is a small price to pay for the easier maintenance.

## If You Think That Your Class Is Never Copied, Declare the Copy Operators as Private and Omit Defining Them

Very often in an application, you will have some complex classes containing pointers which ought to have a copy constructor and an assignment operator, except that you are pretty sure that the application never copies instances of the class. You do not want to write what might be a complex routine for nothing, but what if after all the class is copied somewhere, or your successor adds some code that copies it?

The solution is to declare the copy constructor and the assignment operator as private and not to define them:

```
class Example {
public:
  Example(){pArray = NULL; nSize = 0;}
  virtual ~Example(){delete pArray;};
  void Init(int n){pArray = new int[n]; nSize = n;}

private:
  int* pArray;
  int nSize;

  // this class is not to be assigned
  Example(const Example&);
  Example& operator = (const Example&);
};
```

Now if the program does try to copy the class, the compiler will issue an error message, because the operators are private. It is possible that one of the member functions in the **Example** class itself might try to copy an instance: the compiler will allow this, but then the linker will generate an error, because the operators are not defined anywhere.

## When Redefining the Assignment Operator, You Must Copy All the Members

Once you decide to write an assignment operator, you must copy all of the members yourself. This can be a nuisance if you have a class with fifty members, two of which are pointers. You have to write an assignment operator to copy the contents of the pointers, but then you have to copy explicitly the other forty-eight members as well.

```
class Example {
public:
  // default constructor
  Example(){pArray = NULL; nSize = 0;}

  // copy constructor
  Example(const Example&);

  // assignment operator
  Example& operator = (const Example&);
  virtual ~Example(){delete pArray;};
  void Init(int n){pArray = new int[n]; nSize = n;}

protected:
  int * pArray;
  int nSize;
  int a;
  int b;

  // . . .

  int z;
};
```

```
  // . . .

Example& Example::operator = (const Example& RightSide)
{
  nSize = RightSide.nSize;

  // create a new buffer and copy the contents
  int* pTemp = new int[nSize];
  memcpy(pTemp, RightSide.pArray, nSize*sizeof(int));

  // delete the old buffer
  delete pArray;
  pArray = pTemp;
  a = RightSide.a;
  b = RightSide.b;
  . . .
  z = RightSide.z;
  return *this;
}
```

There is no way of calling a default assignment operator to copy all the members, and then to copy just the buffers. This is a nuisance: every time you add a member to the class, you need to update the assignment operator.

The solution here is to put the normal members in a base class and the pointers in a class derived from that base class. You can then let the default assignment operator copy the normal members, and provide an assignment operator in the derived class to copy the pointers:

```
class ExampleBase {
// base class contains normal members
public:
  int a;
  int b;
  // . . .
  int z;
  int nSize;
};

class Example : public ExampleBase {
public:
  Example(){pArray = NULL; nSize=0;}
  virtual ~Example(){delete pArray;};
```

```
    Example(const Example&);
    Example& operator = (const Example&);
    void Init(int n){pArray = new int[n]; nSize = n;}

protected:
    int * pArray;
};

// Other members are the same as before

Example& Example::operator = (const Example& RightSide)
{
    // copy the base class members
    (ExampleBase&)*this = RightSide;

    // now copy the members in the derived class
    // as before
    int* pTemp = new int[nSize];
    memcpy(pTemp, RightSide.pArray, nSize*sizeof(int));
    delete pArray;
    pArray = pTemp;
    return *this;
}
```

Notice the syntax for casting the instance to its base class. There are other ways of casting the instance, but the method shown here is probably the simplest. There is no need to cast the right-hand side to **ExampleBase**: the compiler will automatically truncate it.

## The Assignment Operator Is Not Inherited

Another problem when using the assignment operator is that it is not inherited. If a derived class does not redefine the operator, then the compiler will use the member copy on all the members, even those in the base class which had defined an assignment operator.

When a base class redefines the assignment operator, all the derived classes must do so as well. The assignment operator in the derived classes can use the method shown in the previous tip to call the assignment operator in the base class, before copying their own members.

# Before Assigning to a Pointer Other Than in a Constructor, Delete the Previous Contents

A common cause of memory leaks is overwriting a pointer that already points to an allocated memory block. This effectively orphans the block. Errors of this sort frequently occur in code that the programmer intended to be called only once, but which is for some reason called twice or more. Before assigning to a pointer, delete its contents first. If the pointer is indeed empty, nothing will happen.

The only times when this is not necessary are in a constructor when initializing members, and when you are declaring a local scope pointer in a function. Here is an example of an initialization routine in a class:

```
class Example {
public:
  Example(){pBuffer = NULL;}
  ~Example(){delete pBuffer;}

  void SetUp(unsigned nSize){
    delete pBuffer;  // guard against calling SetUp twice
    pBuffer = new char[nSize];
  }

private:
  char* pBuffer;
};
```

Although the **SetUp** function is intended to initialize the instance, a program might call it twice. In case that happens, **SetUp** deletes the previous buffer. If there is no buffer and **pBuffer** is null, then **delete** will have no effect.

# If You Delete a Pointer Other Than in a Destructor, Set it to Null Afterwards

It is an error to delete a pointer twice: once the memory pointed at has been freed, the pointer is invalid. If you ever delete a class pointer member in any function other than the destructor, you should immediately set the pointer to null. There is no need to do this in the destructor, because the member will cease to exist once the destructor has finished:

```
class Example {
public:
  Example(){pBuffer = NULL;}
  ~Example(){delete pBuffer;}

  void SetUp(unsigned nSize){
    delete pBuffer;  // guard against calling SetUp twice
    pBuffer = new char[nSize];
  }
  void CloseDown(){
    delete pBuffer;
    pBuffer = NULL;
  }

private:
  char* pBuffer;
};
```

In the class above, **CloseDown** sets the pointer to null so that the destructor, or the **SetUp** function, does not delete the allocated memory a second time.

## Provide an Initialization Function for a Class Instead of Using the Constructor

A class becomes more flexible if you give it a separate initialization function instead of obliging users to initialize the class with the constructor. If there is an initialization function, the constructor will simply set the contents of the class to zero.

When a class has a separate initialization function, other classes can declare an instance as a member and initialize it later. If the instance is a class member, it will be destroyed with the class instance that declared it. When a class does not have a separate initialization function, other class are often obliged to use **new** to initialize the instance, and **delete** to destroy it.

For example, the **iostream** classes have separate initializers. You can declare a stream and later associate it with a file:

```
class Example {
public:
void Setup(const char* pFile);

private:
ifstream InFile;  // the input stream
};

void Example::Setup(const char* pFile)
{  // open the stream
  InFile.open(pFile);
}
```

Here **Example** can construct the input stream in two stages. It first declares the stream as a class member, and later opens the file. The file will be closed and the stream destroyed when the instance of **Example** is destroyed. If the **ifstream** class had not provided a separate initialization function **open**, and instead relied on the constructor, then **Example** would have been obliged to use **new** and **delete**.

```
class Example {
public:
  Example(){pInFile = NULL;}
  ~Example(){if (pInFile) delete pInFile;}
  void Setup(const char* pFile);

private:
  ifstream* pInFile;
};

void Example::Setup(const char* pFile)
{
  delete pInFile;
  pInFile = new ifstream(pFile);
}
```

This code is already more complex. The **Example** class must now provide a constructor and a destructor to handle the input stream. Since the class contains a pointer, **Example** should also provide a copy constructor and an assignment operator, as explained in Tip 143.

C/C++

# Try to Localize new and delete Operations in a Separate Class

When **new** and **delete** are unavoidable, they can often be isolated in a separate class, so that you only need them once. Thereafter, you only need to declare an instance of the class.

Often in a function you need a temporary buffer of an unknown size. You cannot declare the buffer as a local array, because local arrays must have a constant size. The traditional solution is to use **new** and **delete** (or **malloc** and **free** in C programs):

```
void test(char* pMsg)
{
   // allocate a buffer
   char* pString = new char[strlen(pMsg)+1];

   // use it
   strcpy(pString, pMsg);

   // . . .

   // hope test does not return prematurely

   // free the buffer
   delete pString;
 }
```

It would be much neater to write a class to allocate and free the buffer—something like this:

```
class SimpleString {
public:
  // constructor allocates the buffer
  SimpleString(int nSize) {pBuffer = new char[nSize];;}
  SimpleString(const char aString[]){
    pBuffer = new char[strlen(aString)+1];
    strcpy(pBuffer, aString);
  }

  // destructor frees the buffer
  ~SimpleString(){delete pBuffer;}
```

```
  // type conversion to char*
  operator char* (){return pBuffer;}

  // copy operators
  SimpleString(const SimpleString& Right)
    {pBuffer = NULL; *this = Right;}
  SimpleString& operator = (const SimpleString& Right){
    char* pTemp = new char[strlen(Right.pBuffer)+1];
    strcpy(pTemp,Right.pBuffer);
    delete [] pBuffer;
    pBuffer = pTemp;
    return *this;
  }

private:
  char* pBuffer;  // the buffer
};
```

The type conversion allows other classes to treat this class as a **char*** type. An application might use the class in this way:

```
void test(char* pMsg)
{
   // declare the buffer of required size
   // and copy pMsg into it
   SimpleString aString(pMsg);

   // use it as if it were a char array pointer
   int n = strlen(aString);
}
```

Since **aString** is an automatic item, the function **test** will call the destructor when **aString** is no longer in scope, and that includes the case when **test** returns prematurely. With the **SimpleString** class, there is no longer any danger of accidentally omitting to delete the buffer. In addition, classes that contain **SimpleString** members do not need to define copy operators to copy the **SimpleString** instances. When the compiler does a default member copy, it will invoke the **SimpleString** copy operator.

Note that while **SimpleString** illustrates this principle succinctly, you will probably find a more useful **String** class in the class libraries included with your compiler.

# How to Redefine new and delete Globally

It is possible to replace the default **new** and **delete** operators with your own version. You would not want to do this for normal programming, but it can be useful for debugging or when you need to modify the default memory algorithm. Here is an example of redefined **new** and **delete** functions:

```
#include <stdlib.h>

static unsigned long nCalled;  // an allocation counter

// overloaded new and delete
extern void* operator new(size_t siz)
{
  ++nCalled;
  return malloc(siz);
}

extern void operator delete(void* obj)
{
  if (obj) {
    --nCalled;
    free(obj);
  }
}
```

These redefined operators maintain a counter while allocating and deleting memory. Notice that you need to call the standard C routines **malloc** and **free** to allocate and release the actual memory.

The routines above are useful for determining whether a program has a memory leak. If you have a debugger, you can examine the contents of the variable **nCalled** just before the program terminates. If there is a memory leak, it will be positive. You can also check the contents of **nCalled** before and after calling functions that should release any memory that they allocate, to make sure that the value of **nCalled** has not changed.

Remember that in a large project with many developers, there will be problems if each one tries to redefine **new** and **delete**.

# A Class May Have Its Own new or delete Operator

A class may define **new**, **delete** or both as a public member function. If so, the compiler will use the redefined class operator whenever a program creates or deletes an instance of that class, or of any class derived from it.

The compiler will use the redefined class operator even when a program has overloaded **new** and **delete** globally. The class version of **new** may call the globally defined **new** (or the default **new**) by using the scope operator **::operator new(size_t s)**.

The **new** and **delete** operators will be static functions, even if they are not explicitly declared as static. This means that they may only access other static class members.

Here is a class that redefines **new** and **delete** so that they add the name of the class to the memory block. The overloaded **new** operator allocates some extra space and writes the class name at the beginning of the block. It returns the address just after the name. The **delete** operator receives a pointer to the address of the block following the name. It backs up this pointer to point to the beginning of the name, clears the name text, and frees the block. This class can be useful for debugging. Using a debugger, or by scanning a memory dump, a developer can determine whether any instances of **Example** remain allocated.

```
class Example {
public:
  virtual ~Example(){};
  void *operator new(size_t s);
  void operator delete(void*);

protected:
  int Data;
  static char Name[];
};

char Example::Name[]="Example";

void *Example::operator new(size_t s)
{
  // allocate extra space for name
  // using global new
```

```
  void* p = ::operator new(s + sizeof Name);

  // copy name into memory
  strcpy((char*)p, Name);

  // return address following name
  return (void*)(((char*)p) + sizeof Name);
}

void Example::operator delete(void* pObj)
{
  // the pointer may be NULL !
  if (!pObj) return;

  // find the name.
  char* pName = ((char*)pObj) - sizeof Name;
  pObj = pName;

  // overwrite the name
  while (*pName) *pName++ = 0;

  // call global delete
  ::operator delete(pObj);
}
```

Notice that the functions can use the class member **Name**, because **Name** is defined as static. Also notice how the functions call the globally defined versions of **new** and **delete**. Remember that the pointer given to **delete** may be null.

Tip 165 will show another use of class-specific versions of **new** and **delete**, optimizing memory allocation for certain classes.

## An Overloaded Delete Operator Can Accept an Optional Size Argument

When a class redefines the **delete** operator, it may declare the operator in one of two ways; either as:

```
  void operator delete(void*);
```

or as:

```
void operator delete(void*, size_t);
```

If the operator is declared with a **size_t** argument, the compiler will provide the size of the object being deleted. The compiler will calculate this from the type of the pointer provided in the statement. However, if the class is a base class, and has a virtual destructor, the compiler will provide the size of the derived object. This underlines the importance of declaring a virtual destructor for a public base class.

Often the **delete** function will not need to know the size of the object, since **malloc** will store the size so that **free** can deallocate it. Knowing the size can, however, be useful for a class that wants to implement its own specialized memory allocation scheme. The following example class keeps track of the amount of memory used by instances of the class:

```
class Example {
public:
  // virtual destructor
  virtual ~Example(){};
  void *operator new(size_t s);
  void operator delete(void*, size_t);

private:
  int Data;
  static int TotalMemory;
};

int Example::TotalMemory;

void *Example::operator new(size_t s)
{
  // get the memory
  void* p = ::operator new(s);

  // add size to total
  if (p) TotalMemory += s;

  // return address
  return p;
}

void Example::operator delete(void* pObj, size_t s)
{
  // the pointer may be null!
```

```
    if (!pObj) return;

    // remove size from total
    TotalMemory -= s;

    // delete the block
    ::operator delete(pObj);
}
```

## How to Specify Placement Arguments for the new Operator

When you redefine **new**, you may specify extra arguments after the obligatory **size_t** argument. These arguments are known as placement arguments, because they are usually used to control the placement of the allocated memory; but they can be anything that you need. You might, for instance, want to specify a flag that serves as a hint for the memory allocation scheme.

To specify extra arguments, just add them after the first **size_t** argument, for example:

```
void* operator new(size_t s, unsigned Flags);
```

When a program invokes **new**, it adds the extra arguments like this:

```
Object* pObj = new(HighUsageFlag) Object(23);
```

Here, **HighUsageFlag** is the argument to **new**, and 23 is an argument for the **Object** constructor. Note that the compiler still provides the first **size_t** argument.

## When a Class Redefines new to Use a Placement Argument, It Should Also Provide a new Without Arguments

Usually, redefinitions of **new** with placement arguments are found in classes. If you define **new** to take a placement argument, you will not be able to use **new** to create an instance of the class without a

placement argument. The redefinition hides the global version of **new** completely and the compiler will give an error, for example:

```
class Example {
public:
  // virtual destructor
  virtual ~Example(){};
  void *operator new(size_t s, unsigned Flags);
  void operator delete(void*, size_t);
protected:
  int Data;
  static int TotalMemory;
};

void test()
{
  Example* pEx = new(MyFlags) Example;  // OK
  pEx = new Example;     // error!!
```

If you decide that the placement argument must be obligatory for the class, then this is OK. If you would like to call **new** without a placement operator, then you can either specify a default for the placement argument:

```
void *operator new(size_t s, unsigned Flags = 0);
```

or add an additional definition without a placement argument:

```
void* operator new(size_t s){return ::operator new(s);}
```

## How to Allocate Class Instances in a Fixed Buffer

The default **new** operator will allocate space for a class instance in the global heap. Occasionally, you would like to allocate an instance of a class in a block of memory that you provide. You would not do this in everyday programming, but there are circumstances under which it is necessary. You might need to use a special block of memory for interprocess communications. The Microsoft Windows Dynamic Data Exchange protocol, for example, requires memory blocks that have been allocated with a special

DDE flag. You might need to use a fixed block in a time-critical function to avoid the overhead of the standard **new** operator.

In C, you can allocate variables and structures in buffers with a simple cast, for example:

```
char Buffer[100];
MyStruct* pStruct;

pStruct = (MyStruct*)&Buffer;
// pStruct now points to buffer
```

In C++, this will work with simple structures, but if the item is a more complex class, the class constructor will not be called. To allocate class instances in buffers, define a **new** operator with a placement argument for the address, and return that address in the **new** operator. For example:

```
class Example {
public:
  Example(){Data = 13;}  // complex constructor
  virtual ~Example(){};

  // new simply returns the address given
  void* operator new(size_t s, void* pBuf){return pBuf;};

  // conventional new
  void* operator new(size_t s){return ::operator new(s);}

protected:
  int Data;
};
```

A program would allocate an instance of **Example** in a buffer like this:

```
char Buffer[100];
Example* pEx = new(Buffer) Example;
```

Note that this class also redefined the **new** without an argument so that a program can still allocate instances of **Example** in the normal heap.

## Redefine Delete When You Redefine the new Operator

If you have redefined **new** to allocate space in memory other than the standard heap, you must not delete those instances unless you have also redefined **delete** to do something appropriate. In many cases the redefined **delete** operator will just do nothing and return. What you must not do is call the default **delete** when the instance is not in the standard heap: this will cause the **delete** operator to either corrupt memory, or provoke an operating system memory protection fault.

## How to Redefine a Delete Operator When the new Operator Is Overloaded

When a class redefines **new**, it may overload **new** with different placement arguments. Frequently, there will be a version of **new** with no placement arguments which simply calls the global **new**.

C++ will not allow you to overload the **delete** operator in a similar way, and even if it did, there would be no guarantee that the program would always invoke the **delete** operator that corresponded to the **new** operator used to create the object. Since there can be only one **delete** operator, a good idea might be to set a class member flag in the **new** operators. The **delete** operator could consult this flag to decide what to do:

```
class Example {    // this will not compile !!!
public:
  Example(){Data = 13;}  // complex constructor
  virtual ~Example(){};

  // new simply returns the address given
  void *operator new(size_t s, void* pBuf)
    {bFlag=TRUE; return pBuf;};  // error!

  // conventional new
  void *operator new(size_t s)
    {bFlag=FALSE; return ::operator new(s);}  // error !

  void operator delete(void* pObj)
```

```
    {if (bFlag) return; ::operator delete(pObj);}  // error !

protected:
  int Data;
  BOOL bFlag;
};
```

Unfortunately, this will not work, because **new** and **delete** are static functions and can only access static data members. Instead of using a class member, **new** can allocate some extra memory and store the flag there. For efficiency, the extra memory should be the size of the machine's natural word: this ensures that the rest of the class stays aligned on a word boundary. Here is how to do it:

```
class Example {
public:
  virtual ~Example(){};
  void* operator new(size_t s, void* pBuf);
  void* operator new(size_t s);
  void operator delete(void* pObj);
protected:
  int Data;
};

void *Example::operator new(size_t s, void* pBuf)
{
  int* pInt = (int*)pBuf;
  *pInt = TRUE;  // set flag
  return pInt+1; // advance address
};

void* Example::operator new(size_t s)
{
  // allocate space for an extra int
  int* pInt = (int*)::operator new(s + sizeof(int));
  *pInt = FALSE;  // set flag
  return pInt+1;  // advance pointer
};

void Example::operator delete(void* pObj)
{
  int* pInt = (int*)pObj;
  if (! *--pInt)  // back up pointer and check flag
    ::operator delete(pInt);
};
```

Note that the functions use **sizeof(int)** rather than a numerical value. With a polyvalent **delete** operator like this, a program can safely delete all instances of the class that have been allocated with **new**.

## The Global new Is Always Used for Creating Arrays of Instances, Even If the Class Redefines new

If you create an array of instances, the compiler will always use the global **new** operator, even when the class has redefined the **new** operator. This may be a nuisance if you have redefined **new** in the class to do something clever, but there it is:

```
class Example {
public:
  virtual ~Example(){Data = 13;};
  void* operator new(size_t s, void* pBuf);
  void* operator new(size_t s);
  void operator delete(void* pObj);
protected:
  int Data;
};

// creates an array of 5 instances using the global new
Example* pExArray = new Example[5];

// cannot create arrays with MyBuffer::new
pExArray = new(MyBuffer) Example[5];  // compiler error!
```

If you need an array of class instances, you may be better off using a special purpose array or collection class. There is probably a library of collection classes included with your compiler.

Alternatively, if you really need an array of instances in your own buffer, you can use a placement argument and initialize the instances in a loop:

```
void test()
{
  char Buffer[100];
  Example* pStart = (Example*)&Buffer[0];
  Example* pEnd = (Example*)&Buffer[100];
```

```
  // initialize elements
  while (pStart < pEnd) new(pStart++) Example;
}
```

## Use the Delete [] Operator for Deleting Arrays

When you have created an array of instances using **new**, you should **delete** it using the [ ] form of **delete**.

```
pExArray = new Example[5];

  . . .

delete [] pExArray;
```

When you use this form, the operator will destroy each element in the array, calling the destructor, before deallocating the memory.

On most compilers, you will not see an error if you leave out the [ ] operator, because the compiler is usually unable to tell whether the item points to an array or not. If you do omit the [ ] operator, however, the program will simply call the destructor for the first element before deallocating the block.

If you use standard C arrays for C++ classes, you are responsible for deleting them in the correct manner. To avoid the possibility of a mistake, you should use a C++ container class. Unfortunately, there is not yet a standard C++ container class, although there will usually be a container or an array class included with the compiler package.

## How a Redefined new and delete Can Cope with Derived Classes

When you redefine the **new** and **delete** operators in a class, the compiler will use the redefined operator whenever a program uses **new** and **delete** to create or destroy an instance of any derived class, unless the derived class has also redefined the operators. Depending on what your redefined **new** and **delete** does, this may be OK; but it is possible that the redefined operators can only cope with instances of the base class itself, perhaps because they implement a special memory allocation scheme that relies on the allocation having a certain size. Remember that instances of a derived class will typically be larger than instances of the base class.

If your redefined operators cannot handle derived classes, they can check the value of the size argument. If the size is greater than the size of the class itself, the redefined function can pass the request off to the global **new** or **delete**.

```
void* Example::operator new(size_t s)
{
  // deal with instances of derived classes
  if (s > sizeof(Example)) return ::operator new(s);

  // rest of function here
};

void Example::operator delete(void* pObj, size_t s)
{
  // deal with instances of derived classes
  if (s > sizeof(Example)) ::operator delete(pObj);

  // rest of function here
};
```

## How to Redefine new to Find Memory Leaks

If you think that your program has a memory leak and is calling **new** without calling **delete** afterwards, it can be difficult to find just where in the application source you are leaking memory. Fortunately, there is a way of redefining **new** so that after running your application you can see the source file name and the line number of the statement causing the memory leak!

This trick relies on the predefined macros __FILE__ and __LINE__ which most compilers provide. These macros give the current source file name and line number. If you redefine **new** to accept these values as placement arguments, you can add the values into the memory heap. If, in addition, the

**delete** operator erases the values, then when the application has run, you only need to scan through the memory heap with a debugger to see the memory leaks tagged with the line number in the source that allocated them. Here is how to redefine **new** and **delete**:

```
class DebugSpec {
public:
  char Sign[4];  // makes it easy to spot leaks
  char Module[16];
  int LineNo;
};

extern void* operator new(size_t siz,
                          char pModule[],
                          int LineNr)
{
  // allocate some extra space
  DebugSpec* pSpec
    = (DebugSpec*)malloc(siz + sizeof(DebugSpec));

  // an attention grabber
  strcpy(pSpec->Sign,"!!!");

  // this is for MS DOS and Windows,
  // in UNIX search back for a '/' character
  pModule += strlen(pModule);  // go to end of name

  // search back for a directory
  while (*pModule !='\\') pModule--;
  pModule++;  // start of module name
  strncpy(pSpec->Module, pModule,9);
  pSpec->Module[9] = 0;

  // could also convert line number to text
  pSpec->LineNo = LineNr;

  // return the address just past the structure
  return pSpec+1;

}

extern void operator delete(void* pObj)
{
  if (!pObj) return;
```

```
    DebugSpec* pSpec = (DebugSpec*)pObj;
    // back up to actual block
    pSpec--;

    // clear the fields
    strcpy(pSpec->Sign,"    ");
    strcpy(pSpec->Module,"            ");
    pSpec->LineNo = 0;
    // free the memory
    free(pSpec);
}

// redefine new as a macro to add the placement operators
#define new new(__FILE__ , __LINE__)
```

The **new** operator allocates some extra memory and copies the module name and line number into it. The actual module name will be the complete path specification with directories. Usually, it is enough to know just the file name, so **new** searches for the file name at the end of the string and copies that. This is for the PC. UNIX and Mac programmers will need more space for the name. This version leaves the line number in binary: you could convert it to text, but then you would need six bytes instead of two.

The **delete** operator scrubs out the debug text by overwriting it with spaces. The **#define** statement will cause the compiler to replace all occurrences of **new** with the call using the placement arguments. You must arrange to have the **#define** included in all the modules, perhaps by inserting it in a standard header file, and then you must recompile.

After you have run the program, any leaks will be tagged in the memory heap. You should use a debugger to stop the application just before it returns to the operating system and scan through the heap looking for the !!! tags.

Most programmers will have no problem scanning through memory with a debugger to find the leaks, but a more luxurious system will do it for you and print out a list.

## TIP 165 Optimizing new for Certain Classes

The general purpose version of **new** in most systems allocates blocks of memory in a large heap. At first, the routine will allocate the blocks one after the other, but as the application begins to

delete blocks, holes will appear in the allocated memory. When the application makes a **new** request, **new** will look at all the holes to see if there is one big enough for the amount of memory requested.

As a general purpose algorithm this works well enough, but you will notice its deficiency when you want to allocate and deallocate blocks of a fixed size at frequent intervals. Each time the application needs a new instance, the **new** operator will begin a laborious search through the heap, even though the application might have just deleted an instance of the appropriate size. This situation might arise in an event driven system, where one module creates instances of an event class and passes them on to other modules where they are eventually processed and deleted.

For these special cases, it may be worth redefining **new** and **delete** for a certain class to help the standard memory allocation routine along. Exactly how you do this will depend on how the class is used. One possibility, for instances that are allocated and deleted very often, is to keep a small cache of blocks, so that if there is a block in the cache, the redefined **new** can return it immediately. If the cache is empty, the redefined **new** will call the global **new** in the normal way. Similarly, the redefined **delete** would just add the block to the cache, and only when the cache is full will the redefined **delete** call the global **delete**. Here is an example that does this:

```
class Example {
public:
  void* operator new(size_t s);
  void operator delete(void* pObj, size_t s);
  enum{CacheSize = 5};
private:
  static Example* Cache[CacheSize];
  static int nCache;
};

Example* Example::Cache[Example::CacheSize];
int Example::nCache = 0;

void* Example::operator new(size_t s)
{
  // deal with instances of derived classes
  if (s > sizeof(Example)) return ::operator new(s);

  // if there is something in the cache return it
  if (nCache) return Cache[--nCache];

  // otherwise call global new
  return ::operator new(s);
 };
```

```
void Example::operator delete(void* pObj, size_t s)
{
  // deal with null pointers
  if (!pObj) return;

  // deal with instances of derived classes
  if (s > sizeof(Example)) ::operator delete(pObj);

  // if there is space, put the object in the cache
  if (nCache < CacheSize) Cache[nCache++] = (Example*)pObj;

  // otherwise delete it
  else ::operator delete(pObj);
};
```

The size of the cache will depend on the application. A small cache will be sufficient when the total number of instances in use is fairly static. Where the turnover is high, one option would be to have the redefined **new** increment a counter whenever it calls the global **new**. You could then use the counter to tune the cache size. Each time you increase the cache size, you run the application and examine the counter. When the counter does not decrease significantly after you have increased the cache size, then the last cache size was the optimum size.

## How new Can Cause Page Thrashing on Virtual Memory Systems

In a virtual memory system, an application has access to far more memory than is physically available. The operating system maps virtual memory onto the physical memory and an external page file. If an application tries to access memory that is not mapped to physical memory, the operating system will swap out a page of physical memory and swap in the appropriate page from the external file. This system works well, provided that applications stay within certain regions of memory and do not jump about too much. In general this is the case. In most applications, there are a host of functions that users rarely access, and the system will page out the code and data for these functions.

The **new** function will allocate virtual memory to satisfy requests, but the **new** function searches through the heap to find a space big enough for the request. Each time that an application creates an instance, **new** will access locations scattered all over the heap. In addition, the instances created will also be scattered over the heap.

The operating system will be obliged to keep all of the heap in physical memory, leaving less space for the rest of the application and for other tasks. This in itself will result in increased paging activity. At the limit, when the application heap grows to the size of the physical memory, the system will be obliged to page memory in and out while **new** searches for a free block. At that moment, the system will grind to a halt while the disc drive hammers away furiously.

The solution here is to redefine **new**, either globally or for certain classes, so that it allocates memory within a relatively small region. For example, a document processing application might allocate a block of memory for each page of the document and have any instances associated with that page allocated in that part of memory. This might well use more memory overall, but in virtual memory systems the total amount of memory used is not very important, provided that accesses are localized.

## Overload new Rather Than Using set_new_handler

The **set_new_handler** function lets a program specify a function which **new** should call if it fails to satisfy a request to allocate memory. The intention is that this function should take appropriate action, perhaps displaying an error message, or maybe freeing some allocated memory so that **new** can try again.

The **set_new_handler** function was introduced in C++ 1.2, but with C++ 2.0 or later, you can achieve the same result by overloading **new**. Because overloading **new** is more flexible than the **set_new_handler** mechanism, you should consider **set_new_handler** as obsolete.

## If a Class Has No Explicit Constructor, the Compiler Will Supply a Default Constructor

When a user-defined class does not contain an explicit constructor, the compiler will supply a default constructor, having no arguments:

```
class Example {
public:
  void Func(int n);

private:
  int Data;
};

Example anExample;  // uses default constructor
anExample.Func(13);
```

Having a default constructor simply means that an application can declare instances of the class, since C++ requires that whenever an instance of a class is created, its constructor is called. Notice that the default constructor does not do anything specific, and in particular, it does not initialize member data items to zero.

## Declaring a Constructor with Arguments Will Hide the Default Constructor

Once you provide a constructor with arguments, the default constructor, with no arguments, is hidden. This means that you must always specify the arguments when you declare an instance of the class.

```
class Example {
public:
  Example(int n, char* pName);
  void Func(int n);

private:
  int Data;
};

void test()
{
  Example One(13, "Hello");    // OK
  Example Two;  // error! no default constructor
}
```

C/C+

If the class absolutely has to be initialized in the constructor, then this is OK, otherwise you only need to provide an additional default constructor. This constructor may have an empty function body, so that it has the same effect as the compiler-generated default constructor, but it is even better to have a default constructor that initializes the class members to appropriate initial values.

```
class Example {
public:
  Example()       // default constructor
    {Data = 0;}
  Example(int n, char* pName);
  void Func(int n);

protected:
  int Data;
};

void test()
{
  Example One(13, "Hello");     // OK
  Example Two;  // OK, Two.Data initialized to 0
}
```

## A Constructor with Default Arguments is Equivalent to a Default Constructor

When a class has a constructor with arguments, rather than declaring a separate default constructor, you can give the arguments default values in the declaration:

```
class Example {
public:
  Example(int n=0, char* pName=NULL);
  void Func(int n);

protected:
  int Data;
};

void test()
```

```
{
  Example One(13, "Hello");   // OK
  Example Two;  // OK, equivalent to Two(0,"")
}
```

## When a Class Has Hidden the Default Constructor, Derived Classes Must Provide Constructors

If a class has a constructor with arguments, and does not provide its own default constructor, this implies that derived classes must provide a specific constructor that calls the base class constructor in the initialization list:

```
class Example {
public:
  // no default constructor
  Example(int n, char* pName);
  void Func(int n);

protected:
  int Data;
};

class Derived : public Example {
public:
  // default constructor
  // must call Example constructor
  Derived():Example(0,""){}
};

class DerivedAgain : public Derived {
  // OK, compiler-generated constructor
  // will call Derived()
};
```

Notice, however, that once a derived class provides a default constructor, classes derived from this class do not have to provide a constructor, since the compiler-generated constructor will call the default constructor in the class immediately above in the hierarchy.

## Even Primitive Types Have Constructors

Even primitive types, such as integers and floats, have default constructors that you can use to initialize an item:

```
int a(3), b(4), c(5);
float f(1.23), g(4.56);
```

This code defines three integers and two floats, and initializes them to the values shown. You might not care for this notation in normal programming, but some of the following tips will show how this notation might be useful.

## How to Construct Temporary Instances

You can construct temporary anonymous instances and use them in expressions. The compiler will delete them after use:

```
class Complex {
public:
  Complex(float r, float i);
  Complex& operator +(Complex&);
};

void test()
{
  Complex c1(1.0, 2.0);
  // add a temporary instance to c1
  Complex c2 = c1 + Complex(3.0, 1.5);
}
```

In this example, **Complex(3.0, 1.5)** is an anonymous temporary instance.

## Avoid Creating Temporary Instances in Function Calls

If you declare a function argument as being a class instance, like this:

```
void Func(Complex c);

Complex x;
Func(x);  // temporary instance created
```

The compiler will call the class copy constructor to create a temporary item for the function when you call it. It may be that you need a local copy, but if the function does not modify the item, you should declare a constant reference, so that the function can use the original argument directly, without having to construct and delete a temporary item.

```
void Func(const Complex& c);

Complex x;
Func(x);  // passes reference to x
```

## Do Not Call the Default Constructor from Another Constructor of the Same Class

A mistake that most C++ programmers make at least once is to have a class with both a default constructor and a constructor with arguments, and to call the default constructor from the other constructor, in order to carry out some initialization common to both. Here is an example where this happens:

```
class Example {
public:
  Example()
    :a(0),b(0),c(0),d(0){}
```

```
  Example(int n){
    Example();   // not what you think!
    d = n;
  }

private:
  int a;
  int b;
  int c;
  int d;
};
```

Here the intention was to have the second constructor first call the default constructor, which initializes everything to zero, before setting **d** to something specific.

Unfortunately, this will not work, because the call to the constructor **Example**( ) creates a temporary instance of the class and initializes that. It does not initialize the instance calling the constructor.

The solution is to have a separate initialization routine and to have both constructors call that, as in this example:

```
class Example {
public:
  Example(){Init();}
  Example(int n){
    Init();
    d = n;
  }

private:
  int a;
  int b;
  int c;
  int d;

  void Init(){
    a = 0;
    b = 0;
    c = 0;
    d = 0;
  }
};
```

Notice here that there is no reason for not making the initialization function private. Derived classes will not require access to the function, because they will call the **Example** class constructor in any case.

TIP 176

## Understanding Copy Constructors

A copy constructor is a constructor of the form **ClassName(ClassName&)**. The compiler will use the copy constructor whenever you initialize an instance at the same time that you declare it.

```
Example One;          // default constructor used
Example Two = One;    // copy constructor used
```

You do not need to declare a copy constructor. If you do not, the compiler will copy the instances member by member. This means that if any of the members are of a class that has declared a copy constructor, then the compiler will use that constructor for copying the member.

Notice that the compiler-generated copy constructor is not hidden when you declare another constructor in the class. Notice also that the member by member copy is different from the C language copy. In C the compiler just copies the bit image when it copies a structure.

You will probably need a copy constructor if the class contains pointers as members, as explained in Tip 143. You may also need a copy constructor if for any reason you do not want all the members of a class to be copied.

## Copy Constructors Should Take a const Argument

If you declare a copy constructor, you should specify **const** for the argument:

```
Example(const Example&);
```

This way you can use a constant instance of the class to initialize another.

## Copy Constructors May Have Additional Default Arguments

A copy constructor may take additional arguments, provided that they have default values. For example:

```
class Example {
public:
  Example(const Example&, int nValue=0);
  // . . .
};

void Func()
{
  Example One;
  Example Two = One;       // calls copy constructor
                           // with nValue = 0
  Example Three(One, 2);   // calls copy constructor
                           // with nValue = 2
}
```

## Virtual Constructors

C++ does not allow virtual constructors, and the way that the language is implemented means that virtual constructors cannot be provided. Even so, there are many occasions when a programmer would like to write something that means in effect, "Give me another one of these." These situations occur when there is a pointer to a base class available, and the program needs a copy of the actual derived class that the pointer is referencing. For example:

```
class Employee {
public:
  virtual Employee(const Employee&);   // cannot do this
  . . .
};
```

```
class Operator : public Employee{
  . . .
};

void test()
{
  Employee* pEmployee = new Operator;

  . . .

  Employee* pClone = new Employee(*pEmployee);
}
```

The intention here is create a clone of whatever **pEmployee** references. Because virtual constructors are not allowed, **pClone** will end up pointing to an instance of the base class **Employee**. Even though C++ does not provide virtual constructors, it does provide facilities that let you simulate the effect of a virtual constructor, as the next tip shows.

## A Virtual Cloning Function as a Virtual Constructor

If you simply want to clone an instance, given a pointer to a base class, you can write a virtual clone function and redefine it in each derived class. For example:

```
class Employee {
public:
  virtual Employee* Clone()
    {return new Employee(*this);}
  //  . . .
};
```

The **Employee** class is the base class, and it defines the virtual function **Clone** that returns a copy of the instance.

```
class Operator : public Employee{
public:
  Employee* Clone()
    {return new Operator(*this);}
```

```
  //  . . .
};
```

The **Operator** class is a typical derived class that also defines the **Clone** function to return a copy of the instance of **Operator**. Here is an example that calls the **Clone** function to duplicate an instance of **Operator**:

```
void test()
{
  Employee* pEmployee = new Operator;

  //  . . .

  Employee* pClone = pEmployee->Clone();
  // both pEmployee and pClone point to
  // instances of Operator.
}
```

Notice how the derived class defines the **Clone** function. It must declare the function as returning a pointer to the base class (otherwise it will not redefine the base class virtual function) but it creates an instance of its own class, **Operator** in this case. The **Clone** function calls the copy constructor so that the members of the new instance will have the same values as the members of the existing instance. Another possibility would be to write a virtual function that just returns an instance of the class type, without copying the members:

```
class Employee {
public:
  virtual Employee* InstanceOf()
    {return new Employee();}
  //  . . .
};

class Operator : public Employee{
public:
  virtual Employee* InstanceOf()
    {return new Operator();}
  //  . . .
};
```

# TIP 181 Why is a Destructor Not Being Called?

C++ beginners often discover that a class destructor is not being called, even though the application deletes the instance, and the memory allocated for the class is being freed. Here is a case where that happens:

```
class Employee{
  // definition of Employee
};

class Vehicle {
public:
  void ReturnToPool();
};

class Driver : public Employee {
public:
  // allocate new driver a vehicle
  Driver(Vehicle& aVehicle):aVehicle(aVehicle){}

  // return vehicle to pool
  ~Driver(){aVehicle.ReturnToPool();}

protected:
  Vehicle& aVehicle;
};

void test()
{
  Vehicle Van;  // a Vehicle

  // create a new employee of type driver
  Employee* pDriver = new Driver(Van);

  // remove the employee at a later time
  delete pDriver;
 }
```

For some reason the vehicle does not get returned to the pool. The reason is that the base class **Employee** did not declare a virtual destructor. Although the compiler deallocates the memory for the **Driver** class

instance, it calls the destructor only for **Employee**, because **pDriver** is declared to be a pointer to **Employee**.

The solution is to make the **Employee** destructor virtual, or if **Employee** does not have a destructor, define a dummy virtual destructor:

```
class Employee {
 virtual ~Employee(){};
};
```

## How to Initialize Member Items in a Constructor Initialization List

A common problem in constructors is that the constructor takes an argument, and the constructor uses this argument to initialize a member. You would like the argument and the member to have the same name, but then you run into problems with scope rules:

```
class Example {
public:
  int nMaxSize;
  Example(int nMaxSz)  // can't have same name
    {nMaxSize = nMaxSz;}
};
```

You could use the same name and then qualify the member with the class name, **Example::nMaxSize**, but the simplest solution is to call the member's constructor in the initialization list. Remember that even simple items have a constructor:

```
class Example {
public:
  int nMaxSize;
  Example(int nMaxSize)
    :nMaxSize(nMaxSize){}
};
```

Using the initialization list is more efficient than assigning to members in a constructor. When you initialize members in the initialization list, as in the last tip, the compiler will initialize the member as it is constructed. If you assign to the member in the body of the constructor, the compiler will first construct a default instance and then assign to it. Of course, for primitive types and simple classes without a constructor, there is no difference between the two methods of initializing members, but it is well worth initializing member items of more complex classes in the initialization list:

```
class Example {
public:
  Example(const Complex& x){
    Example::x = x;}  // first constructs a default x
                      // and then copies into it.

private:
  Complex x;
};

class Example {
public:
  Example(const Complex& x)
   :x(x){}            // initializes member while
                      // constructing it.

private:
  Complex x;
};
```

It is common to see constructors which use the initialization list to initialize base classes and which use assignments to initialize member items, but this only reflects the programmer's upbringing in a C environment.

Remember that items in an initializer list are not initialized left to right: the compiler will initialize first the base classes and then the members in the order they are declared in the class (not the list). This can cause problems when one member depends on another. It is especially easy to forget this when converting assignments to initializations. Consider this:

```
class Example {
public:
  Example(int nBufferSize){  // OK
    nSize = nBufferSize;
    pBuffer = new int[nSize];
  }

private:
  int* pBuffer;
  int nSize;
};
```

This is perfectly correct: the compiler will initialize first **nSize** and then **pBuffer** by assignment. Now assume that a programmer converts this to initialization. It is easy to write something like this:

```
class Example {
public:
  Example(int nBufferSize)    // wrong!!
   :nSize(nBufferSize),pBuffer(new int[nSize]){}

private:
  int* pBuffer;
  int nSize;
};
```

Although this compiles correctly, the compiler will first try to initialize **pBuffer**, since it is declared first, using an uninitialized value of **nSize**. You could swap the positions of the two members, so that **nSize** is first in the class, but note that there is no problem if the member has the same name as the argument:

```
class Example {
public:
  Example(int nSize)    // OK
   :nSize(nSize),pBuffer(new int[nSize]){}

private:
  int* pBuffer;
  int nSize;
};
```

Now, although the compiler still initializes **pBuffer** first, it uses the argument **nSize**, which is correct, rather than the member **nSize**.

## You May Not Use an Initializer List to Initialize Inherited Members

A derived class constructor may initialize members inherited from the base class, but not in the initializer list. It has to initialize them by assignment:

C/C+

```
class Base {
private:
  int a;
  int b:
};class Derived : public Base {
public:
  Derived():a(0),b(0){}  // not allowed
  Derived(){a=0; b=0;}   // OK
};
```

Notice that in general it is the job of the base class constructor to initialize the base class members, so if you need to initialize a base class member in a derived class, this may indicate that the base class should have a constructor capable of initializing the members.

## TIP 184 How to Call a Destructor Explicitly

If you have copied an instance of a class into a private block of memory, you will probably need to destroy the instance at some later time. You cannot use the global delete operator on the instance, because the block of memory that contains the instance is not allocated in the standard heap. If the class has its own delete operator that can detect where the memory has been allocated and take appropriate action, then this is fine, but the class might be a library class or a class that you do not want to modify.

Since the memory that the instance uses is your own, there is no need to free the space occupied by the instance. The problem is that if you do not delete the instance, the class destructor will not be called and the class will not be able to free any resources that it has allocated.

In that situation you can call the class destructor directly, using this syntax:

```
Example* pExample;

  . . .

pExample->Example::~Example();
```

An explicit call to a destructor is allowed even when the class does not define a destructor. In this case the compiler will use the default destructor, which does nothing.

You should also be able to use the syntax:

```
pExample->~Example();
```

but many compilers do not support this. This is a virtual call to the destructor, and should invoke the virtual destructor in a derived class, if there is one. The first notation was a static call, and would only call the destructor in **Example**, even if there was a virtual destructor in a derived class.

## Automatic Instances Are Only Deleted on Exit from Their Block

When you declare an automatic class instance in a function, the compiler will call the class constructor to allocate the object at the place where it is declared, and will only call the destructor when control passes out of the scope in which the instance was declared. It will not delete the object earlier, even if the object does not appear to be used after a certain point.

This property allows you to use a class as a lock or to set an operating mode. If the destructor releases the lock or restores the mode, you can be sure that the destructor will be called at the end of the block. For example:

```
class CriticalArea {
public:
  CriticalArea()
    {/* inhibit interrupts */}
  ~CriticalArea()
    {/* restore interrupts */}
};

void CriticalFunction()
{
  CriticalArea ToEndOfFunc;

  // critical processing here

  // interrupts restored here
}
```

The instance will be deleted only at the end of the block, even though it appears to be unused after its declaration. The advantage of using a class to release a lock or resource is that the destructor will be called if the function returns early, perhaps because of an error:

```
enum ErrorCode{OK, NoMemory, DiskFull};

ErrorCode CriticalFunction()
{
  CriticalArea ToEndOfFunc;

  // critical processing here

  // interrupts restored if error
  if (/* condition */) return NoMemory;

  // more critical processing

  // interrupts restored here
  return OK;
}
```

## Temporary Instances are Deleted When They Are No Longer Referenced

The last tip showed how to use a class to release a lock or resource in its destructor. Although automatic variables exist until the end of their scope, temporary variables are deleted as soon as they are no longer referenced. Do not write something like this:

```
ErrorCode CriticalFunction()
{
  CriticalArea(); // wrong! instance deleted immediately

  // critical processing here

  if (/* condition */) return NoMemory;

  // more critical processing
```

```
  return OK;
}
```

The item must be named if you want it to exist throughout a block.

## Use a Block to Delete Automatic Instances Early

You might prefer that an automatic instance be deleted before the end of its scope. The instance, for example, may be claiming some resources that you want to be released. The way to do this is to limit the scope of the instance with an inner block. Using the **CriticalArea** class described in Tip 185, for example, you can limit the **critical area** to part of a function:

```
void CriticalProcessing()
{

  // non-critical processing here
  {
    // disable interrupts
    CriticalArea ToEndOfBlock;

    // critical processing here

  }// interrupts enabled

  // more non-critical processing
}
```

## Make Sure Global Instances Are Initialized Before Use

When you declare static class instances in a module, the compiler will ensure that each instance is initialized before use, even if the instance is used in the constructor of another static instance.

Things are more complex when you have static instances in different modules, and the instances refer to each other. Since there is no way of knowing which module will be initialized first, there is a danger that one instance will use an uninitialized instance of another class in its constructor.

If you have a static instance in a module, and you know that other classes might use it during their initialization, there is a way of ensuring that your instance is initialized first. You must declare a class in the header file for your instance:

```
class InitCounter {
public:
  InitCounter(){
    if (!nCount++){
      // initialize your static instance
    }
  }
  ~InitCounter(){
    if (!--nCount){
      // destroy your static instance
    }
  }

private:
  static nCount;
};

static InitCounter anInitCounter;
```

Now any other module that includes your header file will declare a static instance of **InitCounter**. The compiler will initialize this instance first, and call the **InitCounter** constructor. The constructor will then initialize your global static instances. The count variable **nCount** is to ensure that your instances are initialized only once. If another module includes your header file, **nCount** will be non-zero, and nothing will happen.

When the application terminates, a similar process occurs in reverse, so that your instance will be destroyed after all the others.

Jerry Schwarz used this technique in the iostream library to initialize **cin**, **cout**, and other instances.

# Type Conversions and Overloading

TIP 189

## Converting to a Class

If a class has a constructor that takes a single argument of a certain type, then the compiler will use the constructor to convert from the type of the argument to the type of the class. For example:

```
class Complex {
public:
  Complex();  // default constructor
  Complex(float R, float I);  // explicit constructor
  Complex(float R);  // type conversion from float
};

void Func()
{
  Complex A = 3.0;  // calls constructor directly
  Complex B;
  B = 3.0;    // creates a temporary and copies it to B
  B = 3;  // OK, compiler promotes int to float
}
```

Recall that a complex number has a real and an imaginary part. The real part corresponds to simple "everyday" numbers. The imaginary part is the square root of a negative number. Complex numbers provide solutions to many mathematical problems. The instance **Complex(1.0, 0)** corresponds to the normal value 1.0, while the instance **Complex(0, 1.0)** corresponds to the square root of –1.0.

The class **Complex** defines a type conversion from **float** to **Complex**. Notice that the program can also assign ordinary integers to the class: the compiler will consider promoting primitive types when it is looking for a match. Notice also that unless you declare the item and assign a value in the same statement, the compiler will create a temporary instance of the class, and then copy that to the destination.

## A Constructor with Default Arguments Can Also Serve for Type Conversion

The **Complex** class in the last tip could be written with just one constructor with default arguments:

```
class Complex {
public:
  Complex(float R = 0.0, float I = 0.0);   // explicit constructor
};
```

The compiler would still find a conversion from a **float** to **Complex**, because it can call the **Complex** constructor with a single **float** argument, and the default value of 0.0 for the imaginary part of the complex number.

## Avoid the Overhead of a Temporary Instance with a Typed Assignment

Tip 189 pointed out that when a class has defined a conversion to that class using a constructor, the compiler may generate a temporary instance, copy that instance to the destination and then delete the instance, so that an expression like:

```
Complex A;

A = 3.0;
```

when the class **Complex** defines a conversion from a float, is really equivalent to:

```
A = Complex(3.0);
```

If the class constructor and destructor are quite simple, then it may not matter that the compiler creates a temporary instance. If, on the other hand, the constructor allocates extra resources that are deleted by the destructor, or if the class has redefined the copy constructor to do something more involved than a simple member by member copy, then the overhead of the temporary instance may be unacceptable.

To avoid the overhead of the temporary instance, define an assignment operator in the class for the type. For example:

```
class Complex {
public:
  Complex(float R=0.0, float I=0.0);   // constructor
  Complex& operator =(float f);   // assign float to Complex
```

```
private:
  float r,i;
};

Complex& Complex::operator =(float f)
{
  r = f;
  return *this;
}
```

## Converting from a Class to Another Type

You may also define conversions away from the class by means of a conversion operator. A conversion operator is declared as:

```
operator conversion-type ();
```

Neither a return type nor an argument may be specified by the conversion operator. Imagine that you wanted to specify a conversion between the **Complex** class and a **float**, such that the float is assigned the real part of the complex number, and the imaginary part is ignored. You would define the operator like this:

```
class Complex {
public:
  Complex(float R=0.0, float I=0.0);  // explicit constructor
  operator float (){return r;}  // conversion to float

private:
  float r,i;
};

void Func()
{
  Complex A(3.0, 4.5);
  float f = A;  // f = 3.0
}
```

If necessary, you may define a number of conversion operators for different types.

# When Possible, Provide Conversion Operators for Primitive Types and Library Classes Only

As a general rule, write conversion operators for conversions to primitive types and general purpose classes provided in libraries. Rather than declaring a conversion operator to another of your own classes, you should declare a conversion constructor in the other class. For example, rather than writing this:

```
class MyOtherClass;

class Complex {
public:
  Complex(float R=0.0, float I=0.0);  // explicit constructor
  operator MyOtherClass ();  // conversion to MyOtherClass

private:
  float r,i;
};
```

it is better to write this:

```
class MyOtherClass {
public:
  MyOtherClass(const Complex& C); // conversion from Complex
}
```

There are several reasons why this is preferable. First, it is easier for a class to initialize itself in a constructor. If **Complex** needed to initialize **MyOtherClass**, it might need access to the private members of **MyOtherClass**. Second, once you start writing operators to convert to other classes, there is a danger that you will end up with a list of conversions to all the other classes in the system.

# An Ambiguity Will Arise If You Declare Both a Conversion Operator and a Conversion Constructor Between Two Classes

The ambiguity arises when you write something like this:

```
class X {
public:
  X(const Y&);
};

class Y {
public:
  operator X();
};
```

If you now try to convert between X and Y, the compiler will not know which of the two conversions to try. This is another reason for not writing conversion operators for other classes.

# Remember That Conversion Operators May Be Virtual

A conversion operator may be virtual. ( Conversion constructors may not, because virtual constructors are not allowed.) Whether you need a virtual conversion operator depends on how the class hierarchy is designed. If the base class declares the data members and the derived classes simply treat the data in their own way, then a non-virtual conversion operator in the base class is usually sufficient.

If the derived classes instead redefine data members that are used in the conversions, then you may well find that you will have to redefine the conversion operators as well. In that case you should make the operator virtual.

# Watch Out for Ambiguities When you Declare Type Conversions and Overload Expressions

When you declare both type conversions and other operators, ambiguities may arise. When they do, the compiler will issue an error message and you will have to disambiguate the expression. Here is a class that can give rise to an ambiguity:

```
class Complex {
public:
  // constructor defines conversion from float
  Complex(float R=0.0, float I=0.0);

  // conversion to float
  operator float (){return r;}

  // addition of complex numbers
  Complex operator+(const Complex& c);

private:
  float r,i;
};

void Func()
{
  Complex C = 2.0;
  Complex A = C + 3.0;    // ambiguous!
}
```

What should the compiler make of the last statement? Should it convert **C** to a **float**, add the **float** to 3.0, and convert the result to a **Complex**? Or should it convert 3.0 to a **Complex**, add that to **C**, and store the result in **A**? Both are valid. To disambiguate the expression, you need to state one of the conversions explicitly. For example:

```
Complex A = C + Complex(3.0);   // OK
```

Now there is no ambiguity: the compiler will convert 3.0 to a **Complex** and add it to **C**.

# Be Wary of Overusing Type Conversions

Although user defined type conversions, as discussed in the preceding tips, are a useful feature, there is a danger of overusing them. By specifying more type conversions than are necessary, you increase the risk of the compiler accepting expressions that have been written incorrectly.

Remember that an alternative to a type conversion is a member function that returns a result of the appropriate type. Because the program has to call the member function explicitly, the meaning of the expression is much clearer. Type conversions should be reserved for types that are conceptually close to the class itself. For example, a character string class could specify conversions to and from the **char*** type. A Binary Coded Decimal (BCD) number class might specify conversion from integers and longs.

Even the conversion between the **Complex** class and the **float** type, in the examples accompanying the previous tips, is overdone. A proper implementation of a **Complex** class would define a conversion from **float** to **Complex**, but instead of providing a conversion from **Complex** to **float**, it would provide member functions to extract the real and imaginary parts of the complex number, like this:

```
class Complex {
public:
  //  constructor
  Complex(float R=0.0, float I=0.0);

  // assign from float
  Complex& operator =(float f);

  // arithmetic operators
  Complex operator+(const Complex& c);

  // return components
  float RealPart(){return r;}
  float ImaginaryPart(){return i;}

private:
  float r,i;
};

void Func()
{
  Complex A(3.4, 5.6);
```

```
// . . .
float f = A.RealPart();
```

Now the code is more explicit. In addition, the compiler will detect type mismatch errors caused, for instance, by accidentally calling a function that takes a **float** argument instead of one that takes a **Complex** argument.

## When to Overload Functions

An overloaded function is one that is declared two or more times in the same scope. The overloaded functions have the same name, but different arguments. For example:

```
long Sqrt(long n);          // overloaded for long integers
double Sqrt(double f);      // and double floats
```

An overloaded function is useful for allowing alternative argument types in a function, especially if there is a way of optimizing the function for the argument type. In the square root example above, we could assume that the integer version of **Sqrt** uses integer arithmetic internally, which on most machines would make it much faster than the double float version of **Sqrt**. Of course, the floating point version of **Sqrt** is more exact. Remember that the square root of an integer is generally not an integer itself.

A more subtle form of overloading for the **Sqrt** function would be:

```
float Sqrt(float n);          // overloaded for single floats
double Sqrt(double f);      // and double floats
```

The idea is the same: single float arithmetic is faster than double float arithmetic, so if single float accuracy is sufficient, it makes sense to provide a fast version of the routine for single floats. The compiler will call whichever of the two functions matches the arguments supplied:

```
double d = 81.0;
float f = 144.0F;
d = Sqrt(d);        // calls Sqrt(double)

f = Sqrt(f);        // calls Sqrt(float)
```

```
d = Sqrt(144.0F); // calls Sqrt(float),
                  // converts result to double

f = Sqrt(81.0);   // calls Sqrt(double),
                  // but truncates result to float

f = Sqrt(81.0F);  // calls Sqrt(float)
```

## Use Constant Suffixes When Calling Overloaded Functions

The example accompanying the last tip used the **F** suffix on some constants to indicate that the constant was a float, and not a double. These suffixes were rarely needed in ANSI C programming (provided of course, that you used prototypes,) but they are useful for indicating which overloaded function should be called.

An ordinary floating constant (123.45) has the double type, while adding the **F** suffix (123.45F) makes it a float. The suffix **L** (123.24L) makes it a long double. Similarly for integers, a constant without a suffix is a signed int. The **U** suffix makes the constant unsigned and the **L** suffix makes it long. The two can be combined, **UL** or **LU** means unsigned long.

All of these suffixes may appear in either upper or lower case.

## Avoiding Ambiguity When Calling Overloaded Functions

The compiler may give an ambiguity error message when you try to use an overloaded function. Usually these errors arise when you call an overloaded function with arguments that do not exactly match any of the function declarations. The compiler could apply conversions to the arguments to match a function, but it does not know which function to choose. For example:

```
float Sqrt(float n);
double Sqrt(double d);
```

```
double d = Sqrt(81);    // ambiguous
```

The expression is ambiguous, because 81 is an integer. The compiler could promote the integer to either a float or a double, but it does not know which one. Remember that the compiler never looks at return types when choosing an overloaded function, so it will not choose the **double Sqrt** function simply because the destination is a double.

The solution is to explicitly convert the argument to one of the defined types. With a constant, it is enough to rewrite the constant as either a float (81.0F) or a double (81.0), but with variables, you need to convert the variable using a constructor.

```
float Sqrt(float n);
double Sqrt(double d);

int n = 81;
double d = Sqrt(n);    // ambiguous
d = Sqrt(double(n));   // construct a double around n
float f = Sqrt(float(n));
```

## The const Property Is Sufficient to Distinguish Overloaded Function Arguments

Overloaded function arguments need only differ in the **const** (or **volatile**) property. You can make use of this property to give the **const** property to the result, for example:

```
// functions overloaded on const arguments
char* SubString(char aString[], int nPos);
const char* SubString(const char aString[], int nPos);
```

Here is a function **SubString** that returns a pointer to a substring within the argument string. Without overloading, you would declare this function as:

```
char* SubString(const char aString[], int nPos);
```

You would be able to pass the function either a constant or a normal string, but the result would lose any constant property that it had, so you would be able to write to the substring returned, even though the original string was constant. However, if you were to make the result type **const**, then you would be prevented from writing to the substring returned by the function, even when the original string was not constant.

With overloading, the substring has the same constant property as the argument. If the argument is **const**, the result is also **const**. If the argument is not **const**, then the result is also not **const**.

## The const Property of the Instance Is Sufficient to Distinguish Overloaded Member Functions

Overloaded member functions need only differ in the **const** (or **volatile**) property of the instance calling them. As with the last tip, this property is useful for specifying the return type of the function. If the instance is **const**, you may make the return type **const** also:

```
class Example {
public:
 // if instance is const, return const
 const char* Buffer() const {return pBuffer;};

 // otherwise not
       char* Buffer()       {return pBuffer;};

private:
  char* pBuffer;

};

void Func(){
  // const instance
  const Example One;
  const char* pOneBuf = One.Buffer();

  // modifiable instance
  Example Two;
```

```
   char* pTwoBuf = Two.Buffer();
}
```

In this example, **One** is a constant instance that returns a pointer to a constant buffer, while **Two** is a modifiable instance and returns a pointer to a writable buffer.

Notice how you specify the function as applying to a **const** instance: you add the **const** specifier after the argument list. (In the example there are no arguments.)

## Remember That Function Overloading Does Not Work Through Function Pointers

You may assign the address of an overloaded function to a function pointer, and the compiler will choose one of the functions according to the type of the pointer. Thereafter, when you dereference the pointer, you will always get the same function. You cannot use the function pointer with different types of argument, hoping to call one of the other overloaded functions.

That is reasonable when you think how pointers would have to be implemented to make indirect overloading work. (I don't know how either, but it wouldn't be easy!) All the same, it is easy to accidentally hide overloading with a function pointer, as the following example shows:

```
float Sqrt(float f);          // overloaded functions
double Sqrt(double d);

void test(){
   double(*pFunc)(double);    // pointer to a function
   pFunc = &Sqrt;             // points to double Sqrt(double)
   float f = (*pFunc)(3.4F);  // calls Sqrt(double)
}
```

The code assigns the double version of **Sqrt** to **pFunc**, because that is how **pFunc** is defined. The compiler will promote the float argument to a double before calling the contents of **pFunc** if necessary, but there is no way of calling **float Sqrt(float)** through **pFunc**.

# Using Overloading in Place of Default Arguments

Using default arguments gives the appearance of overloading, because the function may be called with an optional number of arguments. For example:

```
class Complex {
public:
  Complex(double R, double I=0.0);
  // . . .
};
```

This allows an instance of **Complex** to be constructed using either one argument or two. If only one argument is provided, the compiler supplies a default value for the second.

The default argument works well for the **Complex** class, but sometimes you are better off declaring an overloaded function rather than using a default argument. Typically this would be when the function has no further need of the argument after checking that it has a default value. By declaring an overloaded function, you save the compiler the trouble of pushing the default argument on the function call stack, and you save the function the trouble of testing the default value. A function with a default argument like this:

```
void Func(const char* pValue = NULL);

void Func(const char* pValue)
{
  if (pValue) {
    // do something
  }
  else {
    // do something else
  }
}
```

would be better written as an overloaded function like this:

```
void Func(const char* pValue);
void Func();
```

```
void Func(const char* pValue)
{
    // do something
}

void Func()
{
   // do something else
}
```

## Consider Using Overloaded Functions to Set or Return Values in a Class

Overloaded functions can be useful to either set or retrieve a value from a class.

```
class Person {
public:
  int Age(){return nAge;}     // retrieves Age
  void Age(int n){nAge = n;} // sets Age
  // . . .

private:
  int nAge;
};
```

This makes **Age** appear as a property of a **Person** to outside classes, but you still have the freedom to completely re-implement the class internally, for example:

```
class Date;
Date ToDay;

class Person {
public:
  // retrieves age at end of this year
  int Age(){
    return ToDay.Year() - YearOfBirth;
  }
```

```
  // Sets age at end of this year
  void Age(int n){
    YearOfBirth = ToDay.Year()-n;
  }
  // . . .

private:
  int YearOfBirth;
};
```

Here the programmer has rewritten the class so that the age is calculated from the birth date and the current date, but the public interface is unchanged.

## List of Operators

The following operators may be overloaded:

```
+    -    *    /    %    ^    &    |    ~    !
=    <    >    +=   -=   *=   /=   %=   ^=   &=
|=   <<   >>   >>=  <<=  ==   !=   <=   >=   &&
||   ++   --   ,    ->*  ->   ()   []   new  delete
```

The operators

```
.  .*  ::  ?:  sizeof
```

and the preprocessing operators # and ## may not be overloaded. The reason is that the first three operators already have a well-defined meaning for any class, and it was thought unnecessary to overload the others.

Notice that the operators

```
+  -  *  &
```

are available in both unary and binary forms.

You may not invent new operators, nor may you redefine operators for primitive types.

## When to Overload Operators

TIP 207

Good programming practice requires that if you redefine any of the operators for a class, the operator's original meaning should be preserved. If you redefine the + operator for a class, the operator should still have the sense of adding something to the class instance.

Remember that operators are not any more efficient than member functions, and it is usually better to give a class operation a well chosen name rather than to force an inappropriate operator onto it.

The shift operators >> and << are conventionally overloaded to perform input and output with streams. This topic is covered in Chapter 12 of this book. Overloading **new** and **delete** allows a class to control its own memory management. This topic was covered in Chapter 5.

## Take Care with Operator Precedence

TIP 208

If you work with floating numbers rather than with bits and bytes, you might be tempted to redefine the bitwise exclusive OR operator, ^, as an exponentiation operator for double types or perhaps for a **Complex** class. You cannot redefine an operator for primitive types such as **double**, but you can for a closely related class. The following example shows what might happen if you redefine the ^ operator for a **Real** class:

```
#include <math.h>

class Real {
public:

  // constructor for conversion from double
  Real(double Value):Value(Value){};

  // type conversion to double (note const)
  operator double() const {return Value;}
```

```
  // overload ^ operator
  friend Real operator ^(const Real& base,
                         const double exponent);

private:
  double Value;
};

// define ^ operator
Real operator ^ (const Real& base, const double exponent)
  {return pow(base, exponent);}
```

Here is some code that uses the ^ operator:

```
Real f = 4.5;
printf("The value is %g\n", f^2.0);
```

This works correctly and prints out "The value is 20.25". So far so good. Here is another piece of code:

```
Real f = 4.5;
Real g = 3.5;
printf("The sum of the squares is %g", f^2.0 + g^2.0);
```

This prints a completely erroneous result. The ^ operator has a very low precedence, lower than all the other arithmetic operators, including the + operator. The expression is compiled as (f^(2.0+g))^2.0. To see the correct result, 32.5, you must bracket the expression as (f^2.0) + (g^2.0).

As you see, the overloaded ^ operator is dangerous, because programmers expect the exponentiation operator to have a higher precedence than the other arithmetic operators, and there is no way to change the precedence.

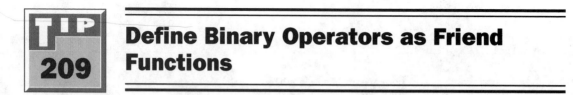

## Define Binary Operators as Friend Functions

Many operators may be defined either as a member function or as a global function. If the operator is a global function, it must usually be defined as a friend, so that it can have access to the class members. Here is how a class might define the addition operator as a member function.

C/C++

```
class BCDNum {
public:
  BCDNum(long n=0); // conversion from long
  BCDNum operator +(const BCDNum& RightSide) const;
};
```

and as a global friend function:

```
class BCDNum {
public:
  BCDNum(long n=0); // conversion from long
  friend BCDNum operator +
    (const BCDNum& Left, const BCDNum& Right);
};
```

When the operator is defined as a member function, the compiler calls the function for the instance on the left side of the expression, so in the function, the left-hand side will be **this**, and the right-hand side will be the argument.

In general, operators should be member functions, but for the binary operators, using a friend function allows for a more flexible type conversion. You will notice that the example class **BCDNum** above defined a conversion from a long integer to the class. Writing the + operator as a member function would allow expressions like:

```
BCDNum N1=10;
BCDNum N2;
N2 = N1 + 5;
N2 = N1+ N2 + N1;
```

but not:

```
N2 = 5 + N1;
```

because the left-hand side would have to be an instance of **BCDNum**, and not the integer 5. When the function has been defined as a global friend, the compiler can convert integers on either side of the expression to an instance of the **BCDNum** class.

## The =, (), [], and -> Operators Must Be Member Functions

The =, (), [] and -> operators must be defined as non-static member functions. They may not be declared as a global function, friend or otherwise.

Notice also that the assignment operator is the only operator that is not inherited by derived classes, and it is the only class operator to be defined by default. (The default is to do a memberwise copy.)

## Declare the Operator Arguments as Constant References

Unless the arguments are primitive types, you should declare them as constant references. When the operator function is a member function, you should declare the function constant, except for operators such as ++ that modify the operand.

Using references avoids the overhead of creating temporary instances when calling the function, and defining arguments as **const** lets you call the operator with constant operands.

## Differentiating Between the Prefix and the Postfix Increment and Decrement Operators

The postfix forms of the increment (++) and the decrement (– –) operators take an extra argument with value zero.

```
class BCDNum {
public:
   BCDNum& operator++();    // prefix
```

```
   BCDNum  operator++(int); // postfix
};
```

The argument serves solely to distinguish the two forms of the expression. Note that this is a comparatively recent extension to C++, and you might still come across an early compiler that does not support this feature. See the next tip if you wonder why the postfix operator cannot return a reference.

## The Prefix Operators Are More Efficient for Incrementing or Decrementing Instances

It is common in programming to use the increment and decrement operators on their own in a statement. If you use these operators on primitive types, it does not matter very much whether you use the prefix or the postfix form of the expression. In C programming, the postfix form is more common.

```
int C;
// two ways to increment C

  C++;  // postfix form
  ++C;  // prefix form
```

When you redefine these operators for a class, you will find that the prefix form is more efficient, at least in the case where you simply want to increment or decrement an instance. To see why, consider how the two forms of the increment operator might be implemented:

```
class Example {
public:
   Example & operator++();     // prefix
   Example operator++(int); // postfix
};

Example& Example::operator++()  // prefix
{
  // add one to this
  return *this;  // return reference
}
```

```
Example Example::operator++(int)  // postfix
{
  Example Temp = *this;  // make a copy of this
  // add one to this
  return Temp;  // return copy
}
```

The prefix form need only return a reference to the instance after having incremented it. The postfix form must first copy the instance to a temporary before incrementing the instance, and then it must return a copy of the temporary. It cannot return a reference, because the temporary copy is going out of scope. The copy operation may be quite time consuming, especially if the class has redefined the assignment operator.

## The Return Type of Overloaded Operators is not Defined

You have complete freedom to specify the return type of overloaded operators. In particular, the class of the return type need not be the same as the class defining the operator. If you write a **Vector** class, you might decide that the result of multiplying two instances of **Vector** should be an instance of an **Area** class.

```
class Area{
  // . . .
};

class Vector {
public:
  // . . .
  friend Area operator *(const Vector& x, const Vector& y);
  // . . .
};

Vector Width;
Vector Height;

// . . .
```

```
Area theArea = Height * Width;
```

## Understanding the Function Call Operator

The function call operator is interesting, because it lets you use a constructor-like syntax on an instance that already exists. Here is an example of the function call operator:

```
class BCDNum {
public:
  BCDNum(long n=0);          // a constructor
  void operator()(long n); // the function call operator
  // . . .
};


void test2()
{
   BCDNum N1(10);  // call constructors
   BCDNum N2(20);
   N1(20);         // use function operators
   N2(10);         // on existing instances
}
```

As with the constructors, you may overload the function call operator several times with a different set of arguments. In contrast with constructors, the function call operator may take a return type. It does not need to return **void**, as in the example above.

One advantage in using the function call operator for assignments is that it is inherited by base classes, while the ordinary assignment operator is not inherited. The following example makes use of this to create some simple derived classes for type checking:

```
// A very simple number class
class ULong {
public:
  // the function call operator
  void operator()(unsigned long n){nValue = n;};

  // a type conversion
  operator unsigned long(){return nValue;}
```

```
private:
 unsigned long nValue;
};


// two classes used for type checking

class Age : public ULong {};

class Salary : public ULong {};

void func(Age theAge, Salary theSalary);
};

void test()
{

   Age a;
   Salary s;
   a(23);
   s(45000);
   func(a, s);  // OK
   func(s, a);  // wrong! compiler reports an error
}
```

By using classes instead of simple unsigned long arguments, this program can detect errors where one value is used in place of another.

## Using Non-Integer Arguments with the Subscript Operator

The subscript operator [] is often used to implement intelligent array or vector classes. In contrast to a simple C array that has no bounds checking and always starts at index 0, an array class can incorporate array bounds checking, and may have array bounds starting and ending at arbitrary indexes.

A general purpose array class will define the subscript operator with an integer argument to resemble C array subscripting. It is possible, however, to use a non-integer type for the subscript argument. Here is an example that uses a character string as a primary key to retrieve records from a table class.

C/C+

```
class Record;
class String;

class Table {
public:
  Record& operator[](const char* PrimaryKey);
};


void Test()
{
  Table NameTable;

  // get a record
  Record& APerson = NameTable["Joe Soap"];

}
```

In fact, a class such as this might also define a subscript operator that takes an integer argument, to provide the effect of a table cursor.

# Inheritance and Member Access Control

TIP 217

# In C++ a struct Is a Public Class

Many C programmers believe that in C++ a **struct** is a collection of public data members, as in the C language, and a class is a superstructure with function members, inheritance and access control. In fact, C++ promotes the structure to have the same status as a class, except that its members and base classes are public by default, whereas the members and base classes of a class are private by default.

C++ structures may contain member functions, and may be derived from another class or structure:

```
struct Base {
};

struct Derived : Base {
  Derived();
  ~Derived();

private:
  int a;
  int b;
};
```

The structure **Derived** is derived publicly from **Base**, and the constructor and destructor are public. The structure is functionally identical to the class:

```
class Derived : public Base {
public:
  Derived();
  ~Derived();

private:
  int a;
  int b;
};
```

## There Is No Need to Use the typedef Trick When Declaring Structs

In C you must use the keyword **struct** when declaring an instance of a structure.

```
struct Record {
  /* body */
};

struct Record aRecord;
```

To avoid this, C programmers declare the structure with a **typedef** so that they can declare instances without writing "struct".

```
typedef struct Record {
  /* body */
} Record;

Record aRecord;
```

There is no need to do this in C++. Because a structure is equivalent to a class, except that the members are public by default, you can just declare an instance of a structure as you do a class:

```
struct Record {
  // body
};

Record aRecord;
```

## Member Order Need Not Be Maintained Across an Access Specifier

If you have a class or a structure with an access specifier in the middle, the language only guarantees that members with the same access privileges will be kept together. If you write:

C/C+

```
struct s {
  int a;
  int b;
private:
  int x;
  int y:
}
```

the compiler may keep the members in this order, or it may put **x** and **y** before **a** and **b**.

For C++ programming this does not matter, but if you want to pass the structure to a function compiled with a C compiler, you should avoid inserting access specifiers between members.

## Restricting Member Access Does Not Affect Visibility

Making a member private does not affect its visibility. The member is still visible, even though the compiler will not allow access to it. For example:

```
int Item;    // global scope


class Base {
  int Item; // private member
};

class Derived : public Base {
public:
  void func(){Item++;}   // not allowed
};
```

The compiler will not allow the class **Derived** to access **Item**, because **Item** has been declared private by the base class. The fact that there is another variable called **Item** at the file scope does not make any difference.

# How to Selectively Allow Access When Deriving Privately

When you derive a class privately from a base class, users of the derived class will not have access to any members defined in the base class. Usually, you do not want to deny access to all the base class members, just some of them. To do that, derive the class privately and then selectively declare some of the base class members in the derived public section of the derived class. Here is an example:

```
class Base {
public:
  int a;
  int b;
  int c;
};

class Derived : private Base {
public:
  Base::b;  // allows access to b
  int d;
};
```

Here the class **Derived** inherits privately from **Base** and then selectively allows access to **b** in **Base**. Users will be able to access **b** and **d**:

```
Derived d;
d.a = 0;    // illegal!
d.b = 0;    // OK
```

The same applies to member functions as well.

## You Cannot Deny Access to Certain Members of a Base Class When Inheriting Publicly

The last tip explained how to selectively allow access to a private base class. Note that you cannot do things the other way around and selectively deny access to base members by declaring them in the derived private section of the derived class.

```
class Base {
public:
  int a;
  int b;
  int c;
};

class Derived : public Base {
public:
  int d;
private:
  Base::b;  // you cannot do this!
};
```

There would be no point in doing this even if it were possible, because one could still gain access to the members in **Base** by assigning the instance of **Derived** to a **Base*** pointer.

TIP 223

## Avoid Making Member Data Public

When designing a class, the general rule should be to avoid making member data public. Instead, you should make the data private and provide public functions to access it. The main reasons for hiding class data are:

- To give yourself the possibility of replacing the data by a function that calculates the value of the data. It frequently happens that rather than trying to maintain some data item, it is more efficient to provide a function that calculates the data value when needed.

- To have a consistent interface. It can be confusing if your class has a mixture of public functions and data members. It is more consistent if all access to the class is via member functions.
- To have a finer control over access. With data members, an external class either has complete access or none at all. If you use function members to access data, you can decide whether you want to allow read access or write access, or both.

## When a Class Inherits from a C struct, Consider Deriving Privately

In many systems there is a legacy of C structures that are widely used in system interfaces. When programming in C++, it is useful to derive C++ classes from the structures, to provide a simpler programming environment while keeping the original structures for the interface.

A C **struct** has a public interface, and of course all of its members are data members. For this reason, consider deriving privately and supplying function members to access the data.

```
typedef struct Point{
  int x;     // the original C struct
  int y;
} Point;

// C++ class derived from C struct
class CPoint : private Point {
public:
  CPoint(int x=0, int y=0):x(x),y(y){}
  // access functions
  int X(){return x;}
  void X(int n){x=n;}
  int Y(){return y;}
  void Y(int n){y=n;}

  // type conversion
  operator Point&(){return *this;}
};

void Test(Point& p);
```

```
void func()
{
  CPoint C(4,5);
  int a = C.X();
  C.Y(10);   // C is now (4,10)
  Test(C);   // call function that
             // expects the C struct
}
```

Deriving privately uncouples the C++ class from the old C structure. If necessary, the C interface could be overhauled at some later date without affecting users of the derived C++ classes.

TIP 225

## When to Derive Publicly

When you derive a class from an existing base class, it may inherit from the base class publicly, privately, or with protection. If you specify nothing, the class will inherit privately.

If you look at existing C++ class hierarchies, you will notice that most classes are derived publicly, and that it is rare to find a class that is not derived publicly. In fact many programmers always derive classes publicly, as a matter of course.

You should derive a class publicly when you want the derived class to have all the attributes of the base class, plus some extra attributes that are defined in the derived class. Deriving publicly is a way of saying "is a type of." Obviously, public inheritance is appropriate to most well designed object-oriented systems, so it is not necessarily bad that so many classes inherit publicly.

To take an example, in a personnel database, there may be a base class **Employee** and a number of other classes—**Driver**, **Manager**, **Loader**, **SalesPerson**—derived from the base **Employee** class. The intention here will be that the derived class will inherit all of the attributes of the base **Employee** class. For example, the **SalesPerson** class will inherit from **Employee**, because a **SalesPerson** is a type of **Employee**. The **SalesPerson** class may add extra functions appropriate to the class, perhaps a function for calculating bonuses based on the number of units sold by that employee. Because all of the derived classes are a type of **Employee**, they will all inherit publicly from the base **Employee** class.

## When to Derive Privately

TIP 226

Private inheritance should be reserved for classes that cannot be viewed as a type of their base class. These classes are derived from a base class simply because there may be some member functions in the base class that the derived class would like to use. Private inheritance does not reflect the object-oriented design of the system—it simply reflects an implementation shortcut. There is nothing wrong with taking these shortcuts, provided that they are hidden from the rest of the implementation.

As an example, if a system had the **Employee** hierarchy discussed in the last tip, a programmer might wish to add a **PensionScheme** class. The **PensionScheme** class might be derived from the **Employee** class, not because a **PensionScheme** is a type of **Employee**, but because the **Employee** class contains some useful functions for calculating pension fund contributions. In that case, the **PensionScheme** class would be derived privately from **Employee** so that the implementation of **Employee** is invisible to any user of the **PensionScheme** class.

## Deriving from a Private Base Class When Writing Template Classes

It is possible to write a template class in one go, perhaps something like this:

```
template <class type> class List  {
public:
    List(){
      pLast = 0;
    };
    List(type *pItem){
     if ((pLast = new Link(pItem))!=0)
       pLast->pNextLink = pLast;
    }
    int insert(type *pItem) {
      // code for insert
    }
    int append(type *pItem) {
      // code for append
```

```
    }
    int unlink(type *pItem) {
      // code for unlink
    }
    type *get() {
      // code for get
    }

private:
  class Link {
    Link* pNextLink;
    type *pItem;

    Link(type *pItem):pItem(pItem){pNextLink = NULL;}
    ~Link() {delete pItem;}
  };
  Link* pLast;
}; // class List
```

There are two disadvantages in doing things this way. First, the class definition is burdened with all the source for the class. With template classes it is impossible to put the source of a member function in a separate file, because the compiler needs access to the source whenever a program declares an instance of the template. The second disadvantage is that there will be one or more copies of the object code of the class for each type of template included in the application. Templates give you reusability of source code, but not reusability of object code.

To avoid these problems, you can write a general purpose class, using void types or void pointers. The source of the member functions may be in a separate file, and the compiler will only generate one copy of the object code for this class. Here is a general list class:

```
class VoidList {
protected:
  VoidList();
  VoidList(void *a);
  ~VoidList() { clear(); }
  void clear();
  int insert(void *);
  int append(void *);
  int unlink(void *);
  void *get();

private:
  class VoidLink {
```

```
    VoidLink* pNextLink;
    void *pItem;

    VoidLink(void *pItem):pItem(pItem){pNextLink = NULL;}
    ~VoidLink() {delete pItem;}
  }; // class VoidLink
  VoidLink* pLast;
}; // class VoidList
```

You then write a template class that casts specific objects or pointers to the void type and calls the general corresponding routine in the general class, like this:

```
template <class type> class List : private VoidList {
    public:
    List():VoidList(){};
    List(type *a):VoidList(a){};
    int insert(type *a) { return VoidList::insert(a); };
    int append(type *a) { return VoidList::append(a); };
    int unlink(type *a) { return VoidList::unlink(a); };
    type *get() { return (type *) VoidList::get(); };
}; // class List
```

The template class inherits the base class privately because it is simply making use of the implementation of **VoidList**.

If you now declare a list of some type:

```
   List(Complex) ComplexList;
  ComplexList.append(new Complex(13.5, 4.87));
```

the compiler will use the template to generate a **List <Complex>** class. The size of this generated class is almost nothing, because the member functions are all inline. There is also little run-time overhead, because the compiler can replace calls to the template member functions with calls to the base class. In fact, the result is about the same as using the base class directly, except that the compiler is able to provide proper type checking.

# Use Protected Members in Template Base Classes

The previous tip showed how to derive a template class **List<type>** from a base class **VoidList** that deals only with void types. The template class simply casts types to void and calls functions in the base class. Implementing template classes in this way is much more efficient than trying to write a complete stand-alone template class.

The member functions of the base class should be at least protected, but not public. The base class is not intended for general use: it only serves to implement the template classes. Even the constructor should be protected, to ensure that the class users do not inadvertently declare an instance of the base class.

Note that if a user really wants a list of void types, perhaps in order to interface with some old C code, there is no disadvantage in simply declaring a template class instance of type void. For the preceding example, this would be:

```
List<void> vList
```

TIP 229

# Use Multiple Inheritance with Care

Think twice before you start using multiple inheritance. There are advantages to using multiple inheritance in the right circumstances, but using multiple inheritance can be complex, and it is not always the most efficient way to solve a problem. Many experienced C++ programmers do not use multiple inheritance at all, and it is well to remember that some object-oriented languages, including Smalltalk, do not provide multiple inheritance.

You might also have problems using multiple inheritance with certain commercial class libraries. These libraries may not have been designed to support multiple inheritance efficiently.

# Resolving Ambiguities in Multiple Inheritance

If you derive a class from one or more other classes, you may find that there is a member that has the same name in two or more of the base classes. The member need not have the same function in the classes—it may just be coincidence that it has the same name. If you use this name in the derived class, it will be ambiguous, and the compiler will issue an error message.

```
class Window {
protected:
  void Setup();
  // other functions
};

class CommPort {
public:
  void Initialize(){
    Setup();
    // more code
  }
  // other functions
private:
  void Setup();
};

class CommWindow: public Window, public CommPort {
public:
  CommWindow(){
    Setup(); // ambiguous
  }
};
```

The **CommWindow** class wants to set up the base **Window** class, but the call is ambiguous, because there is also a **Setup** function in the **CommPort** class. Notice that the call is ambiguous even though the **Setup** function in the **CommPort** class is private and cannot be accessed.

To disambiguate the call, you will have to specify which base class you mean:

```
class CommWindow: public Window, public CommPort {
public:
```

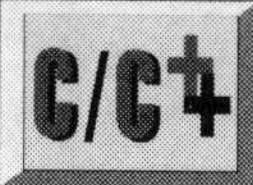

```
  CommWindow(){
    Window::Setup(); // OK
  }
};
```

TIP 231

## Using Virtual Base Classes

You may find that the multiple classes from which you want to inherit are themselves derived from a common base class. This is not uncommon, and is very likely if you use a commercial class library.

Imagine that you have two classes derived from a **Window** class:

```
class Window {
public:
  Window() {nStyle = SNone;}
  enum Styles{SNone = 0,
          SPopUp =0x0001,
          SEdit =0x0002,
          SButton = 0x0004};
protected:
  int nWindowNumber;
  int nStyle;
  void Setup(){
   nWindowNumber = Create(nStyle);
  }
  // other functions
private:
  int Create(int nStyle);
};

class PopupWindow : public Window {
public:
  PopupWindow(){nStyle |= Window::SPopUp;}
protected:
  //  functions
};

class EditWindow : public Window {
```

```
public:
  EditWindow(){nStyle |= Window::SEdit;}
  //  functions
};
```

The base **Window** class does most of the work, and the derived classes add in whatever is specific to a certain type of window. Here, the constructors of the derived class simply set the style flag, so that the **Window** class will later create the correct type of window.

Imagine now that you wanted a popup type of edit window. You might consider using multiple inheritance to define a new class.

```
class PopupEditWindow : public PopupWindow, public EditWindow {
public:
  PopupEditWindow(){
    Setup();
  }
};
```

The problem here is that an instance of **PopupEditWindow** will contain two copies of the base **Window** class, one in **PopupWindow** and the other in **EditWindow**. Apart from the problem of some wasted storage, the class will not function properly. If the **Window** instance on the **PopupWindow** side creates the actual window, it will initialize **nWindowNumber** for itself, but the **nWindowNumber** in the instance on the **EditWindow** side will be invalid, and in all likelihood the functions in the **EditWindow** class will not work correctly.

To solve this problem, both the **EditWindow** and the **PopupWindow** classes can declare **Window** as a virtual base class like this:

```
class PopupWindow : virtual public Window {
 // . . .
};

class EditWindow : virtual public Window {
 // . . .
};
```

Now these classes will share the same copy of a **Window** instance if they are used in multiple inheritance. Note also that there will no longer be any ambiguity if **PopupEditWindow** refers to a member of the **Window** class, because there is now only one instance of **Window**.

The only snag is that because the **Window** class must be declared virtual by its immediate descendants, there is no way of declaring it virtual from the **PopupEditWindow** class. This is a problem if the classes are declared in a library, because library classes should be treated as read-only. Even when you have access to the source of the base classes, you should read the following tips before you make them virtual.

## TIP 232 Do Not Declare All Classes Virtual

The last tip explained how to declare base classes as virtual, when they are used in multiple inheritance. You might think of declaring all base classes as virtual, just in case another class needs it for multiple inheritance. Unfortunately, there is an overhead in declaring virtual base classes.

In order to implement the virtual base class, the compiler will put a pointer to the base class in instances of the derived class. Normally the derived and base classes would be contiguous in memory. The compiler will use the pointer whether there is multiple inheritance or not. If there is multiple inheritance, different derived classes will point to the same copy of the base class.

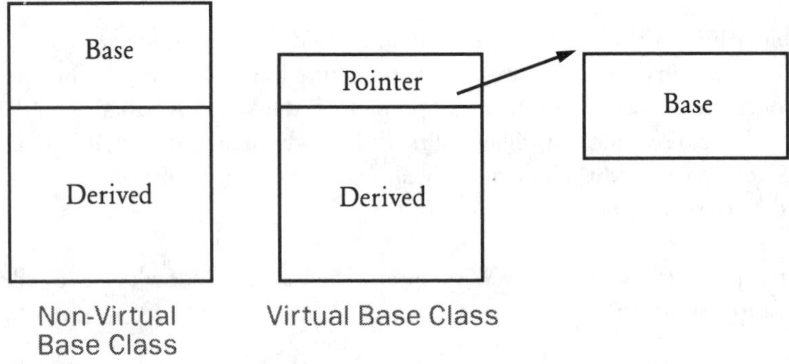


It follows then that multiple inheritance is something that should be planned for in advance, and the designer of a class library will have to decide whether or not to support it. For most libraries, the decision will be not to support multiple inheritance.

## Resolving Ambiguous Virtual Function Calls in Multiple Inheritance

If a virtual base class declares a virtual function, this function may be redefined in two or more derived classes when multiple inheritance is used. Consider this:

```
class Window {
public:
  Window() {nStyle = SNone;}
  enum Styles{SNone = 0,
         SPopUp =0x0001,
         SEdit =0x0002,
         SButton = 0x0004};
protected:
  int nWindowNumber;
  int nStyle;
  void Setup(){
   nWindowNumber = Create(nStyle);
  }
  virtual void MouseClicked();
  // other functions
private:
  int Create(int nStyle);
};

class PopupWindow : virtual public Window {
public:
  PopupWindow(){nStyle |= Window::SPopUp;}
protected:
  virtual void MouseClicked();
  //  functions
};

class EditWindow :  virtual public Window {
public:
  EditWindow(){nStyle |= Window::SEdit;}
  virtual void MouseClicked();
  //  functions
};


class PopupEditWindow : public PopupWindow, public EditWindow {
public:
  PopupEditWindow(){
    Setup();
    nWindowNumber;
  }
};
```

Both the **PopupWindow** class and the **EditWindow** classes redefine the virtual function **Mouse-Clicked**. When the user clicks the mouse in a window, we assume that the system will call **Mouse-Clicked**: but which function will the compiler use, the one in **EditWindow**, the one in **PopupWindow**, or both?

In fact, the function is ambiguous and the compiler should report this as an error. The compilers I am using now do not detect this error and call one function or another, but future versions may detect this error. It is a very difficult error for a compiler to detect, so have some patience.

Whether the compiler detects the error or not, you should disambiguate the virtual function in the derived class like this:

```
class PopupEditWindow : public PopupWindow, public EditWindow {
public:
  PopupEditWindow(){
    Setup();
    nWindowNumber;
  }
  virtual void MouseClicked(){
    // call both parent functions
    PopupWindow::MouseClicked();
    EditWindow::MouseClicked();
  }
};
```

This class elects to call both functions, but it could have called one or another of the functions. It could even have done nothing at all, if it wanted to suppress mouse clicks.

## How To Avoid Redundant Virtual Base Class Function Calls

The previous tip showed how a class derived from multiple bases could call a virtual function defined in both base classes. In the example, the function **MouseClicked** in the **PopupEditWindow** class called **MouseClicked**() in both the **PopupWindow** and the **EditWindow** base classes.

The virtual function in the base classes may in turn call a function in their own base class. In the example, both **EditWindow::MouseClicked** and **PopupWindow::MouseClicked** might call a **Mouse-**

**Clicked** function in the **Window** class. If the base class is a virtual base class, as it was in the example, the function would be called twice. The following example illustrates the problem more clearly:

```
class Window {
public:
  // . . .
protected:
  // . . .
  virtual void MouseClicked(){
    // processing relevant to windows
  }
  // other functions
};

class PopupWindow : virtual public Window {
public:
  // . . .
protected:
  virtual void MouseClicked(){
    // popup processing
    Window::MouseClicked();
  }
  //  functions
};

class EditWindow :  virtual public Window {
public:
  // . . .
protected:
  virtual void MouseClicked(){
    // edit processing
    Window::MouseClicked();
  }
  //  functions
};


class PopupEditWindow : public PopupWindow,
                        public EditWindow {
public:
  // . . .
protected:
  virtual void MouseClicked(){
    // call both parent functions
```

```
    PopupWindow::MouseClicked();
    EditWindow::MouseClicked();
    // causes Window::MouseClicked
    // to be called twice
  }
};
```

Depending on the function, this might just be an inefficiency, but it could cause the program to function incorrectly.

The solution is to separate out the local code from the virtual functions in the immediate base classes, and to place it in a protected member function. The derived class then has the option of calling either the virtual function or the broken out function:

```
class Window {
public:
  // . . .
protected:
  // . . .
  virtual void MouseClicked(){
    // processing relevant to windows
  }
  // other functions
};

class PopupWindow : virtual public Window {
public:
  // . . .
protected:
  virtual void MouseClicked(){
    MClickAction();
    Window::MouseClicked();
  }
  void MClickAction();
  //  functions
};

class EditWindow :  virtual public Window {
public:
  // . . .
protected:
  virtual void MouseClicked(){
    MClickAction();
```

```
    Window::MouseClicked();
  }
  void MClickAction();
  //  functions
};


class PopupEditWindow : public PopupWindow,
                        public EditWindow {
public:
  // . . .
protected:
  virtual void MouseClicked(){
    // call both parent functions
    PopupWindow::MouseClicked();
    EditWindow::MClickAction();
    // causes Window::MouseClicked
    // to be called once only
  }
};
```

Now the derived class has complete control over the function call sequence. In the example, the **PopupEditWindow** class calls first **PopupWindow::MouseClicked**, which in turn calls **Window::MouseClicked**. It then calls **EditWindow::MClickAction**, which executes the actions for the edit window, but does not call **Window::MouseClicked**.

## Virtual Base Classes Must Be Initialized By Any Derived Classes

Once a class is virtual, any class derived from it must explicitly initialize it in its member initializer list, or the virtual class must have either a default constructor or no constructor at all. Consider this code:

```
// virtual base class
class VirtualBase {
 public:
   VirtualBase(int i){SomeValue = i;};
 protected:
   int SomeValue;
```

```
};

// base class
class Base : virtual public VirtualBase {
public:
   Base(int i):VirtualBase(i){};
};

// class derived from Base
class Derived : public Base {
public:
   Derived():Base(13){}; // wrong!
};
```

The class **Derived** is trying to initialize **VirtualBase** through **Base**. This code would be correct if **Base** had not declared **VirtualBase** to be virtual, so most programmers are puzzled to find that it does not work here.

The reason this is not allowed is that the compiler must initialize the virtual base class before any of the others. Although in this case the **Base** class does initialize **VirtualBase**, it need not, and in general the compiler would have no way of knowing what **Base** did, because the code of the **Base** class constructor might be in a separate file.

The are two ways to correct the code. The first is to add a default constructor to **VirtualBase**:

```
class VirtualBase {
 public:
   VirtualBase(int i){SomeValue = i;}
   VirtualBase(){SomeValue = 0;}
 protected:
   int SomeValue;
};
```

Now the compiler will first call the default constructor for **VirtualBase** before calling the constructor for **Base**. **Base** will not initialize **VirtualBase** a second time, so the final value for **SomeValue** will be 0. This is probably not what the programmer intended. The alternative is to have **Derived** initialize **VirtualBase** explicitly:

```
class Derived : public Base {
public:
   Derived():VirtualBase(13), Base(13){};
};
```

This code will result in **SomeValue** having the value 13. Notice that in this particular case there is no longer any need for **Derived** to call the **Base** constructor explicitly.

## Casting a Class with Multiple Inheritance May Change the Value of the Pointer

With single inheritance class hierarchies, a pointer to a derived class instance may be cast to be a pointer to the base class, but the actual value of the pointer will not change. Given a hierarchy of classes as follows:

```
class Base {};
class Derived : public Base {};
class Bottom : public Derived{};
```

pointers to instances of **Base**, **Derived**, and **Bottom** will look like this:

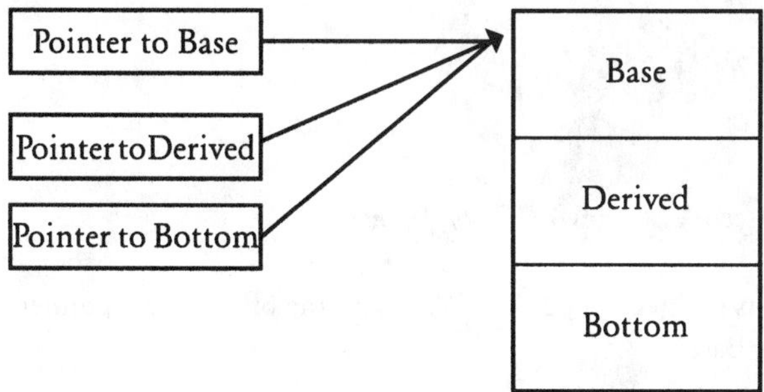


With multiple inheritance, things are rather different, because the derived class has more than one base class. Given the hierarchy:

```
class Base1 {};
class Base2 {};
class Derived : public Base1, public Base2 {};
```

pointers to instances of **Base1**, **Base2**, and **Derived** would look like this:

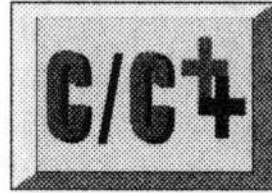

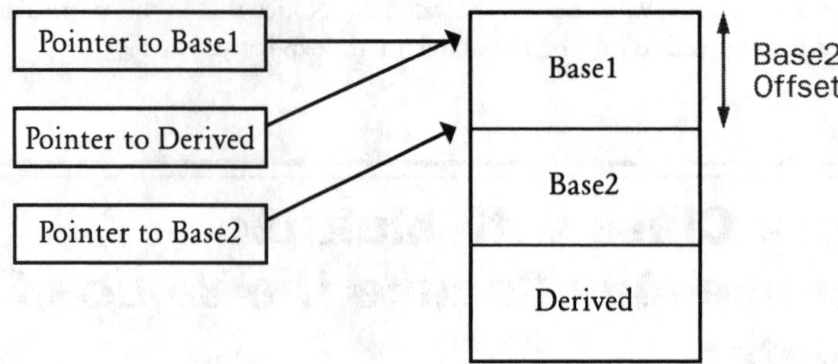


If a pointer to an instance of the **Derived** class is cast to be a pointer to **Base2**, the compiler will have to add the offset of **Base2** to the pointer.

Normally, the fact that the pointer changes does not matter very much. The exception is when you cast the pointer via a third type, perhaps a void pointer. Code like the following is never recommended, but while it will work with single inheritance, it will not work with multiple inheritance.

```
void* pObject;

  // . . .

  Derived d;
  pObject = (void*) &d;

  // . . .

  Base2* p2 = (Base2*)pObject; // wrong!
```

When the compiler casts **pObject** to **p2**, it will not add the offset to the pointer, and **p2** will be left pointing to the data for **Base1**.

## Multiple Inheritance Is Easier When Deriving from Unrelated Base Classes

Many of the problems and complexities of multiple inheritance arise when a class derives from two or more base classes that are related in some way. If the two base classes are themselves derived from a common class, you have the problems associated with virtual base classes; but even when this is not the case, you will often need to deal with ambiguity. These problems were discussed in preceding tips.

When the base classes are conceptually different, you are much less likely to have problems. It is still possible that there will be an ambiguous name in the base classes, but this is unlikely.

## Using a Wrapper Class Instead of Multiple Inheritance

A common use of multiple inheritance is to access useful functions in another class. When these functions are protected, they can only be accessed by derived classes. Here is a definition of a **Manager** class. A **Manager** is a type of **Employee**, but this implementation also tries to derive from the **SalesPerson** class, because this class contains some useful functions for calculating travelling expenses. Because the **SalesPerson** class is only an implementation base class, **Manager** derives it privately. The class hierarchy would look something like this:

```
class Employee {
protected:
int nId;
};

class Auto {
};

class SalesPerson : public Employee {
public:
  void Automobile(Auto& anAuto){theAutomobile = anAuto;}
  Auto Automobile(){return theAutomobile;};
```

```
protected:
  unsigned AutoExpenses(int nMiles);

private:
  Auto theAutomobile;
};

class Manager : public Employee, private SalesPerson {
public:
  Manager(int nID, Auto& anAuto){
    Employee::nId = nId;  // Error!
    Automobile(anAuto);
  }
  int CalcExpenses(int nMiles){
    // ...
    int n = AutoExpenses(nMiles);
    // . . .
    return n;
  }
};
```

This seemed like a good idea, but there are some errors. The **Salesman** class also inherits from **Employee**, so that if the **Manager** class refers to a member of **Employee**, such as **nID**, the reference is ambiguous, because there are two instances of the **Employee** class. It is impossible to disambiguate the reference, and the **Employee** base class is effectively inaccessible.

It would be better in this case to give up on multiple inheritance, and to declare an instance of **SalesPerson** as a member of the **Manager** class. The problem here is that the routines needed in **SalesPerson** are protected.

The solution is to derive a class from **SalesPerson** privately and have this new class make **Manager** a friend. The **Manager** class would then be able to access both the public and the protected members of **SalesPerson**. It would have the same privileges that it hoped to gain through inheritance. The new class and the modified **Manager** class would look like this:

```
class SalesPersonImp : private SalesPerson {
friend Manager;  // Manager access
};

class Manager : public Employee {
public:
  Manager(int nID, Auto& anAuto){
    Employee::nId = nId;
```

```
    SPImp.Automobile(anAuto);
  }
  int CalcExpenses(int nMiles){
    // ...
    int n = SPImp.AutoExpenses(nMiles);
    // . . .
    return n;
  }

private:
  SalesPersonImp SPImp;
};
```

Now there are no more headaches with multiple inheritance, and the **Manager** class still has access to the **SalesPerson** functions.

Note that if the **SalesPerson** class was able to declare the **AutoExpenses** function as static, with the **Automobile** instance as an extra argument, then the **Manager** class would not have needed to declare an instance of **SalesPerson**. Instead it would have declared an instance of **Automobile** and used it to call the static function:

```
class Manager : public Employee {
public:
  Manager(int nID, Auto& anAuto){
    Employee::nId = nId;
    theAuto =anAuto;
  }
  int CalcExpenses(int nMiles){
    // ...
    int n = SalesPersonImp::AutoExpenses(nMiles, theAuto);
    // . . .
    return n;
  }

private:
  Auto theAuto;
};
```

# Designing Classes for Multiple Inheritance

The last two tips showed different ways of implementing a **Manager** class using functions from a **SalesPerson** class to calculate travelling expenses. In a real-life application, as opposed to an example, this might not be an efficient solution. The **SalesPerson** class might be quite big, and it might contain data structures for recording sales, commission, contacts and so on. It would be a pity for other classes to carry all this baggage around simply in order to calculate travelling expenses.

A better idea might be to create a new class, **Traveller**, and derive both the **Manager** and the **SalesPerson** classes from this. The **Traveller** class would contain all the functionality to do with travelling, automobiles, fuel expenses and so on. Other classes—perhaps the **Deliverer** class for delivery personnel—could also be derived from the **Traveller** class.

You could use single inheritance through the **Traveller** class, like this:

```
class Employee {};

class Traveller : public Employee {};

class SalesPerson : public Traveller {};

class Manager : public Traveller {};

class Deliverer : public Traveller {};
```

That might not be a good idea in the end. What if you introduced a new class, **PCUser**? Both salespeople and managers use PCs, at least in this organization, while delivery people do not.

In this case it is better to use multiple inheritance. Each type of employee derives from the **Employee** class, and if necessary from the **Traveller** or the **PCUser** class, or both, like this:

```
class Employee {
  // general data and functions
  // common to all employees
protected:
  int nId;
};
```

```
class Auto {
};

class Traveller {
  // functions related to business travel
public:
  void Automobile(Auto& anAuto){theAutomobile = anAuto;}
  Auto Automobile(){return theAutomobile;};
protected:
  unsigned AutoExpenses(int nMiles);

private:
  Auto theAutomobile;
};

class PCUser {
  // functions related to PC use
};

class SalesPerson : public Employee,
            public Traveller,
            public PCUser {
  // a salesperson is an employee who travels
  // and uses PCs
};

class Deliverer :   public Employee,
            public Traveller {
  // a deliverer is an employee who travels
};

class Manager : public Employee,
        public Traveller,
        public PCUser {
  // a manager is an employee who travels
  // and uses PCs
public:
  Manager(int nID, Auto& anAuto){
    nId = nId;
    Automobile(anAuto);
  }
  int CalcExpenses(int nMiles){
    // ...
    int n = AutoExpenses(nMiles);
```

```
    // . . .
    return n;
  }
};
```

Multiple inheritance works well here, because the base classes are completely unrelated. The **Traveller** and **PCUser** classes are not derived from the **Employee** class, because they are designed for multiple inheritance.

# C++ Techniques

TIP 240

## When Two Classes Refer to Each Other

Often, two classes may refer to each other. In most cases, each class will contain a function that takes an instance of the other class as a parameter:

```
class ClassA {
public:
  Func(ClassB& b);
};

class ClassB {
public:
  Func(ClassA& a);
};
```

A problem that arises in this case is that the compiler will complain that one or another of the references was used before it was declared. In this example, **ClassB** on the third line has not yet been declared, and this will cause a compiler error.

A similar problem arises when each class has its own header file. If each header file included the header file for the other class, you would have the "chicken and the egg" problem: one of the two classes will be undefined.

The solution is simply to declare the classes without defining them:

```
// declare the classes
class ClassA;
class ClassB;

// define them
class ClassA {
public:
  Func(ClassB& b);
};

class ClassB {
public:
  Func(ClassA& a);
};
```

When the compiler encounters a reference or a pointer to a class, it does not need to know how the class is defined, it just needs to know that the pointer is a pointer to a class. (Remember that some compilers implement pointers to different types in different ways. In particular, pointers to characters need to be treated in a special way on word-addressed machines.)

Note that although the compiler does not need a class definition for a pointer to a class instance, it does need a full class definition for base classes and member class instances.

When you have a header file that contains a large number of classes, it is useful to declare them all at the beginning of the file, even if they do not refer to each other. This will act as a sort of table of contents for the file.

## Including Referenced Classes in the Implementation File

The previous tip showed how to declare classes, rather than defining them, when two classes refer to each other. When a class **ClassA** refers to another class **ClassB** that is defined in a header file, it is better for **ClassA** to simply declare **ClassB** in its own header file, and to include the **ClassB** header file only in the **ClassA** implementation (cpp) file. That is, rather than writing this:

```
// classa.h
#ifndef CLASSA_INC
#define CLASSA_INC

#include "classb.h"

class ClassA {

  // . . .

  void Func(ClassB&);
};

#endif // CLASSA_INC
```

write this:

```
// classa.h
#ifndef CLASSA_INC
#define CLASSA_INC

class ClassB;

class ClassA {

  // . . .

 void Func(ClassB&);
};

#endif // CLASSA_INC
```

and include the file in **classa.cpp**.

```
// classa.cpp
#include "classa.h"
#include "classb.h"

void ClassA::Func(ClassB& theB)
{
  // . . .
}
```

Doing this will speed up compilation for any class that includes the **ClassA** header file, because this header file will no longer include the **ClassB** header file along with all the header files that **ClassB** might include in turn.

## Layering Classes to Hide Implementation Details

When you write a class library, you can compile all the implementation files into a library, but you have to give users both the library and the header files that define the classes.

The class definition in the header files will contain all the private data and functions, as well as the public interface. Although the user cannot access the private interface, you cannot remove it from the

class definition. The compiler will need details of the private interface to calculate the size of a class instance, and for generating virtual function tables.

Having to include details of the private interface in the header files is a nuisance. You might have a class that looks like this:

```
class Account;
class Amount;
class Status;

class FundTransfer {
public:
  FundTransfer();
  FundTransfer(const FundTransfer&);
  ~FundTransfer();
  FundTransfer& operator = (const FundTransfer& Copy);
  Status StartTransaction();
  Status SetDebitAccount(Account& DebitAccount);
  Status SetCreditAccount(Account& CreditAccount);
  Status Transfer(Amount& theAmount);
  Status CloseTransaction();
  Status RollBack();

private:
  int JoesHack;
  void Kludge();
  int CuddlyBear;
  Status* JustForTest;
  void CreamOffCents(Amount);
};
```

Many classes are like this. They have a polished professional looking public interface, and a less professional private interface that hints as to how the class might be implemented.

There are other reasons, apart from hiding unprofessional code, for hiding the private interface. The private interface might change frequently, and you would like to distribute new libraries without users having to rebuild the complete system. The private interface may declare instances of other private classes. If so, you will need to distribute header files for these classes as well.

If you need to hide the private interface for whatever reason, you can use the layering technique. This technique involves two classes, a private class and a public class. The private class is an "all-in-one" class, like the one just shown. The public class contains just the public interface functions and a pointer to an instance of the private class. Because it is only a pointer, the header file for the public class only needs to declare the private class as a class: it does not need to include its header file.

The implementation of the public class will pass all function calls on to the private class through the pointer. The public class constructor must create an instance of the private class, and the destructor will destroy it. Because the class contains a pointer, the public class will need a copy constructor and an assignment operator to duplicate the instance of the private class. If it were layered, the previous example class would look like this:

```
class Account;
class Amount;
class Status;
class PrivateFundTransfer;

class FundTransfer {
public:
  FundTransfer();
  FundTransfer(const FundTransfer&);
  ~FundTransfer();
  FundTransfer& operator = (const FundTransfer& Copy);
  Status StartTransaction();
  Status SetDebitAccount(Account& DebitAccount);
  Status SetCreditAccount(Account& CreditAccount);
  Status Transfer(Amount& theAmount);
  Status CloseTransaction();
  Status RollBack();

private:
  PrivateFundTransfer* pTransfer;
};
```

This looks much more professional. The implementation of **FundTransfer**, which the user will not see, will look something like this:

```
// include definition of FundTransfer
#include "fundtran.h"

// include definition of PrivateFundTransfer
#include "prvfndtr.h"

FundTransfer::FundTransfer()
{
  pTransfer = new PrivateFundTransfer;
```

```
}

~FundTransfer::FundTransfer()
{
  delete pTransfer;
}

Status FundTransfer::StartTransaction()
{
  return pTransfer->StartTransaction();
}

// . . .
```

Layering classes has some disadvantages. There is a slight overhead in passing function calls through the pointer, and the public class cannot contain inline functions that refer to members of the private class.

## Keeping Reference Counts for Pointers

TIP 243

As some of the previous tips have pointed out, if a class contains a pointer to data allocated on the heap, you cannot use the default copy operators for that class, because that would result in two instances of the class containing a pointer to the same data. If one of the instances deleted the data, the other instance would be left with a pointer to invalid data. The usual solution is to redefine the class copy operators to copy the data being pointed at, so that each instance points to a separate copy of the data.

All this copying of the data can be inefficient, especially if the data is large. Another technique is to keep a reference count with the pointer, and to increment it every time a class copies the pointer. Instead of deleting the pointer's data, classes would just decrement the reference count, and only delete the data when the reference count reached zero.

Reference count pointers are especially efficient if the data they contain is relatively constant. If a class wishes to change the contents of a referenced pointer, it must first decrement the reference count of that pointer and then create a new pointer containing the address of the new data.

A reference count pointer is easier to implement as a class. Here is a class for a void pointer with a reference count:

```
class VoidRefPtr {
public:

  // constructor allocates memory for data
  VoidRefPtr(void* pData, int nSize){
    ptr = malloc(nSize);
    memcpy(ptr, pData, nSize);
    nCount=1;
  };

  // increment the reference count
  VoidRefPtr* Ref(){nCount++;return this;};

  // decrement the count and delete if zero
  void Deref(){if (!--nCount) delete this;}
  ~VoidRefPtr(){delete ptr;}
  void* Ptr(){return ptr;}

private:
  void* ptr;          // the data
  unsigned nCount;  // the reference count
};
```

The class contains the actual pointer and member functions to increment and decrement the reference count. The instance destroys itself when the reference count reaches zero. Here is a class for referenced character strings that makes use of **VoidRefPtr**:

```
class RefCountCharPtr {
public:
  RefCountCharPtr(const char* pData= ""){
    // constructor creates a ref pointer
    pRef = new VoidRefPtr((void*)pData, strlen(pData)+1);}

  RefCountCharPtr(const RefCountCharPtr& a){
    // copy constructor increments ref count
    pRef = a.pRef->Ref();
  }

  ~RefCountCharPtr(){
    // destructor decrements ref count
    pRef->Deref();
  }
```

```
  const RefCountCharPtr& operator =(const RefCountCharPtr& a){
   // assignment
   // decrement ref count of existing pointer
   pRef->Deref();
   // increment that of assigned pointer
   pRef = a.pRef->Ref();
   return a;
  }

  RefCountCharPtr& operator = (const char* pData){
    // char string assignment
    // decrement ref count of existing pointer
    pRef->Deref();
    // make new pointer
    pRef = new VoidRefPtr((void*)pData, strlen(pData)+1);
    return *this;
  }

  // type conversion to a char string
   operator const char*(){return (char*)pRef->Ptr();}

private:
  VoidRefPtr* pRef;
};
```

This class takes care of the copying and assignments. Notice that the type conversion on the last line declares the result as **const**. That is to prevent other classes from modifying the shared data without first copying it. Finally, here is a simple class that makes use of **RefCountCharPtr**:

```
class Person {
public:
  Person(const char* pName, unsigned Number):
    pName(pName),Number(Number){};
  const char* Name(){return pName;}

private:
  RefCountCharPtr pName;
  unsigned Number;
};
```

This class does not need to worry about assignments and copying, because the **RefCountCharPtr** class takes care of everything. The following code is valid and makes two clones of an instance of **Person**:

```
Person Joe("Joe Soap",5923);
Person* pPerson = &Joe;
Person Clone1 = *pPerson;
Person Clone2 = Joe;

cout << Clone2.Name();
```

Alternatively, this is also valid:

```
Person* pPerson = new Person("Joe Soap",5923);
Person Clone1 = *pPerson;
delete pPerson;
Person Clone2 = Clone1;

cout << Clone2.Name();
```

In this last example, the two clones are valid even after the original has gone. Because the name reference count is still 2, it will not have been deleted.

# Preprocessing

# Using Macros for Conditional Compilation

The macro processor allows conditional compilation. The simplest form of conditional compilation is the **#if- -#endif** block. The **#if** is followed by a constant integer expression, and usually this expression itself contains a macro, for example:

```
#if OP_SYS_VERSION >= 410
  /* only available in V4.10 onwards */
  NewOpSysCall();
#endif
```

The compiler will compile the function call only if the value of **OP_SYS_VERSION** is greater than or equal to 410. The macro **OP_SYS_VERSION** might be defined in a header file somewhere:

```
/* Version 4.30 */
#define OP_SYS_VERSION 430
```

The **#if** block has an **#else** part which the compiler will compile if the condition is false or equal to zero. The **#if** block may also be followed by a number of **#elif** statements, each with a constant expression and a block. The compiler will evaluate each condition in turn until it finds one that returns true. It will then compile the following block. If none of the conditions is true, the compiler will compile the **#else** block, and if that is not present, the compiler will resume compiling after the **#endif** statement. For example:

```
#if OP_SYS_VERSION >= 410
  /* only available in V4.10 onwards */
  NewOpSysCall();
#elif OP_SYS_VERSION >= 350
  /* available in V3.50 but superseded in V4.10 */
  OpSysCall();
#else
  /* must simulate call with versions prior to V3.50 */
  SimulateOpSysCall();
#endif
```

Conditional preprocessing statements such as these can be useful when you need to support different environments, but you should take care to localize them in your application. Resist the temptation to cut and paste conditional blocks all over the application, because you or your successor will certainly need to change them one day. Remember that the compiler does not check the syntax of any blocks that it does not compile, so it is possible to make a syntactic error in a conditional block that will only be detected when the condition for that block is true. If you have already duplicated the block many times, you will need to go back and correct each block.

A useful technique for localizing these statements is to define another macro in the **#if** blocks and then to use that macro within the application, so the previous example could be written as:

```
#if OP_SYS_VERSION >= 410
  /* only available in V4.10 onwards */
  #define OPSYSCALL() NewOpSysCall()
#elif OP_SYS_VERSION >= 350
  /* available in V3.50 but superseded in V4.10 */
  #define OPSYSCALL() OpSysCall()
#else
  /* must simulate call with versions prior to V3.50 */
  #define OPSYSCALL() SimulateOpSysCall()
#endif
```

A conditional block like this can be localized in a header file, and the application will use the **OPSYSCALL( )** macro to call the operating system.

## Using Macros as Flags

TIP 245

A common use of macros is simply to define a macro name, without assigning it a value, and then to test whether or not the macro is defined. To test the macro, use the **defined** operator in the **#if** statement:

```
#define TEST_BED

/* . . . */

#if defined TEST_BED | defined DEBUG
  /* call function if either TEST_BED */
  /* or DEBUG are defined */
  DebugTrace();
#endif
```

You can define the macro with a **#define** statement as in the example, or you can define it with the compiler. Exactly how you do this is compiler dependent, but it is frequently a `'D'` switch, for example: **/DTEST_BED** or **–DTEST_BED**.

The **defined** operator is new to ANSI. An alternative if you only have one macro to test is the **#ifdef** or **#ifndef** statement. These statements:

```
#ifdef TEST_BED
#ifndef DEBUG
```

are equivalent to:

```
#if defined TEST_BED
#if !defined DEBUG
```

The identifier after the **defined** operator may also be enclosed in brackets:

```
#if defined (TEST_BED)
```

## TIP 246 Comment Out Code with #if 0

It is common practice when maintaining production source code to "comment out" redundant code rather than removing it. If the text of the original code remains, other maintenance programmers will be able to follow the modification history more easily.

One problem with commenting out code is that the code may itself contain comments, and comments cannot be nested. Another problem is that the code following the code to be removed may be a comment block, so it may not be clear exactly where the "maintenance" ends.

The best way to disable redundant code is with an **#if 0** block. Comments within the block are unaffected, and it is clear that the maintenance ends with the **#endif** statement, for example:

```
#if 0 /* removed by Joe Soap 03/05/98 */
  int DummyValue; /* not used */
  int TestFlag;   /* used for prototype */
#endif

/* Variables used for Widget interface */
int WidgetStatus;
/* . . . */
```

# Offering a Choice Between a Macro and a Function

Macros may be undefined with the **#undef** directive:

```
#undef DEBUG

/* . . . */

#if defined DEBUG
  /* this code is not compiled */
#endif
```

It is not an error to undefine a macro that is not defined. A common trick, used in the standard libraries, is to define a function both as an ordinary function and as a macro. If the programmer does nothing but call the function, the compiler will take the macro version, but if the programmer first undefines the macro, the compiler will take the function version. Here is an example, taken from the **ctype.h** header file:

```
/* declare function prototype, isascii is defined in
   ctype.c */
int isascii (int __c);

/* define a macro */
#define isascii(c)   ((unsigned)(c) < 128)
```

The macro would normally override the function, so if a programmer includes **ctype.h** and writes:

```
  int c = getchar();
  if (isascii(c)) { /* . . . */ }
```

the compiler will use the macro instead of the function. If the programmer first undefines the macro:

```
  #undef isascii
  int c = getchar();
  if (isascii(c)) { /* . . . */ }
```

the compiler will call the function instead.

## The Difference Between #include "file name" and #include <filename>

There are two ways of including a file. If the file name is enclosed between angle brackets as in **#include <stdlib.h>**, the system will search for the file in a predefined sequence of places. Exactly how this sequence of places is defined depends on the implementation, but it is usually a list defined by an environment variable named INCLUDE.

If the file name is enclosed in quotes, as in **#include "mylib.h"**, the system will first search for the file in one predefined place, and if the file is not to be found there, the system will search as if the file were enclosed in angle brackets. The first predefined place is usually the directory that contains the source file being compiled, but it is possible for an implementation to define another location. This could be the case in a project source control system that maintained all source in a database.

You can use quotes with standard library header files like **#include "stdlib.h"**, and in general the compiler will find the correct file. You should avoid doing so, however, because you may have a local header file with the same name as a library header file. If the compiler picks up the local header file instead of the library file, you will see some puzzling error messages. Of course, you are not likely to have a local header file called **stdlib.h**, but you may well have one with the same name as one of the less common library header files.

## The include File Name Can Be a Macro

Instead of including a file directly, you may include a macro, provided that this macro evaluates to one of the two forms **<filename>** or **"file name"**.

This trick can be useful when you want to include a file and specify the file name at compile time. If you write:

```
#include INCFILE
```

in the source, you can define **INCFILE** using perhaps a compiler switch. Many compilers have some sort of define switch that allows you to add something like **/DINCFILE="myfile.h"** to a compiler command line.

## Include Files May Be Nested

TIP 250

An include file may itself include another file. In the past, this was considered bad form. There is still debate as to whether nesting header files is good practice or not. The advantage of nesting is that a header file for a module can include the header files of additional modules that the first module needs. This is especially useful when writing C++ classes. A relatively complicated C++ class may use a number of other existing classes. It makes sense for the complicated class to include these headers:

```
// header file for ComplicatedClass
// complcat.h

#include <nuts.h>
#include <bolts.h>
#include <brick.h>
#include <block.h>

class ComplicatedClass {
  // . . .
```

Another class or module that needs to include the header for the **ComplicatedClass** need only include **complcat.h**. It does not have to know which other classes **ComplicatedClass** uses.

One disadvantage of nesting is that it is easy to include certain header files twice, leading to redefinitions and errors. For example, if another class **SimpleClass** also included **bolts.h** in its header, a program that included both **ComplicatedClass** and **SimpleClass** would indirectly include **bolts.h** twice. The following tip shows a simple way of dealing with this problem.

Another problem with nesting is that it complicates the task of maintaining dependency files for the MAKE utility. It is difficult to see exactly which header files any given source file is dependent on. Fortunately, there are project management systems that either replace MAKE or generate dependency files for MAKE automatically.

# How to Avoid Including Header Files More Than Once

In C, header files typically contain a list of functions and perhaps some definitions. They do not in general include other header files. In C++, the header file that defines a derived class will include the header file that defines the parent class. Here are three abridged header files, beginning with **base.h**:

```
class Base {
   . . .
};
```

and then the header for a class derived from **Base**, **classa.h**.

```
#include "base.h"

class ClassA : public Base {
   . . .
};
```

and now the header for another class derived from **Base**, **classb.h**.

```
#include "base.h"

class ClassB : public Base {
   . . .
};
```

If another module wishes to use both **ClassA** and **ClassB**, it will need to include both **classa.h** and **classb.h**. This means that it will indirectly include **base.h** twice, and the compiler will object that the class **Base** is being defined twice.

An alternative would be not to include **base.h** in the derived class header files, but to include it once whenever a module needed the **Base** class of any class derived from **Base**. A module that used both **ClassA** and **ClassB** would include all three headers like this:

```
#include "base.h"
#include "classa.h"
#include "classb.h"
```

This would ensure that each header was included just once. The problem is that in complex class hierarchies, it quickly becomes almost impossible to keep track of all the **include** files, especially if the files are being developed by different people who keep changing the class dependencies.

A simpler solution is to put a conditional statement in each header file, so that if the file is included more than once, the compiler will only parse the body once. The conditional statement would look like this:

```
#ifndef BASE_INC
#define BASE_INC

class Base {
   . . .
};

#endif // BASE_INC
```

If the symbol **BASE_INC** has not been defined, the compiler defines it and parses the body of the file. The second and subsequent times that the compiler encounters the file, **BASE_INC** would already be defined, and so the compiler just skips the file.

You should also add a condition of this sort to C header files, if they are likely to be included in C++ programs.

## Header Files Should Not Contain Variable Data

Header files should not contain variable data, since the storage for this data would be declared by every module that includes the header file. If the data is accessible externally, this will cause a linker error. If the data is static, there will not be an error, but the application will not run correctly, because each module would have its own copy of the data. Define the data in the implementation file, and if it is global data, declare it in the header file with the **extern** specifier.

Remember that global data is a thing to avoid. Applications that make heavy use of global data are difficult to understand and maintain. It is better to make data static in a module and provide a function to access the data.

Constant initialized data may be declared in the header files of C++ programs and used as named constants. In C++ constant data of a primitive type does not occupy any space in memory.

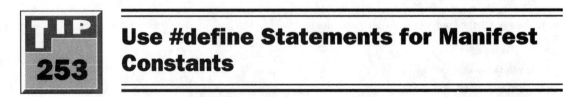

## Use #define Statements for Manifest Constants

The most common use of the **#define** statement is to define constants for a program, for example:

```
#define ARRAYSIZE 50
#define MAXFILES 10

/* . . . */

int Array[ARRAYSIZE];

/* . . . */

while (nFiles < MAXFILES){
/* . . . */
```

The advantage of using macros for these constants is that the value is defined in one place, and changed very easily if need be. Notice that it is a convention to write the names of these constants in uppercase—this indicates to anyone reading the program that the name is that of a **#define** macro. Unfortunately, these macro names are not generally visible in a debugger.

C++ programmers do not need to use **#define** statements for constants: an initialized **const** item works much better (see Tip 136 for an explanation).

C programmers can use the **enum** statement to declare integer constants.

## Using Function Macros

Another popular use of macros is as a function replacement, for example:

```
#define max(a, b) ((a)>(b)?(a):(b))

void func()
{
  int x = 13;
  int y = 99;
  printf("The maximum of %d and %d is %d\n", x, y, max(x,y));
}
```

There are two advantages to using function macros. The first is that the macro is expanded inline, so there is no function call overhead. The second is that there is no type checking, so a macro such as **max** as defined in the example will work with integers, shorts, floats, doubles—anything that can be compared.

Function macros are not without disadvantages. The first disadvantage is that the macro is expanded inline, so the amount of object code generated will be greater than it would with a simple function call. The second is that if the argument is an expression, it may be evaluated many times in the macro. This may be inefficient, and it may also cause errors. Consider this example:

```
#define max(a, b) ((a)>(b)?(a):(b))

/* . . . */

int x = 13;
int y = 99;
printf("The maximum is %d\n", max(x,y++));
```

This reports that the maximum is 100. Note that after the print statement, **y** contains 101. Since the macro evaluates each argument twice, it has incremented **y** twice.

C++ programmers do not need to use macros in place of functions, since they have many other facilities available.

## Use Parentheses When Defining Function Macros

When defining function macros, place a pair of parentheses around the replacement text, and around each occurrence of a macro argument. These are necessary because the argument might be an expression such as **a** >>2 or **b** > **c**. It is important that the precedence of the operators does not change when the argument is an expression, and that can only be ensured by using parentheses around the arguments.

In the same way, the macro itself may be part of an expression, and the replacement text must be placed in parentheses to ensure proper precedence. The example in the previous tip used parentheses in the correct manner:

```
#define max(a, b) ((a)>(b)?(a):(b))
```

This macro will work even in expressions like:

```
if (d > max(e+1, bFlag?x:y)){
  /* . . . */
}
```

## Extending a Macro over More Than One Line

A macro ends with the end of the line. If you have an especially long or complex macro, you can extend it over several lines if you terminate each line except the last with the '\' character. If the '\' character appears as the last character in the line, it acts as a continuation character. For example:

```
#define max(a, b) \
  ((a)>(b)?(a):(b))
```

You may not put anything after the '\' character if you intend it to be a continuation character, not even a comment.

TIP 257

## Using the Stringizing Operator

Imagine that you wanted to define a macro that output trace messages, so that you could insert calls to the macro within your program like this:

```
void func()
{
  TRACE(entered func);

  /* . . . */

  TRACE(leaving func);
}
```

You could try writing a macro like this:

```
#define TRACE(Text) printf("Trace: " "Text" "\n")
```

That compiles, but when you run the program, the output is:

```
Trace: Text
Trace: Text
```

The argument **Text** between quotes is treated as a string, and is not replaced by the macro argument. In this situation you need the stringizing operator #. The stringizing operator expands the next token and then places string quotes around it. The **TRACE** macro above should be written as:

```
#define TRACE(Text) printf("Trace: " #Text "\n")
```

Notice that this macro makes use of string concatenation, as explained in Tip 259.

## Expanding Macros with the Stringizing Operator

Look at this example, which uses the **TRACE** macro discussed in the previous tip:

```
define VALUE 13

#define TRACE(Text) printf("Trace: " #Text "\n")

/* . . . */

  TRACE(constant is VALUE);
```

When you run the program, it outputs:

```
Trace: constant is VALUE
```

How can you get the **TRACE** macro to expand the **VALUE** macro as well? One way is to use a nested macro:

```
define VALUE 13

#define TTRACE(Text) printf("Trace: " #Text "\n")
#define TRACE(Text) TTRACE(Text)

/* . . . */

  TRACE(constant is VALUE);
```

The **TRACE** macro will expand the macros in the argument, including **VALUE**, and pass it on to **TTRACE**, which will print it out, displaying:

```
Trace: constant is 13
```

## Using the Concatenation Operator

The concatenation operator ## will concatenate two tokens into one:

```
#define concat(a, b) a##b

concat(C, lock);
```

This will generate **Clock**. As with the stringizing operator, if you want to concatenate expanded macro names, you will need to go through an intermediate macro, as explained in the previous tip.

ANSI C added the ## operator. In some classic C compilers it was possible to concatenate tokens using a comment:

```
#define concat(a, b) a/*unreliable trick*/b
```

The compiler would remove the comment, leaving the tokens concatenated. ANSI C has killed off this unreliable trick by stating that a comment is equivalent to a white space. You might still come across this trick when recompiling some old code with an ANSI C or C++ compiler, so at least you know what to do about it.

## Defining Typed Functions with the Concatenation Operator

Sometimes you need a series of functions that are identical, except that each function takes a different type of argument, or returns a different type of result. If you wanted a function **max** that returned the maximum of two values, you would need a function for integers, a function for floats, and so on.

The quick way out is to define a macro function, as described in Tip 254. The macro is completely untyped, so it will accept everything. As the tip explained, there are disadvantages in using a macro function, so it could be better to define a proper function to do the job.

The problem is that each function of a certain type must have a unique name, so you need to write something like this:

```
int maxint(int a, int b)
  { return a>b?a:b;};

float maxfloat(float a, float b);
  { return a>b?a:b;};

long maxlong(long a, long b);
  { return a>b?a:b;};
```

With the concatenation operator, you can simplify this work. Here is an example:

```
#define declaremax(type) type max##type(type a, type b){\
  return a>b?a:b;}

#define max(type) max##type
```

The **declaremax** macro declares a function of a certain type. In this example, it defines the function as well. The macro adds the type to the token **max**, to generate a unique name for the function. If type is **int**, the macro will generate a function called **maxint** with an integer result and arguments. The

other macro **max(type)** will be used to call the correct function. To use these macros for finding the maximum of two integers, first declare the function once and then use it, as in this example:

```
/* declare a function max for integers */
declaremax(int);

/* . . . */

int x = 13;
int y = 99;
printf("The value is %d\n", max(int)(x, y++));
```

In contrast to the macro function in the earlier tip, this version prints the correct value, 99, and only increments y once, as expected.

## Using Predefined Macros

Certain macros are predefined. The following macros are mentioned in the ANSI standard, and are always available:

| Macro Name | Purpose |
|---|---|
| __LINE__ | The current source line number as a decimal integer |
| __FILE__ | The file specification of the current module |
| __DATE__ | The date of compilation in the form "mmm dd yyyy" |
| __TIME__ | The time of compilation in the form "hh:mm:ss" |
| __cplusplus | Defined when compiling a C++ program |

The **__LINE__** and **__FILE__** macros are useful for trace and debug macros. The values of these macros change when compiling **#include** files, and then change back afterwards. The **TRACE** macro in Tip 257 could be rewritten as:

```
#define TTRACE(Text) printf("Trace Line: %d File:%s " #Text "\n",\
    __LINE__,__FILE__)
#define TRACE(Text) TTRACE(Text)
```

This adds the line number and source file to the message. The following example:

```
int main()
{
TRACE(entered main);

/* . . . */

TRACE(leaving main);
 return EXIT_SUCCESS;
}
```

produces this result:

```
Trace Line: 18 File:test.cpp entered main
Trace Line: 22 File:test.cpp leaving main
```

Remember that the **__DATE__** and **__TIME__** macros give the time of compilation, not the time that the program is run. These macros are useful for identifying different versions of an application or library.

The **__cplusplus** macro can help if you want to write code that can be used with either a C or a C++ compiler. Tip 139 explains how to make header files portable between C and C++ compilers.

## Using the #error Directive

The **#error** directive causes the compiler to issue an error message and stop. The error message will contain the text that appears after the **#error** directive.

The main use of this directive is in detecting wrong configurations, revealed by the presence or absence of certain macros. A common use is to check for the **__cplusplus** macro in C++ header files, for example:

```
#if !defined __cplusplus
  #error  requires a C++ compiler
#endif
```

You can also use it to check your own macros:

```
#if defined DEBUG && defined TEST_BED
  #error Cannot use DEBUG and TEST_BED together
#endif
```

TIP 263

## Being Pragmatic About Pragmas

The preprocessor supports the **#pragma** directive. Pragmas are completely implementation dependent. The tokens following **#pragma** may be interpreted by the compiler to mean something, otherwise the compiler will ignore the statement.

Pragmas are often used for turning compiler options on and off, for generating form feeds in listings, and for generating warning messages. A typical pragma might look like this:

```
#pragma optimize off
/* The following code is not optimized */
```

You will have to check your compiler documentation for a list of supported pragmas. If you use more than one compiler, you may put pragmas for the different compilers one after the other and each compiler will take its own pragma and ignore the others, for example:

```
/*switch off optimization for compilers X, Y and Z */
#pragma optimize off
#pragma options nooptimize
#pragma -O
```

## The Reason for the #line Directive

The **#line** directive has the form:

```
#line constant "filename"
```

This directive resets the value of the internal **__LINE__** macro to the value of the constant, and it resets the value of **__FILE__** to "file name". The compiler will also use these new values for error and warning messages. After the line number has been reset, it will be incremented as usual at each line.

The main use of this directive is for programs that translate source written in some other language to C or C++. A well known example is **yacc**. **yacc** is a program for generating compilers: its name is an abbreviation of "Yet Another Compiler-Compiler." **yacc** source is a mixture of grammar and C routines that should be executed when the new compiler recognizes a particular construct. **yacc** takes this source and generates the C source of a compiler that will parse source according to the grammar.

When this source is compiled, the compiler may find errors in the C routines that were included in the original **yacc** input. **yacc** only checks the grammar, not the C routines. To help the programmer find the errors in the original **yacc** source, **yacc** inserts **#line** directives before the C routines, resetting the line number to that of the original **yacc** source.

If the C compiler finds any errors in the C routines, it will report the error using the source line and the name of the original **yacc** source file, not that of the C source generated by **yacc**.

## Identifying #endif Directives

When an **#if**- -**#endif** block is long, or if there are nested blocks, it is useful to identify the **#endif** or **#else** directives with the condition of the matching **#if** directive. For example:

```
#if defined DEBUG

/* . . . */

#if defined TEST_BED

/* . . . */

#endif /* TEST_BED */

/* . . . */
#endif /* DEBUG */
```

You should use a comment to identify the **#endif** directive. Some implementations allow uncommented tokens after these directives, but the ANSI standard disallows this. You should use comments for portability.

# TIP 266 How to Write a Multistatement Macro

If a macro contains more than one statement, you could enclose the statements in braces { }. For example, a **TRACE** macro might print out a message and place the current line number and message in global variables. This could help with debugging:

```
unsigned LastLine;
char* pLastTrace;

#define TRACE(Text)   { \
   printf("Trace Line: %d File:%s " #Text "\n",\
     __LINE__,__FILE__); \
   LastLine = __LINE__; \
   pLastTrace = #Text; \
}
```

This would appear to work quite well when used like this:

```
int main()
{
TRACE(entered main);

/* . . . */

TRACE(leaving main);
 return EXIT_SUCCESS;
}
```

but the following code produces an error:

```
BOOL bFlag;

/* . . . */
if (bFlag) TRACE(condition TRUE);
else TRACE(condition FALSE);
```

Because the **TRACE** macro expands to a block, the semicolon at the end of the **if** statement is in error. To avoid this error, declare the macro as a **do** loop with a false condition.

```
#define TRACE(Text) do { \
```

```
printf("Trace Line: %d File:%s " #Text "\n",\
__LINE__,__FILE__); \
LastLine = __LINE__; \
pLastTrace = #Text; \
} while (0)
```

Because the condition is false, the statements will be executed just once. If the statement had been a **while** statement instead of a **do** statement, it would not have been executed at all. Note that the last line does not have a semi-colon. The compiler will consider the complete macro to be a single **do** statement, and so this macro will work with **if** statements as well.

## How to Compile Conditionally on the Size of an Integer

If you have compilers that generate different size integers, you may need to compile conditionally depending on integer size. There are both 16-bit and 32-bit compilers available for DOS. If the code is being compiled with a 16-bit compiler, you may need to use the long type for certain variables, while if it is a 32-bit compiler, an integer would be sufficient. You are not allowed to use the **sizeof** operator in an **#if** directive, because the compiler evaluates **#if** directives before it checks and evaluates types.

```
#if sizeof(int) == 2  /* wrong!*/
long a,b;
#else
int a,b;
#endif
```

Instead, you should use the macros defined in **limits.h**. There is a macro **INT_MAX** that gives the maximum value of an integer, so you can write:

```
#include <limits.h>

#if INT_MAX==0x7fff
long a,b;
#else
int a,b;
#endif
```

## Simulating C++ Templates with the Preprocessor

Some C++ compilers do not yet support C++ templates. If your compiler does not support templates, you can simulate them with preprocessor macros. The are some macros defined in the standard header file **generic.h** that help with this task. The **generic.h** file is quite simple, and will look something like this:

```
/* generic.h */
#ifndef GENERIC_INC
#define GENERIC_INC

#define name2(n1,n2)                 n1 ## n2
#define name3(n1,n2,n3)              n1 ## n2 ## n3
#define name4(n1,n2,n3,n4)           n1 ## n2 ## n3 ## n4

#define declare(a,type)              a##declare(type)
#define implement(a,type)            a##implement(type)
#define declare2(a,type1,type2)      a##declare2(type1,type2)
#define implement2(a,type1,type2) a##implement2(type1,type2)

#endif
```

The **name** macros simply concatenate a number of names to form one identifier. Notice that although there is some white space between the macro arguments and the concatenation operator ##, the preprocessor will remove this white space before concatenating the names. To declare a template, only the **declare** macro is needed.

Here is an example of a template **List** class declared both with and without templates, so that you can see the difference in style. This example assumes the existence of a class **VoidList** that handles pointers to voids.

```
#ifndef LIST_INC
#define LIST_INC

#include "voidlist.h"

#ifdef __TEMPLATES__
  template <class type> class List : public VoidList {
      public:
      List():VoidList(){};
```

```
      List(type *a):VoidList(a){};
      int insert(type *a) { return VoidList::insert(a); };
      int append(type *a) { return VoidList::append(a); };
      int unlink(type *a) { return VoidList::unlink(a); };
      type *get() { return (type *) VoidList::get(); };
  }; // class List

#else  //  __TEMPLATES__
  #include "generic.h"
  #define List(type) name2(List,type)

  #define Listdeclare(type)\
  class List(type): public VoidList {\
    public:\
      List(type)():VoidList(){}\
      List(type)(type *a) :VoidList(a){};\
      int insert(type *a) { return VoidList::insert(a); }\
      int append(type *a) { return VoidList::append(a); }\
      int unlink(type *a) { return VoidList::unlink(a); }\
      type *get() { return (type *) VoidList::get(); }\
  };
#endif //  __TEMPLATES__

#endif // LIST_INC
```

The two declarations are quite similar. If the compiler does not support templates, this example will declare two macros, **List(type)** and **Listdeclare(type)**. A program will use **Listdeclare** to define a class of a certain type, and **List** to declare an instance of the class. With templates, it is sufficient to declare an instance of the template class for a certain type, and the compiler will generate the code for the class.

Notice that there is a continuation character `'\'` at the end of each statement of the macro, except the last. The macro must also use the **List** macro to declare the constructor and destructor, so that the name of the generated function matches the name of the generated class. This example does not have a destructor, but if it did, it would be declared as:

```
  ~List(type)(){/* actions */}
```

A program that wanted to declare a list of pointers to instances of a **Complex** class would look something like this:

```
// declare a class for lists of Complex pointers
Listdeclare(Complex);
```

```
// . . .

// declare an instance of a Complex list
List(Complex) aComplexList;

// . . .

// Use the instance
aComplexList.insert(new Complex(3.5,-4.5));
```

# CHAPTER 10

# A Question of Style

# Indicating an Item's Type in Its Name

A common and useful convention is to indicate the type of an item in its name. For example:

```
int         nValue;
unsigned    uCounter;
BOOL        bOpen;
double      dTemperature;
long        lValue;
int         anVector[100];
char        szBuffer[80];
int*        pnValue = &nValue;
int*        panVector;
char*       pszBuffer;
```

The lower case letters prefixing each item indicate the type, so the "n" in **nValue** indicates that the item is of type **int**. Similarly, the "an" in **anVector** indicates an array of integers, and the "pan" in **panVector** indicates a pointer to an array of integers. The "sz" prefix indicates a zero-terminated string.

This is the so-called "Hungarian" notation. One problem with this notation is that it cannot be easily extended to cope with **typedef**s and C++ classes. Windows programs used to make extensive use of a **HANDLE typedef** and would use an "h" to indicate handles, as in:

```
HANDLE hBluePen;
HANDLE hStripedBrush;
```

More recent Windows programs use one of a number of handle **typedef**s, HPEN, HBRUSH, HWND and so on, and programmers are no longer sure how to name these things. As a result, you are more likely to see a relaxed Hungarian notion where ordinary items have no prefix, but where pointers are prefixed by a "p" and handles of any type are prefixed by an "h". The practise of using "b" for values that should either be true or false is also common. For example:

```
int       Counter;
unsigned  Value;
char*     pBuffer;
HPEN      hBluePen;
BOOL      bInUse;
```

This is the style used in this book, but do not take that as a recommendation to abandon the more rigorous Hungarian style if you are using it now.

## Use Long Descriptive Names

TIP 270

Early compilers, back in the Sixties and Seventies, were constrained to run in what today seems a ridiculously small amount of memory. In the late Seventies a compiler might have 8K to 16K available for code and data. Many compilers in those days, such as the FORTRAN compiler, imposed a six character limit on the names of identifiers, which often had to be in upper case. Others were more flexible, and would allow longer names, provided that the total for the module did not exceed a certain limit, perhaps 500. Either way, the limit encouraged programmers to write in this style:

```
int rctmxt;   /* reactor - maximum temperature */
int rctmnt;   /* reactor - minimum temperature */
int rctcut;   /* reactor - current temperature */
int rctdtm;   /* reactor - down time in minutes */

  /* check current temperature is within limits */
  if (rctcut > rctmnt && rctcut < rctmxt) {
  /* . . . */
```

These days, although the restrictions have gone, the tendency to cramp names has lived on. If you use longer names there is less need to add comments, since the code itself is more descriptive:

```
/* reactor parameters */

int ReactorMaxTemp;
int ReactorMinTemp;
int ReactorCurrentTemp;
int ReactorMinutesDown;
```

## Two Naming Conventions

TIP 271

There are two widely used naming conventions. The first is the capitalized word convention, used in this book, where the words describing the item are giving an initial capital letter and concatenated. The result may have a Hungarian type prefix:

```
int DefectCounter;
char* pRecordPrimaryKey;
```

The other convention is the underscore convention, where the words are in lower case and separated by underscores, with perhaps a Hungarian suffix:

```
int defect_counter;
char* record_primary_key_p;
```

It does not matter which of these you use as long as you are consistent. One factor which will help you make up your mind is the style of the most important libraries that you use. If you adopt the same style, the program will be more homogeneous. In the PC world, many libraries, including Windows, use the capitalized word style, and so most PC applications do likewise. The underscore convention is common in UNIX applications, and PC users will sometimes see it in packages ported from UNIX.

TIP 272

## Naming Loop Counters

You will have noticed that the counter variable in a **for** statement is almost invariably called **i**. If there are nested **for** statements, the counters for the inner loops will be called **j**, **k**, and so on.

```
int Array[10][10];

for (i=0; i<10; i++){
  for (j=0; j<10; j++){
    Array[i][j] = 0;
  }
}
```

This is another relic from the bygone FORTRAN days. In FORTRAN, only identifiers beginning with the letters *i, j, k* and so on, could be integers. If the identifier began with the letters *a* to *h*, it was of a floating point type.

Although you can use more imaginative names, perhaps **FirstSubscript** and **SecondSubscript**, the chances are that you will use **i**, **j** and **k** like everybody else.

## Naming Macros

Another convention that has taken hold is to name preprocessor macros in upper case. This applies to constant definitions as well as to function macros, for example:

```
#define MSG_MOUSEMOVE        147
#define MSG_MOUSELEFTCLICK   148
#define MSG_MOUSERIGHTCLICK 149

#define ABS(A) ((A)<0?-(A):(A))
```

This convention indicates where the definition of the item can be found. Macros are a special case, because the names do not show up in symbolic debuggers and they are often invisible to source browsers.

An exception to this rule would be a macro that redefined a normal function name, perhaps for debugging purposes:

```
#define MyFunc(A, B)  MyDebugFunc(A, B)
```

Other exceptions are the **min** and **max** macros, which are traditionally written in lower case.

```
#define max(X,Y) ((X) > (Y)?(X):(Y))
```

## Naming typedefs

It is also traditional in C programming to use upper case for **typedefs**. A **typedef** may be used as a shorthand for a type specification:

```
typedef char* PSTRING;
typedef unsigned HANDLE;
```

or to identify structures:

```
typedef struct tagPoint {
   int x;
   int y;
} POINT;

POINT TargetPosition;
```

However, with the advent of C++, there is no clear difference between a structure and a class. A structure is just a class where all the members are public. To reflect this, you will often see structure **typedef**s reuse the structure name like this:

```
typedef struct Point {
   int x;
   int y;
} Point;

Point TargetPosition;
```

The **typedef** here simply saves having to use the **struct** keyword when declaring items.

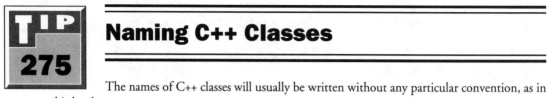

## Naming C++ Classes

The names of C++ classes will usually be written without any particular convention, as in this book:

```
class Employee;
class Manager;
class SalesPerson;
```

If you are providing a class library for others to use, you might consider a conventional name for the classes in that library, perhaps a standard prefix. By doing so, you will lessen the risk of a conflict between the names you use, and the names in other libraries that the user might want to add:

```
//  The Whizzo Object-Oriented Database Library

class WooDatabase;
class WooDataLock;
class WooTransaction;

// . . .
```

There is no need to carry this convention onto the names of the class members, nor is there any need to use it for private classes that the library uses internally.

## Naming Class Instances

TIP 276

This is problematic, since it is difficult to choose a name that gives an indication of the class type of the instance. The Hungarian convention does not help. Often, the best name that springs to mind is the name of the class itself:

```
class Cursor;

Cursor Cursor;   // wrong!

  if (DeskWindow.ContainsPoint(Cursor.Position()) {
  // . . .
```

A useful convention is to use the prefix "the" for the primary instance of the class within a scope, and the prefix "a" or "an" for temporary instances in functions. With other instances, try to use descriptive names that include the class name.

```
Desktop theDesktop;
Cursor theCursor;
Pen BluePen;
File ErrorLogFile;

Window aWindow = theDesktop.GetFirstWindow();
```

## Naming Functions

Function names should usually begin with a verb, followed by a noun, to indicate what they do and what they do it to. For example:

```
void ResetCounter();
void ReleaseLock(Lock& theLock);
Window* CreateWindow();
```

When the function is a class member function, you can omit the noun, since a member function usually acts on the class instance:

```
class Counter {
public:
  void Reset();
  void Increment();
  void Decrement();
};

class Lock {
public:
  BOOL Claim();
  void Release();
};
```

## Naming Function Members That Act as Data Wrappers

Many class function members serve only to access private data:

```
class Rectangle {
int X;
int Y;
int Width;
int Height;

public:
  // . . .
  int GetHeight()
    {return Height;}
  int SetHeight(int NewHeight)
    {Height = NewHeight;}
  int GetWidth()
    {return Width;}
  int SetWidth(int NewWidth)
    {Width = NewWidth;}
  // . . .
};
```

Other member functions simulate class data items that are not kept as data in order to save space, or because the class has been implemented in a certain way, for example:

```
class Rectangle {
int Left;
int Top;
int Right;
int Bottom;

public:
  // . . .
  int GetHeight()
    {return Bottom - Top;}
  int SetHeight(int NewHeight)
    {Bottom = Top + NewHeight;}
  int GetWidth()
    {return Right - Left;}
  int SetWidth(int NewWidth)
    {Right = Left + NewWidth;}
  int GetArea()
    {return GetWidth() * GetHeight();}
  // . . .
};
```

In these cases it would be acceptable to omit the "Get" and "Set" verb prefixes and just use the noun.

```
class Rectangle {
int Left;
int Top;
int Right;
int Bottom;

public:
  // . . .
  int Height()
    {return Bottom - Top;}
  int Height(int NewHeight)
    {Bottom = Top + NewHeight;}
  int Width()
    {return Right - Left;}
  int Width(int NewWidth)
    {Right = Left + NewWidth;}
  int Area()
```

```
    {return GetWidth() * GetHeight();}
  // . . .
};
```

Notice that this is only possible because C++ allows the function to be overloaded so that it either returns a value or accepts a value as an argument.

## Three Different Brace Styles

There are three common brace layout styles. First, there is the Kernighan and Ritchie style:

```
while (bCondition) {

  if (GetFreeMemory() > 500) {
    AdvanceRecord();
    ReadRecord();
  } /* if */

  else {
    ReportError(LOW_MEMORY);
    FreeGarbage();
  } /* else */

} /* while */
```

In this style the opening brace is on the same line as the statement that refers to it. The statements inside the brace are indented, but the closing brace is indented to the same level as the statement containing the first brace. This is the style that Kernighan and Ritchie used in their book *The C Programming Language.* It is also the style used by Ellis and Stroustrup in *The Annotated C++ Reference Manual.*

Two other styles are very common in Europe. There is the Allman style:

```
while (bCondition)
{

  if (GetFreeMemory() > 500)
  {
    AdvanceRecord();
```

```
    ReadRecord();
  } /* if */

  else
  {
    ReportError(LOW_MEMORY);
    FreeGarbage();
  } /* else */

} /* while */
```

Here the opening brace is on a line of its own, indented to the same level as the statement that refers to it. The closing brace is at the same level as the opening brace. In the Whitesmiths style the braces are also indented:

```
while (bCondition)
  {

  if (GetFreeMemory() > 500)
    {
    AdvanceRecord();
    ReadRecord();
    } /* if */

  else
    {
    ReportError(LOW_MEMORY);
    FreeGarbage();
    } /* else */

  } /* while */
```

You may also find variations of these styles, such as the Kernighan and Ritchie style with the closing brace indented the level of the enclosed statements:

```
while (bCondition) {

  if (GetFreeMemory() > 500) {
    AdvanceRecord();
    ReadRecord();
    } /* if */

  else {
```

```
    ReportError(LOW_MEMORY);
    FreeGarbage();
    } /* else */

  } /* while */
```

Although this book uses the Kernighan and Ritchie style, that does not imply that this style is any better than the others. The K&R style is more compact, since it does not require an extra line for the opening brace. Programmers who work with screen displays rather than listings may prefer it because it lets them see more code at one time. If you like to spread program listings out on your desk, you may find the Allman or Whitesmiths style more open and easier to read.

Use the style that you feel most comfortable with, and stick to it. If you join an established project, then use the established style.

TIP 280

## How to Wrap Expressions

Sometimes expressions can get quite long and need to be split over two or more lines. If the expression is especially convoluted, you would be better off rewriting it as several separate statements. Many expressions are not very complex, they are just long, and would not benefit from being split into separate statements.

A useful set of rules for splitting expressions are:

- Split the expression at an operator with a low precedence.
- Place the operator on the new line.
- Indent the line to the level of the operator's left-hand operand.
- If the left-hand operand is the beginning of the statement, indent an extra level.

The ideal would be to split the expression at the operator with the lowest precedence, but if this operator is near the beginning or the end of the expression you are left with a line almost as long as the original. Here are some examples:

```
pDatabaseRecord->Product->Taxcode
    = NewTaxCodes[pDatabaseRecord->Product->Number];
```

The assignment operator has the lowest precedence and also falls in the middle of the expression. Putting the operator on the second line indicates that this line is a continuation, and not a separate statement in its own right. It is easy to overlook an operator at the end of a line. The second line is indented from the statement level.

```
TotalValue = pDatabaseRecord->Product->Value
             + CurrentOrder.Quantity;
```

Here, the second line would still be too long if it were to be split at the assignment operator, so it is split at the operator with the next highest precedence, the addition operator, and indented to the level of the left-hand operand for this operator.

```
bEqualRects =    Rect1.Top == Rect2.Top
              && Rect1.Left == Rect2.Left
              && Rect1.Bottom == Rect2.Bottom
              && Rect1.Right == Rect2.Right;
```

The value being assigned is the result of a Boolean expression, and the logical AND operator has the lowest precedence. Since the lines are similar, the code will look neater if you insert an extra space in the first line, after the assignment, to line up the **Rect1** identifiers.

## Splitting if and while Statements

TIP 281

The rules outlined in the previous tip also apply to **if** and **while** statements. If the body of the **if** or **while** statement is a single statement, first try splitting the line before this statement:

```
if ( Condition == GREEN && Status == OK)
  GrantClearance();
```

When you need to split the expression, the indentation will look odd if you follow the Kernighan and Ritchie style:

```
if (    Condition == GREEN
    && Status == OK
    && ResourceLevel > MinimumResourceLevel)
  GrantClearance();
```

or:

```
if (   Condition == GREEN
    && Status == OK
    && ResourceLevel > MinimumResourceLevel){
  GrantClearance();
  ResetResources();
}
```

It is not really clear where the expression ends and the body begins. In that case you might prefer to always uses braces, even for a single statement, and to place the opening brace on a separate line:

```
if (   Condition == GREEN
    && Status == OK
    && ResourceLevel > MinimumResourceLevel)
{
  GrantClearance();
}
```

Note that many programmers prefer to split one-line **for**, **while**, and **if** statements, even if they are short, so that instead of writing:

```
if ( Status == OK) GrantClearance();
```

they would write:

```
if ( Status == OK)
  GrantClearance();
```

or perhaps:

```
if ( Status == OK) {
  GrantClearance();
}
```

Although this book favors the one-line style, the two-line styles are just as valid.

## TIP 282 How to Split for Statements

The **for** statement is similar to the **if** and **while** statements described in the last tip. If possible, split the **for** statement expression at a semicolon:

```
for ( pCurrentRecord = &FirstRecord;
      pCurrentRecord <= &LastRecord;
      pCurrentRecord = pCurrentRecord->GetNext())
{
  ProcessRecord(pCurrentRecord);
}
```

Often only the second expression, the termination condition, is long, and the other two expressions are **i=0** and **i++**. In that case, you might make an exception and split the statement into two lines, rather than four:

```
for ( i=0; i < ARRAYSIZE && Status == OK
           && ResourceLevel > MinResourceLevel; i++)
{
  /* Loop body */
}
```

# How to Split Long Function Calls

TIP 283

If a function call is part of an expression, it is better to try to split the expression elsewhere and keep the function call intact. When a function has several long arguments, try to split it after an argument.

```
theDatabase.Search( pUserQuery->Criterium,
                    CurrentSession.pDomain,
                    &aSearchCursor);
```

This is an exception to the rule in Tip 280 that recommends placing the operator on the next line in front of the split text. A comma just does not look right with nothing before it.

When only one argument is long and the others are short, you will have to split the argument:

```
SetPoint( XOrigin,   (YOrigin + YOffset + theObject.Y)
                   * YScalingFactor / AspectRatio, FALSE);
```

You might consider rewriting a statement like this as two statements, but often you will still have to split the long expression:

```
int YPosition = (YOrigin + YOffset + theObject.Y)
              * YScalingFactor / AspectRatio;
SetPoint( XOrigin, YPosition, FALSE);
```

Notice that this is easier to do in C++ than in C. In C you would have to declare the temporary value at the head of the block.

## TIP 284 Treat the else if Statements as One

When a statement contains an **else** followed by an **if**, it is more natural to consider them as one and to place the **if** on the same line as the **else**. For example:

```
if (SalesValue > 50000)
  Promote(anEmployee, SALES_MANAGER);
else if (SalesValue > 20000)
  AddBonus(anEmployee, 1000);
else if (SalesValue > 10000)
  AddBonus(anEmployee, 100);
else if (SalesValue < 5000)
  TerminateContract(anEmployee);
```

## Try to Avoid Empty for and while Statements

It is possible to write a **for** or a **while** statement where all the processing is done by the condition. Such statements are often searching for something:

```
/* search for an opening '(' in the text */
while (*++pText != '(');

/* search for element with value 0 */

for (i=0; i< ARRAY_SIZE && Array[i]!=0; i++);
```

Statements such as these are confusing and some compilers will give a warning. A casual reader, not noticing the semi-colon, might assume that the following statement is the loop body. It is better to move something outside the condition just for the sake of appearance.

```
/* search for an opening '(' in the text */
while (*pText != '(') pText++;

/* search for element with value 0 */

for (i=0; i< ARRAY_SIZE && Array[i]!=0; ) i++;
```

## Place the while of a do Statement After the Closing Brace

In a **do—while** statement the **while** condition is better placed on the same line as the closing brace of the **do** statement. That way it will not be mistaken for a **while** loop in its own right.

```
  do {
    /* do body */
  } while ( /* condition */ );
```

## Formatting switch Statements

A common style for **switch** statements is to put the **case** statements on the same level as the **switch** control statement, but to indent the statements following the **case**:

```
switch ( Command ) {
case COM_OPEN_FILE:
  pCurrentFile = OpenFile();
  break;
case COM_SAVE:
  Save(pCurrentFile);
  break;
case COM_SAVEAS:
  pCurrentFile = NewName();
  Save(pCurrentFile);
  break;
}
```

However, as Tip 102 pointed out, if you declare items after a **case** statement, you should enclose the statements in braces, to make the code portable to C++. The code would look odd if these extra braces were at the same level as the **switch** statement, so they should be at the same level as the statements following the **case**:

```
switch ( Command ) {
case COM_OPEN_FILE:
  pCurrentFile = OpenFile();
  break;
case COM_SAVE:
  Save(pCurrentFile);
  break;
case COM_SAVEAS:
  {
    File* pTempFile = NewName();
    if (!pTempFile) break;
    pCurrentFile = pTempFile;
    Save(pCurrentFile);
  }
  break;
}
```

## TIP 288 Writing Function Definitions

Even using the Kernighan and Ritchie style (see Tip 279), the opening brace of the function appears on a separate line:

```
int Function(int Arg1, int Arg2)
{
  /* function body */
}
```

Logically, following the Kernighan and Ritchie style, the opening brace should appear at the end of the first line after the arguments. This is a holdover from classic C, where the argument types were specified separately:

```
int Function(Arg1, Arg2)
  int Arg1;
  int Arg2;
```

```
{
  /* function body */
}
```

The examples in this book have the opening brace on a separate line, following the tradition, but either style would be correct, and it is now common to put the opening brace on the same line as the function declaration when writing inline functions in C++ (see Tip 290.)

Some programmers like to put the return type on a separate line so that the function name is more in evidence:

```
Employee*
CreateNewEmployee(int EmployeeID)
{
  /* function body */
}
```

If the return type is on the same line as the function, you will find it easier to create function prototypes by cutting and pasting the line and then adding the semicolon.

## Two Ways of Laying Out a Class Definition

There are two common ways of laying out a class definition. The first places the private data before the public functions and data. Any members declared in a class before an access specifier are private by default, for example:

```
class Complex {
  double Real;
  double Imaginary;

public:
  Complex();
  Complex(double Real, double Imaginary);
  // more functions
};
```

The other style, used in this book, is to place the public members first, followed by the protected members, followed by the private members. In each section, data members appear before function members:

```
class Complex {
public:
  Complex();
  Complex(double Real, double Imaginary);
  // more functions

private:
  double Real;
  double Imaginary;
  // private functions
};
```

Both of these styles are valid, and you will see both in literature about C++. One advantage in placing the public members first is that anyone using the class will find it easier to browse the header file containing the declaration.

## Laying Out Inline Functions

Most inline functions are only one statement long, and it is common to lay them out in one line:

```
class Counter {
public:
  Counter(int nCount){theCount = nCount;}
private:
  int theCount;
};
```

Notice that the closing brace does not need to be followed by a semicolon, although it makes no difference if you add a semicolon anyway. The statement inside the braces does need to be terminated with a semicolon, even if there is only one statement.

If there is more than one statement, you could still keep them in one line, if they are trivial:

```
class Complex {
public:
```

```
  Complex(){r = 0.0; i = 0.0;}
private:
  double r;
  double i;
};
```

If the statements are too long to write in one line, then you must split them as with a normal function. Since inline functions are a C++ construct, you may wish to break with the C programming tradition of putting the opening brace of a function on a new line (see Tip 288).

```
class Complex {
public:
  Complex(){
    RealPart = 0.0;
    ImaginaryPart = 0.0;
  }
private:
  double RealPart;
  double ImaginaryPart;
};
```

## Separating Out Inline Functions

TIP 291

If you are writing a class library, you might think that it is untidy having the inline statements in the class definition. The class library users will use the class definition in a header file as reference, and they are likely to be confused by the inline statements. In that case, you can separate the inline functions from their definitions:

```
class Counter {
public:
  Counter(int nCount);
  int Value();
private:
  int theCount;
};

inline Counter::Counter(int nCount){ theCount = nCount;}
inline int Counter::Value(){return theCount;}
```

Remember that you must still keep the inline functions in the header file: you cannot put them in the implementation (.cpp) file, because the compiler needs them whenever it compiles the class definition. If the inline functions are in the implementation file and another module includes the header file, the compiler will compile calls to the functions as normal, non-inline, calls, and when you link the application, the linker will give an error because it will not have found these functions.

Although it is not strictly necessary, you can put the inline specifier with the function declaration in the class declaration. This will simply point out to users that the function is indeed an inline function.

```
class Counter {
public:
  inline Counter(int nCount);
  inline int Value();
private:
  int theCount;
};

inline Counter::Counter(int nCount){ theCount = nCount;}
inline int Counter::Value(){return theCount;}
```

## Preprocessor Statements No Longer Need to Start in Column 1

With older C compilers, preprocessor statements, those beginning with #, had to start in column 1. Although this restriction was lifted in ANSI C, as well as in many compilers that predate the ANSI standard, there is still a tradition of placing all preprocessor statements in column 1. This is unfortunate, because in many cases these statements would be better indented.

The following preprocessor statements are better written as:

```
#if defined(DEBUG)
  #define TRACE(TEXT) LogText(#TEXT);
  #if defined(WINDOWS)
    #define TRACE_BUFFER 2000
  #else
    #define TRACE_BUFFER 500
  #endif /* WINDOWS */
#else
```

```
  #define TRACE(TEXT)
#endif /* DEBUG */
```

rather than as:

```
#if defined(DEBUG)
#define TRACE(TEXT) LogText(#TEXT);
#if defined(WINDOWS)
#define TRACE_BUFFER 2000
#else
#define TRACE_BUFFER 500
#endif /* WINDOWS */
#else
#define TRACE(TEXT)
#endif /* DEBUG */
```

## Leave Expression Optimization to the Compiler

C programmers who understand computers at the instruction level are prone to rearranging expressions in an attempt to optimize them. For example, on most processors an arithmetic shift instruction is much faster than a multiply instruction. A programmer who knew that might be tempted to rewrite an expression such as:

```
int a = b * 8;
```

as:

```
int a = b << 3;
```

Shifting a number left by 3 is the same as multiplying it by 2 to the power of 3, which is 8.

Most modern compilers render tricks of this kind unnecessary, since the compiler can optimize the expression itself. If the compiler finds a multiplication by a constant power of two, it will generate code to shift the value rather than multiply it. There are two advantages to leaving the optimization to the compiler.

First, the meaning of the source code is clearer if it is not optimized manually. If the code multiplies by a number, the meaning is clear to everyone, but a shift operation may raise doubts. Not all C programmers realize that a left shift of 3 is equivalent to multiplying by 8, and others may be left wondering why the code uses a shift instead of a multiplication.

The other advantage to leaving the optimization to the compiler is that the compiler can optimize according to the target machine. It is possible, for example, that the next generation of the processor will have a multiply instruction that is faster than a shift.

In spite of that, remember that although the compiler can optimize expressions, it cannot optimize algorithms very much, and it will certainly not replace a poor algorithm with a good one.

PART
2

The
Libraries
Library

# The Standard C Library

## Use the Header Files Delivered with Your Library

If your system has more than one compiler installed, you must make sure that you use the header files that were delivered with the library that you are using. This applies if you only use ANSI standard functions. The header files often contain implementation-dependent code, which means that function calls will either not link or not run with someone else's library. For example, the header file might redefine a function to call some other internal function:

```
/* Whizzo Compiler Header File */

#define StandardANSIFunc WhizzoFunc

int StandardANSIFunc(int nValue);
```

If this is the case, the linker will object if you link with a library that does not contain **WhizzoFunc**.

Remember, when you have two or more compilers, it is easy to leave environment variables like **INCLUDE** pointing to the wrong set of header files.

## Check for Errors After Using a C Library Function

Many C library functions set the global variable **errno** and return an error code if the function encounters a problem. You should check the return code after calling a library function, and if necessary, you can report the error.

Many of the file stream functions return a code that indicates that either an error has occurred or the stream has encountered the end of file. You can distinguish between these conditions by calling either the **feof** or the **ferror** function. If there was an error, the variable **errno** will contain a number indicating the type of error.

If you ever have to debug some code which fails but which does not check for errors, you can still examine the contents of **errno** with the debugger. The contents of **errno** can be especially useful when you are trying to discover why the program was unable to open a file that appears to exist.

The values of **errno** can vary from system to system, but you will find a list of possible error values in the file **errno.h**.

## The Variable errno May Contain an Error Code When a Function Is Successful

The contents of the global variable **errno** are undefined after a successful function call. The variable is only relevant if the function has failed. Some functions simply do not clear the variable **errno** if they succeed, to save time. Other functions put an error code in **errno**, even when they succeed. This may seem bizarre, but a function having one possible type of error and many error paths will first set **errno**, so that it can just return whenever it detects an error.

You cannot check for errors by simply checking whether **errno** is non-zero after calling a library routine.

## There Can Be Life After main

TIP 297

The **atexit** function lets you register functions that will be executed on the normal termination of the program. A program terminates normally if it returns a zero result code from the **main** function, or if it calls the **exit** function with a zero argument. The prototype of **atexit** is:

```
int atexit(void (*func)(void));
```

You may register more than one function, and if you do, they will be called in reverse order: last registered, first called. This program:

```
void f1(){
  printf("A curtain call\n");
}

void f2(){
  printf("A second curtain call\n");
}
```

```
void f3(){
  printf("A last curtain call\n");
}


int main()
{
  /* register exit functions */
  atexit(f3);
  atexit(f2);
  atexit(f1);

  printf("The End\n");

 /* normal exit */
 return EXIT_SUCCESS;
}
```

will produce:

```
The End
A curtain call
A second curtain call
A last curtain call
```

Functions registered by **atexit** are especially useful when the application is likely to call the **exit** function to terminate itself.

## The memcpy Function Does Not Handle Overlapping Areas

The **memcpy** function is not guaranteed to work when the source region overlaps the target region. This situation will arise when you want to move a memory block by a short distance: perhaps when you want to shift a block within a buffer to fill a gap.

On many systems there is an equivalent **memmove** function that copies overlapping areas correctly.

## Using swab to Reverse Byte Order

TIP 299

Some machines, such as the Motorola 68000 series, store integers in memory with the high order byte first. Other machines, such as the Intel 80x86 series and the Digital VAX series, store integers with the low order byte first.

This difference in architecture is only a problem when transferring data between machines of different architectures. In heterogeneous UNIX networks, transfer between different architectures is very common, but there are protocols, RPC (Remote Procedure Call) is one, that will take care of converting the data during transfer. The byte order can still be a problem on UNIX systems when one machine needs to read a binary file that has been created by another machine.

Most PC networks are based on the same Intel hardware, but it is not unusual to find PCs that use the serial port to control equipment containing another type of processor. There are also PC networks that can link with machines running UNIX, VMS, or another operating system.

The best way of dealing with reversed bytes is to reverse them back while reading them, and for that the **swab** function is ideal. The prototype is:

```
void swab(char* pSource, char* pTarget, int nBytes);
```

The source and destination may be the same. You should only use **swab** on the integers in the binary input. Do not use it on character arrays. Note that **swab** only works on 16-bit values. If you need to reverse 32-bit values, take a look at the next tip.

## Reversing byte Order in Long Integers

The **swab** function will reverse bytes in a 16-bit integer, but you may need to reverse bytes in a 32-bit long integer. Here is a function that works with 32-bit long integers:

```
void swali(unsigned long* pSource,
          unsigned long* pTarget,int nNumber)
{
  // first swap byte pairs
  swab((char*)pSource, (char*)pTarget,
      sizeof (unsigned long)* nNumber);
```

```
  // now swap 16-bit integer pairs
  while (nNumber-- >0){
    *pTarget = (*pTarget >> 16)
            | (*pTarget << 16);
    pTarget++;
  }
}
```

The function reverses each element in an array of 32-bit integers. You may call the function like this:

```
unsigned long Array[3] = {0xa1a2a3a4,
                          0xb1b2b3b4,
                          0xc1c2c3c4};

printf("%lx, %lx, %lx\n", Array[0], Array[1], Array[2]);
swali(Array, Array, 3);
printf("%lx, %lx, %lx\n", Array[0], Array[1], Array[2]);
```

This code produces:

```
a1a2a3a4, b1b2b3b4, c1c2c3c4
a4a3a2a1, b4b3b2b1, c4c3c2c1
```

If you want to reverse 64-bit value, you will need to add an additional step that reverses the 32-bit pairs.

## Using getenv to Retrieve an Environment Variable

The **getenv** function will return the value of any system environment variable. This function is used quite often by UNIX programmers, but it is also useful for DOS applications to retrieve the value of system environment variables that the user has set, usually in the **AUTOEXEC.BAT** file.

```
char* pTemp = getenv("TEMP");
cout << "Temporary directory is " << pTemp << endl;
```

If the variable does not exist, **getenv** will return null. Notice that there is also a **putenv** function that sets or changes an environment variable, but only for the current application.

# Using the Character Classification Functions

There are a number of routines that classify characters. Most of these routines begin with the letters "is", for example **isdigit** returns true if the character argument is a decimal digit. There are also two routines that convert characters between lower and upper case, **toupper** and **tolower**. The prototypes for all these routines are in the include file **ctype.h**.

These routines are very efficient, because they use a lookup table. The table contains for each character a set of flags that give that character's properties. The classification routine has only to look up the character and test the flags. Using the routines will be faster than writing tests of this sort:

```
if (c>='0' && c<='9'){ /* it's a digit */
```

Unfortunately, these routines only work with the characters in the range up to 127, so they will not work with any of the 8-bit character sets that include European characters and special symbols. There is one exception, the **isascii** routine returns false if the argument is a character in the extended range of 128 to 255.

These routines are defined both as macros and functions. The macro version is faster, but you forgo the type checking if the argument is not a character.

How do you choose whether to use the macro version or the function? If you call the function normally, the compiler will use the macro version. If on the other hand, you enclose the function name in parentheses, like this:

```
if ((isxdigit)(c))
```

the compiler will not recognize the macro call and will use the function. An alternative would be to undefine the macro definition:

```
#include <ctype.h>
#undef isxdigit

// . . .

if (isxdigit(c)) // use function call
```

## TIP 303 Creating Unique File Names

If you want to create a temporary file, you would like it to have a unique name. The danger with arbitrary names like TEMP.DAT is that the user may have an important file of that name containing details of all the temporary workers in the organization, and then your application goes and overwrites it. Even if you choose a name like XGY85W3K.K2P, you will run into trouble when the user runs two instances of your application, or when two PCs running your application share a common drive on the network.

The **mktemp** function will generate a unique file name in the current directory. You supply a template of the form **prefixXXXXXX**, and the trailing Xs will be replaced by a number, for example:

```
char Template[16] = "hhXXXXXX";
cout << mktemp(Template) << endl;
```

Another alternative is the **tempnam** function. The advantage of this function is that it tries to find a name in the directory specified by the **TMP** environment variable. The user will set this to a directory suitable for temporary files. The current directory might be a slow network drive, or even worse, a CD-ROM! The **tempname** function will look first in the **TMP** directory, then in the directory specified as an argument, if any, and then in the current directory. You may also specify a prefix to **tempnam**. The **tempname** function will use **malloc** to allocate space for the name, so you must free this space after use with **free**. Here is the prototype:

```
char* tempnam(char* pDirectory, char* pPrefix);
```

Here is an example using **tempnam**:

```
char* pName = tempnam(NULL,"hh");
cout << pName << endl;
free(pName);
```

## TIP 304 Getting Information About a File

The **fstat** function will fill a structure with information about an open file, given a file handle. The structure contains the file length, the time it was last modified, and some other information. Here is the definition of the **stat** structure:

```
struct _stat {
    _dev_t st_dev;          // disk drive or device handle
    _ino_t st_ino;
    unsigned short st_mode; // file mode information
    short st_nlink;         // link number, 1 for DOS
    short st_uid;           // owner id
    short st_gid;           // group id
    _dev_t st_rdev;
    _off_t st_size;         // size of the file
    time_t st_atime;        // time of last access
    time_t st_mtime;        // time of last modification
    time_t st_ctime;        // time of creation
    };
```

Here is an example of how **fstat** is used:

```
// open the file
int fh = open("c:\\autoexec.bat",_O_RDONLY);
struct stat sbuf;
fstat(fh,&sbuf); // fill the structure
cout << "The size is " << sbuf.st_size << endl;
close(fh);  // close the file
```

This is well and good, but many applications used buffered file I/O or C++ iostreams. For C streams there is a function **fileno** that returns the file handle associated with a given stream:

```
FILE* aFile = fopen("c:\\autoexec.bat","r");
struct stat sbuf;
fstat(fileno(aFile),&sbuf);  // use fileno here
cout << "The size is "<< sbuf.st_size << endl;
fclose(aFile);
```

## Using seek to Find the File Length

TIP 305

A quick way to find the length of a file is to seek to the end and then use a "tell" function to get the file position of the end of file. This position will correspond to the file length. The advantage of this method is that it works with almost all compilers and systems.

The name of the seek and tell function depends on the type of file: you use **fseek** and **ftell** for C file streams, **lseek** and **ltell** for file handles, and **seekg** and **tellg** for C++ streams:

```
FILE* aFile = fopen("c:\\autoexec.bat","r");
fseek(aFile,0,SEEK_END);  // seek to end
cout << "The size is "<< ftell(aFile) << endl;
fseek(aFile,0, SEEK_SET); // seek to start
fclose(aFile);
```

Remember to seek back to the start of the file afterwards.

## TIP 306 The File I/O Character Routines Use Integers

All the file I/O routines that get or put single characters either return the character in an integer, or expect an integer as an argument. This includes the routines **getc**, **getchar**, **fgetc**, and **fgetchar** for character input; and **putc**, **putchar**, **ungetc**, **fputc**, and **fputchar** for character output.

If you use the character type anyway, the compiler will convert it to and from an integer, but it is better to use an integer type in the first place, for example:

```
int c;
FILE* fin = fopen("comma.txt", "r");

c = fgetc(fin);

while (c!=EOF) {
  fputc(c,stdout);
  c = fgetc(fin);
}

fclose(fin);
```

## Choosing Between Stream and Low-level File I/O

The C library offers two types of file I/O: buffered and formatted stream I/O, and low-level I/O direct to the file or device. The formatted stream I/O functions mostly begin with the letter *f*: **fopen**, **fread**, **fclose**, and so on. The low-level routines work with file handles or descriptors. These are integers that identify the file to the operating system. The formatted I/O routines work with **FILE** pointers. The **FILE** structure contains the status of the internal file buffer as well as the file itself.

The stream routines work in either text or binary mode. In text mode they will convert between new lines and line feed/carriage return pairs on input and output. The low-level routines just do raw I/O and are only suitable for binary data.

In general, it will be more efficient to use the stream routines even for binary data. Because the file access is buffered, these routines minimize the number of actual I/O operations on the file. This is especially important when an application does a large number of small I/O operations, but the stream I/O is still more efficient than low-level I/O when the application is reading or writing up to a kilobyte of data at a time.

One disadvantage of the buffered stream routines is that the buffers may not correspond to the actual contents of the file. This may be a problem when many processes have access to a file simultaneously. An application may flush the stream buffers, but if it needs to do this constantly, this negates the speed advantages of the buffered streams.

## The fopen "w" Mode Truncates Existing Files

If you use the "w" mode with **fopen** to open a file in write mode, the file will be truncated to zero length. This is fine if you are going to write the complete file: your application might be an editor of some sort that saves a complete file from memory.

If you simply want to update a part of the file, you should open it with the "r+" mode. This is the update mode, which means that the file must already exist: **fopen** will not create it if it does not exist.

The "a" mode is the append mode, which means that the file pointer is positioned at the end of the file. If the file does not exist, it is created. This mode is useful for log files. The "a+" mode lets you read the file as well as append data to it, but note that even if you seek within the file to read, data is always written at the end of the file.

TIP 309

## Reading and Writing in Update Modes

If you open a file with **fopen**, specifying either the "r+", "w+", or "a+" modes, the file is opened for update and you can both read and write to the file. Remember that in update mode you must call **fseek**, **fsetpos**, or **rewind** to position the file pointer before changing between reading and writing.

There is no need to move the file pointer to a different position, but you must call one of the functions. If you want to carry on from the current position, you can set the file position to the current position:

```
FILE* fUpdate;

// . . .

fseek(fUpdate, ftell(fUpdate), SEEK_SET);
```

## Redirecting Standard Streams with the freopen Function

The **freopen** function associates a new file with an open stream. The old file associated with the stream is closed. Here is the prototype:

```
FILE* freopen(const char* pFileName,
              const char* pMode,
              FILE* pStream);
```

You can redirect **stdout** to a file like this:

```
if (freopen("test.txt", "w", stdout)){
  printf("This text is redirected to the file\n");
}
```

Redirecting the standard output in this way can be useful not only for debugging, but also as a user option when the output is likely to be voluminous.

You can also redirect **stdin** to read from a file. That is a useful facility, since it lets the user prepare a file in advance and use it as part of the input. Some applications look for the string "@filename" in the standard input. If they see the `'@'` character, they redirect **stdin** to read from the file whose name follows the `'@'` character.

## Redirecting Standard Streams Back Again

The last tip showed how to redirect the standard streams to a file, but how do you redirect them back again? If you redirect **stdin** to read from a file, you will want to restore **stdin** to the original stream when you have read the file. If you have redirected **stdout**, you may have to redirect it back when the user requests it, perhaps by choosing a menu item, or by pressing a certain keyboard key.

One way to redirect a stream is to duplicate the stream's handle with the **dup** function and then to use **fdopen** to reopen the stream. Here are the prototypes of these two functions:

```
int dup(int FileHandle);
FILE* fdopen(int FileHandle, char* pMode);
```

The **dup** function duplicates an existing open file handle, while **fdopen** opens a stream on a file handle that has been duplicated with **dup**. The following program redirects the **stdout** stream to a file, and then redirects it back again:

```
// duplicate the stdout file handle
int fstdout = dup(fileno(stdout));

printf("Writing to stdout\n");
```

```
// redirect to a file
if (freopen("test.txt","w", stdout)){
  printf("This text is redirected to the file\n");

  // close the file
  fclose(stdout);

  // redirect back again
  fdopen(fstdout,"w");
}
printf("redirection finished\n");
```

## When to Use the locking Function

The **locking** function has the prototype:

```
#include <sys\locking>
int locking(int FileHandle, int LockMode, long NBytes);
```

The possible values of *LockMode* are shown here:

| Value | Meaning |
|---|---|
| LK_LOCK | Locks *NBytes* in the file from the current position, tries for ten seconds before giving up |
| LK_NBLCK | Attempts to lock the region, but returns immediately if unsuccessful |
| LK_UNLCK | Unlocks the region (must have been previously locked) |

The function denies both read and write access to other processes on the locked region. You should unlock the region as soon as possible after having locked it.

The function is intended to be used for locking small parts of a file for relatively short periods, and it is useful for reading and writing records in database files. While the region is locked, other processes have free access to the rest of the file. When using this function, it is important to open the file in sharing mode to give read and write permission to other processes, otherwise they will not be able to read or update the file.

Before unlocking a region, you must seek back to the file position where you locked it. Any read or write operations that you may have made will have advanced the file pointer. Here is an example of how to use the **locking** function:

```
int fh = sopen("c:\\autoexec.bat", _O_RDWR, _SH_DENYNO, 0);
if (fh != -1) {
  char Buf[100];
  lseek(fh, 250, SEEK_SET);   // seek to a position
  locking(fh,LK_LOCK, 100);   // lock a region
  read(fh, &Buf,100);         // do an I/O operation
  lseek(fh, 250, SEEK_SET);   // seek back to the position
  locking(fh, LK_UNLCK, 100);// unlock the region
  close(fh);
}
```

You may lock several regions of a file before unlocking them, but they may not overlap. If you lock two contiguous regions in a file, you must still unlock each region separately.

The **locking** function is especially useful for processes that require frequent access to records in a file. If the access is more sporadic, you might consider just opening the file with sharing denied, and then closing it immediately after the I/O action. It is true that this will deny access to the whole file for a short period, but when access is sporadic, the chances of a conflict are relatively low.

## The calloc Function Initializes Data to Zero

The **malloc** function allocates a block of memory on the heap, but does not initialize it. The **calloc** function is intended for allocating arrays. Here is the prototype:

```
void* calloc(size_t NumberOfElements, size_t ElementSize);
```

If you wanted to allocate an array of ten structures you might write:

```
MyStruct* pMyStruct = (MyStruct*)calloc(10, sizeof(MyStruct));
```

A side effect of the **calloc** function is that it also initializes the memory allocated to zero. This can be useful in many cases when you would otherwise have to initialize the data to zero yourself. If you only want to allocate a single structure, just call **calloc** with the first argument set to 1.

```
// allocate a structure and initialize to zero
MyStruct* pMyStruct = (MyStruct*)calloc(1, sizeof(MyStruct));
```

Use the **free** function to release memory allocated by both **calloc** and **malloc**.

## Using calloc or memset to Initialize Structures May Not Work with Pointers or Floating Points

Some architectures or compilers do not represent null pointers, or the floating value 0.0, with a memory location with all the bits set to zero. That means that using the **calloc** or **memset** functions to initialize a structure to zero might not work if the structure contains pointers or floating point numbers.

Many architectures in common use, including the Intel 80x86 architecture used in PCs, do use zero bits for null pointers and floating point 0.0, so in general you can use these functions, but the code might not be portable.

## Using the Time to Seed Random Numbers

The **rand** function will return a number from a sequence of pseudorandom numbers. The sequence will be the same each time the application runs, but you can "seed" the sequence, so that it starts at a different position, using the **srand** function. Even then, if the application uses the same seed, the sequence of random numbers will still be the same each time the application runs.

Often you will want a different set of random numbers each time the application runs. This is usually the case for computer games, for example. In that case you can use the result of the **time** function as the seed. The **time** function has a resolution of one second, so the result will be random enough for most purposes.

```
srand((unsigned)time(NULL));  // seed the sequence

// . . .

int RandNr = rand();  // generate a random number
```

## Sorting Arrays Using the qsort Function

The **qsort** function is useful for sorting arrays in memory. The function uses the quick-sort algorithm, which is a good general purpose algorithm.

The **qsort** function relies on a user-supplied function to compare two elements of the array and return a code indicating their relationship: <0 if the first element is less than the second, 0 if the two elements are equivalent, or >0 if the first element is greater than the second.

One problem in using the **qsort** function, especially with C++ compilers, is that the user-defined function is declared in the **qsort** prototype as taking void pointer arguments. Here is the **qsort** prototype:

```
void qsort(void* pArray, size_t nElements, size_t ElementSize,
  int(*compare)(const void* pElement1, const void* pElement2));
```

This is awkward, because it forces you to cast **void** pointers to array element pointers in the function. It is neater to declare the comparison function with arguments of the same type as the array, but then the compiler will give a type error when you pass this function as an argument to the **qsort** function.

A quick solution is to declare a **typedef** for the **void** function:

```
typedef int(*CompFunc)(const void*, const void*);
```

and then to use this **typedef** to cast the compare function. Here is an example that does that:

```
typedef int(*CompFunc)(const void*, const void*);

// the array element structure
typedef struct MyStruct  {
  char* pLastName;
```

```
  char* pFirstName;
  int a;
  int b;
} MyStruct;


// the comparison function
int MyStructCompare(const MyStruct* pA, const MyStruct* pB)
{
  int result = strcmp(pA->pLastName, pB->pLastName);

  // if last names are equal, compare first names
  if (!result)
    result = strcmp(pA->pFirstName, pB->pFirstName);
  return result;
}

void func()
{
  MyStruct* pMyStruct
    = (MyStruct*)calloc(10, sizeof(MyStruct));

  // fill in the array here

  // sort the array
  qsort(pMyStruct, 10, sizeof(MyStruct),
        (CompFunc)MyStructCompare);
}
```

The comparison routine can be quite complex and may compare several members of a structure.

# Using Templates with the qsort Function

The previous tip showed how to use a cast to call the **qsort** function with a user function that takes typed arguments. The problem with the standard C **qsort** function is that it expects the user-supplied comparison function to have void pointer arguments.

If you have a C++ compiler that supports templates, it is simple to declare a template for the **qsort** function for sorting arrays of a given type:

```
template <class T> void QuickSort
   (T Array[], int nSize, int(*pFunc)(const T*, const T*))
{ qsort(Array, nSize, sizeof(T),
   (int(*)(const void*, const void*))pFunc);}
```

The template **QuickSort** will sort arrays of type **T**. The user-supplied comparison function will take arguments that are pointers to constant **T** items, so you no longer have to use a cast when calling the function. The **QuickSort** template function also relieves you of the burden of having to specify the array element size. The template function can be called like this:

```
// the array element structure
typedef struct MyStruct  {
  char* pLastName;
  char* pFirstName;
  int a;
  int b;
} MyStruct;


// the comparison function
int MyStructCompare(const MyStruct* pA, const MyStruct* pB)
{
  int result = strcmp(pA->pLastName, pB->pLastName);

  // if last names are equal, compare first names
  if (!result)
    result = strcmp(pA->pFirstName, pB->pFirstName);
  return result;
}

void func()
{
  MyStruct* pMyStruct = new MyStruct[10];

  // fill in the array here

  // sort the array using the template function
  QuickSort(pMyStruct, 10, MyStructCompare);
}
```

If you had a C++ **Array** class, you could even dispense with the array size argument: the template would query the **Array** instance for the number of elements in the array.

## Using Arrays of Pointers with the qsort Function

The array sorted by the **qsort** function does not need to be an array of records: it can be an array of pointers to records. In that case the function will sort the pointers, leaving the records themselves where they are.

Sorting pointers is efficient, because the function only has to move the pointers, and this will be faster than moving large structures. The comparison function will be given pointers to the pointers, so you will need to deference them twice to get the record. Here is a sample comparison function for sorting an array of pointers:

```
typedef struct MyStruct  {
  char* pLastName;
  char* pFirstName;
  int a;
  int b;
} MyStruct;


// function for comparing elements when sorting arrays
// of pointers
int MyStructCompare(const MyStruct** pA, const MyStruct** pB)
{
  int result = strcmp((*pA)->pLastName, (*pB)->pLastName);
  if (!result)
    result = strcmp((*pA)->pFirstName, (*pB)->pFirstName);
  return result;
}
```

TIP 319

## Searching in Sorted Arrays

The **bsearch** function searches in an array for an element that matches a given key. The function uses the binary search algorithm, so if the array contains N elements, the function will find the element with at most log2(N) comparisons. The function only works on sorted arrays, but if the

array is not sorted, you might consider using the **qsort** function, discussed in earlier tips, to sort it. Here is the template for the **bsearch** function.

```
void* bsearch(const void* pKey, const void* pArray,
  size_t nElements, size_t ElementSize,
  int(*pCompare)(const void*, const void*));
```

The **bsearch** function needs a user-defined comparison function that compares two elements. If you use the **qsort** function, you can use the same comparison function with both the **qsort** and the **bsearch** functions. The tips for the **qsort** function apply equally well to the **bsearch** function. A C++ template for the function would look like this:

```
template <class T> T*
BinarySearch(T& Key, T Array[], int nSize,
             int(*pFunc)(const T*, const T*))
{
  return (T*)bsearch(&Key, Array, nSize, sizeof(T),
                     (int(*)(const void*, const void*))pFunc);
}
```

and would be used like this:

```
// set up the key
MyStruct Key ={"Soap", "Joe", 0,0};

// search for a match
MyStruct* pMatch
  = BinarySearch(Key, pMyStruct, 10, MyStructCompare);
```

The function returns a null pointer if it does not find a match. If the array contains two or more elements with the same key, the function may return any one of the matching elements.

## Using the assert Function

TIP 320

One of the most useful functions in the C library is the **assert** function. The argument is an expression. If the expression evaluates to non-zero, or to TRUE, nothing happens. If the expression evaluates to 0 or FALSE, the system displays a message and aborts the program. The message will state that an assertion failure has occurred, and will usually quote the expression and give the source module and line number where the assertion failure occurred.

You can use the **assert** function anywhere in an application, but it is intended to catch programming errors that should not occur in a production version of an application. It is especially useful for checking function arguments for reasonable values. For example:

```
void AddMember(char Name[], unsigned Age, unsigned GroupNr)
{
  assert(Name);
  assert(Age < 120);
  assert(GroupNr<=50 || GroupNr==99);

  // rest of function
}

void func()
{
int Age;
int GroupNr;    // uninitialized variables!
AddMember("Joe Soap", Age, GroupNr);
}
```

The program above will probably cause an exception, because the variables **Age** and **GroupNr** are not initialized and probably (but not necessarily) contain invalid values.

The **assert** function is simple to use, and it will catch many of the programming errors that arise during application development. The **assert** function is actually a macro, and it is defined to be nothing when a certain **#define** macro, usually **NDEBUG**, is defined. If you compile the production version of the application with **NDEBUG** defined, the compiler will effectively remove the **assert** statements, so there will be no overhead from them.

## Setting Breakpoints on Assertion Failures

One minor problem with the **assert** function is that it is often difficult to set a breakpoint on an assertion failure using a debugger. With some systems, the debugger may catch the assertion failure, but the procedure call stack is lost and it is difficult to discover how the assertion failure occurred. The message will of course give the immediate cause of the error, but if this is an invalid parameter, it is useful to be able to look in the function that called the function with the **assert** statement.

If you know the assembler language for your machine, it is possible to place a breakpoint inside the code of the **assert** call, just after it has evaluated the expression and the result is true. You will then have to re-run the application to find out what triggered the assertion failure. There is however, an easier way.

Because the **assert** function is a macro, it is possible to redefine it, and in particular, to redefine it to call a function in which you can place a breakpoint:

```
// break function
int AssertBreak(char* pExp){
  int ret = 1;
  return ret;
};

#ifndef NDEBUG
#undef assert
#define assert(exp) \
  if (!exp){ \
    if(AssertBreak(#exp)); \
      _assert(#exp, __FILE__,__LINE__); \
  }
#endif
```

In this redefinition, if the expression is false, the macro calls **AssertBreak** with the expression as a string. If **AssertBreak** returns 1, the macro will call the internal **_assert** function that displays the message and aborts the program. The name and the arguments for this internal function will vary between compilers: this version is for the Microsoft C/C++ V7.0 compiler. You should look at **assert.h** to see how your compiler declares it.

If you place a breakpoint inside **AssertBreak** with your debugger, you will catch any assertion failure before it calls the internal routine, so you will be able to examine the call stack to see what may have caused the assertion failure. If you set the variable **ret** to 0 with your debugger, the macro will not call the internal routine, and will carry on. This may also be useful for finding out what went wrong.

## Formatting the Time with strftime

There is a function **asctime** that converts a **time tm** structure into a formatted text string; but the format is fixed. For example, a typical result of the **asctime** function would be:

```
Wed Jan 02 02:03:55 1980
```

followed by a new line.

The **strftime** function allows you to be much more imaginative when formatting the date and time. The prototype is:

```
size_t strftime(char Buffer[], size_t BufferSize,
                const char* pFormat, const struct tm* pTime);
```

The function will format the text on the buffer supplied. If the buffer is too small, the function will return 0 and the contents of the buffer will be undefined; otherwise the function returns the number of characters inserted in the buffer. The format string contains codes that the function replaces with components of the date and time. Here is an example:

```
char Buf[80];
time_t theTime;

time(&theTime);   // get the time

// format it
if (strftime(Buf, sizeof(Buf),
    "It is %I:%M %p on %A, the %d %B, %Y",
    localtime(&theTime)))
  cout << Buf << endl;   // and print it out
```

This produces output in the following form:

```
It is 08:33 PM on Tuesday, the 01 July, 2003
```

Here is a full list of the format codes:

| Format Code | Meaning |
|---|---|
| %% | The % character |
| %a | The weekday name abbreviated to three characters |
| %A | The unabbreviated weekday name |
| %b | The month name abbreviated to three letters |
| %B | The unabbreviated month name |
| %c | The date and time |
| %d | The day of the month (01—31) |
| %H | The hour (00—23) |
| %I | The hour (01—12) |
| %j | The day of the year (001—366) |

| Format Code | Meaning |
|---|---|
| %m | The month as a number (1—12) |
| %M | The minute (00—59) |
| %p | AM or PM |
| %S | The second (00—59) |
| %U | The week number where Sunday is the first day (00—53) |
| %w | The weekday as a number (0—6) |
| %W | The week number where Monday is the first day (00—53) |
| %x | The date |
| %X | The time |
| %y | The year as two digits (00—99) |
| %Y | The year as four digits |
| %Z | The time zone name |

## Combining strftime with Stream Formatting

With C++, it is quite easy to format a date, partly by using stream formatting and partly by using the **strftime** function. The C++ streams allow extra fine tuning, for example, dates can be displayed without a leading zero.

The trick is to prepare the format string in a buffer before calling **strftime**. Here is an example that prints dates without a leading zero but with a suffix, so that "3" is displayed as "3rd".

```
// function that returns the day suffix
char* DaySuffix(struct tm* ptm)
{
  static char* Suffixes[10]={"th","st","nd","rd",
                    "th","th","th","th","th","th"};
  return Suffixes[ptm->tm_mday % 10];
}

void main()
{

  char Buf[80];
```

```
  time_t theTime;

  time(&theTime);
  struct tm* ptm = localtime(&theTime);

  ostrstream BufStr;
  BufStr << "It is %I:%M %p on %A, the ";

  // add the day and the suffix
  BufStr << ptm->tm_mday << DaySuffix(ptm);
  BufStr << " of %B, %Y" << ends;

  // format the string
  if (strftime(Buf, sizeof(Buf),
      BufStr.str(),ptm))
    cout << Buf << endl;

  // release the buffer
  BufStr.rdbuf()->freeze(0);
}
```

This program produces output similar to this:

```
It is 01:19 PM on Wednesday, the 2nd of July, 2003
```

## Using the strrchr to Extract a File Name from a File Path

A common programming problem is to extract a file name from a file path. You will usually want to do this when displaying user messages such as:

```
"You have modified the file: december89.rpt, do you want to save it?"
```

The user is not generally interested in knowing the complete path of the file, and since the path may easily be over 100 characters long, it is difficult to format properly in a message. You might need to break it in the middle:

```
"You have modified the file:
/usr/sales/central/joesoap/intray/reports/december89.rpt,
do you want to save it?"
```

The **strrchr** function searches a string backwards for a certain character, so it is ideal for searching for the last directory separator in a file specification. The function will return a pointer to this last character, so in the case of a file you will need to increment this pointer to point to the file name itself. It is possible that the file path will not contain any directories and that the **strrchr** function will not find the directory separator. In this case it will return a null pointer, and you should check for that.

```
char* pFileSpec = "/usr/joe/reports/december89.rpt";

 // . . .

 // find the last separator
 char* pFile = strrchr(pFileSpec,'/');

 // if found increment the pointer
 if (pFile) pFile++;
 // otherwise take the filespec
 else pFile = pFileSpec;

 // use the result
 cout << "The filespec is " << pFile;
```

Here is the output of this code:

```
The filespec is december89.rpt
```

Under DOS and Windows, of course, the directory separator is a backslash, and you will need to escape it:

```
 // find the last separator
 char* pFile = strrchr(pFileSpec,'\\');
```

## Allocate Storage Space When Concatenating Strings with strcat

Programmers who come to C via other programming language, such as BASIC, have trouble with the **strcat** function:

```
char* strcat(char* pStr1, char* pStr2);
```

This function concatenates **pStr2** to **pStr1** and returns the result. On the face of things, code like this ought to work:

```
void FormLetter(char* pName)
{ // wrong!!!
   char* pLine = strcat("Contratulations, ", pName);
   pLine = strcat(pLine , " you are the lucky winner...");

   // . . .
}
```

Instead, it causes the application to crash. The problem is that the function copies the contents of the second argument, **pStr2**, to the end of the string pointed to by **pStr1**: it does not allocate any memory. The **strcat** function always returns the address of **pStr1**.

To use this function, the first argument must point to a buffer big enough to hold the result. This may mean allocating or declaring a buffer and copying the first string into it, for instance:

```
void FormLetter(char* pName)
{ // OK
   char Buf[80];
   strcpy(Buf, "Congratulations, ");
   strcat(Buf, pName);
   strcat(Buf, " you are the lucky winner...");

   // . . .
}
```

Notice that the result of the **strcat** function is not useful unless you want to pass the address of the buffer directly to another function, like this:

```
   FormatText(strcat(Buf, "Yours sincerely,"));
```

## The sprintf Function Will Also Concatenate Strings

Rather than using the **strcat** function, which can only concatenate two strings, you might use the **sprintf** function, which can concatenate any number of strings. You will need to provide a format string, which contains an "%s" format code for each string to be concatenated, for example:

```
char Buf[80];

char* pStr1;
char* pStr2;
char* pStr2;

  // initialize strings here

  // concatenate the strings into the buffer
  sprintf(Buf, "%s%s%s", pStr1, pStr2, pStr3);
```

If one or more of the strings are constant text strings, you can put them directly in the format string:

```
void FormLetter(char* pName)
{
  char Buf[80];
  sprintf(Buf,"Congratulations, %s you are the lucky winner...", pName);

  // . . .
}
```

## Using the longjmp and setjmp Functions for Error Recovery

The **longjmp** and **setjmp** function let you implement a long distance goto. Of course, using gotos of any sort is not usually considered good programming, but you can make an exception for severe errors where you would otherwise have to abort the application.

These functions work in conjunction with a buffer of type **jmp_buf**, defined in the include file **setjmp.h**. The **setjmp** function fills this buffer with the current task state. The task state depends on the machine, but it will include at least the contents of all the machine registers. If the program subsequently calls **longjmp** with this buffer as argument, **longjmp** will restore the task state, and immediately after that, the program will return from the original **setjmp** call. The program would have effectively executed a long goto to the place where **setjmp** is called.

Since this pair of functions is often used for error recovery, the **longjmp** function passes a value, an error code perhaps, that will be returned from **setjmp**. The initial call to **setjmp** will return 0. If

**longjmp** attempts to pass the value 0, it will be replaced by the value 1, so you can be sure that if **setjmp** returns any non-zero value, a jump has occurred.

For error recovery, you should call **setjmp** high in the application, perhaps before a loop that processes user commands:

```
#include <setjmp.h>

jmp_buf CommandLoop;


int main()
{
  // set the jump buffer
  int ErrorNo = setjmp(CommandLoop);
  if (ErrorNo) // report error
    ErrMess(ErrorNo);

  // command loop
  int nCommand;
  do {
    nCommand = GetCommand();
  } while (ProcessCommand(nCommand));

  return 0;
}
```

Later on a function that runs into difficulties can jump back to the command loop. Perhaps there is no more memory: at the command level the user can close some functions that consume memory and try again. A typical call to **longjmp** might look like this:

```
  char* pBuffer = (char*)malloc(nSize);

  if (!pBuffer) longjmp(CommandLoop, ERR_LOWMEM);
```

One major problem when using **longjmp** is that if any functions on the call stack have allocated memory with **malloc** or **new**, this memory will not be explicitly released. Not only that, but the destructors of any C++ class instances that were on the stack will not be called. These problems usually preclude using **longjmp** and **setjmp** in C++ applications.

Exception handling in C++ can only be handled reliably by the compiler, but it is a difficult facility to implement, and although an exception handling facility is defined in the C++ language, few compilers have implemented it yet.

# Duplicating Strings

TIP 328

When you have a string, you often need to make a copy of it, so that you can modify the copy without disturbing the original. The original string might be a **const** argument to a function, for example.

The easiest way to duplicate a string in C, is to use the **strdup** function:

```
char& strdup(const char* pString);
```

The **strdup** function allocates space for the duplicate string using **malloc**, copies the string, and returns the address of the new string. Since the function uses **malloc**, you should use **free** to release the memory after having used it.

```
// a function to count the letter e in either case
int CountTheEs(const char* pString)
{
  int nEs = 0;
  // duplicate the string
  char* pUpper = strdup(pString);
  if (!pUpper) return 0;
  // convert to upper case
  pUpper = strupr(pUpper);
  while (*pUpper)
    if (*pUpper++ == 'E') nEs++;
  free(pUpper);   // free the string after use
  return nEs;
}

void test()
{
  char* pTest = "Eastern Edinburgh";
  cout << "There are " << CountTheEs(pTest);
  cout << " occurrences of e in " << pTest << endl;
}
```

This function duplicates a string in order to convert it to upper case. Notice that C++ programmers are better served by a **String** class. There is as yet, no standard **String** class, but most compilers provide one. A **String** class duplicates a string by assignment, and the duplicate string is freed by the **String** class destructor.

## The Case Conversion Functions Do Not Always Work with European Characters

Case conversion functions such as **toupper**, **tolower**, **strupr**, and **strlwr** do not convert European accented characters. The statements:

```
char Buf[10] = "eénñoöaà";
cout << strupr(Buf) << endl;
```

produce the output:

```
EéNñOöAà
```

You should bear this in mind if your application might be used in a European or South American country. The Microsoft Windows SDK contains some functions, **AnsiUpper** and **AnsiLower**, that do convert European characters in the ANSI character set. There are also functions for converting strings between the PC OEM and the ANSI character sets.

## Take Care with Upper Case European Text

It is common to omit accents from upper case text in Europe. The French AZERTY keyboard does not even provide a means of entering accented upper case letters, other than by ALT keypad sequences or special utilities.

This is fine as long as the text stays in upper case, or in a mix of the two cases; but if your application converts the string to lower case, the lack of accents will offend the sensibility of anyone who understands that language. The French word for "star" may be written as "étoile", "Étoile," or "Etoile", but not as "etoile".

You should also be careful when looking up user-supplied words in databases. A user searching for a name "Étienne Étoile" in a database might enter either "Etienne Etoile" or "étienne étoile." The first form is more likely, but users who are more used to computers might use the second form. The safest solution here is to convert accented and upper case letters to lower case unaccented equivalents before

searching or comparing records. Do not let the user see what you have done though: the user should see the original text that was in the database.

## Tokenizing Comma Separated Lists with the strchr Function

Tip 365 shows you how to tokenize comma separated lists using C++ streams. If you are using C, you may use the **strchr** function to read comma separated lists. Of course, you can do much more with the **strchr** function, but comma separated lists are very common in many applications. Most spreadsheets and databases can export data in a comma separated format.

In a comma separated list, commas separate record members, and the new line separates individual records. There may also be white space between the fields and the commas. A field may be missing from the list. If so, this will be indicated by two commas ",," or by a comma followed by a new line. The program should take a default value if a field is missing.

The **strtok** function would be a good candidate for reading comma separated lists, except that this function treats double delimiters as one, and so would not recognize a double comma as a field. The following code reads a comma separated list and prints out the fields between square brackets:

```
// open the file
FILE* fIn = fopen("comma.txt","r");
if (!fIn ) return;

// until end of file
while (!feof(fIn)){
  char Buf[256];
  // read a line
  if (fgets(Buf, sizeof(Buf), fIn)) {
    char* pNext;
    char* pToken = Buf;

    printf("Record: ");

    do {
      // find a comma
      pNext = strchr(pToken, ',');

      // if no comma, find the new line
```

```
        if (!pNext) pNext = strchr(pToken,'\n');

        // overwrite the delimiter with a zero terminator
        if(pNext) *pNext = 0;

        // handle the field
        printf("[%s] ", pToken);

        // advance the pointer past the delimiter
        pToken = pNext+1;
      } while (*pToken); // until there are no more tokens

      printf("\n");

    }
  }

  fclose(fIn);
```

If the file contains the text:

```
East,563,865,973,387,34,276
North,735,287,594,179,745,390
South,274,194,1035,638,837,87
West,389,649,,903,234,
```

the program will display:

```
Record: [East] [563] [865] [973] [387] [34] [276]
Record: [North] [735] [287] [594] [179] [745] [390]
Record: [South] [274] [194] [1035] [638] [837] [87]
Record: [West] [389] [649] [] [903] [234] []
```

Notice that the program has recognized the two empty fields in the last record.

## Parsing Fields in Lists with the strtol and strtod Functions

The previous tip showed a method of reading comma separated lists. If the list has been generated by a database program, your application may know what each record should contain. Perhaps the first

two records are text fields, the third an integer, and the fourth a floating point number. If the list has been generated by a spreadsheet, or by another application, you might not always know in advance what the fields are going to be. Even if most of the fields are numeric, the first record might contain a description of the fields as text, and the last record might contain text indicating the total.

The **strtod** and **strtol** functions convert text to items of the double and long integer types. Here are the prototypes:

```
double strtod(const char* pString, char** pEnd);
long strtol(const char* pString, char** pEnd, int Base);
```

The first argument is a pointer to the string to be parsed. If the second argument **pEnd** is not null, its contents are replaced by a pointer to the first character in the string that could not be parsed. This character may be the terminating zero. The third parameter to the **strtol** function is the expected base of the number: eight for octal numbers, ten for decimal, and so on.

The second argument is useful for parsing fields, especially when the field is null-terminated. If the pointer **pEnd** points to the null terminator, the field has been parsed as expected. If **pEnd** points to a character within the field, then the parse has failed and you can try something else. If you want to check for either a double or a long integer, or for a text string, you should check first for a long integer. If you check first for a double you will parse long integers as well as doubles.

Here is a function that parses a token and prints out the value between parentheses. The type of parentheses will depend on the value type: they will be, "[ ]" for long integers, "( )" for doubles, and "{ }" for strings.

```
void ParseToken(char* pToken)
{
  char* pEnd = NULL;
  double d;
  long l;

  // try for a long integer
  l = strtol(pToken, &pEnd, 10);
  if (!*pEnd) // OK
    printf("[%ld] ", l);
  else {
    // try for a double
    d = strtod(pToken, &pEnd);
    if (!*pEnd)   // OK
      printf("(%.2f) ", d);
    else          // it is a string
      printf("{%s} ", pToken);
  }
}
```

The comma list code described in the previous tip would call the function like this:

```
// open the file
FILE* fIn = fopen("comma.txt","r");
if (!fIn ) return;

// until end of file
while (!feof(fIn)){
  char Buf[256];

  // read a line
  if (fgets(Buf, sizeof(Buf), fIn)) {
    char* pNext;
    char* pToken = Buf;

    printf("Record: ");

    do {
      // find a comma
      pNext = strchr(pToken, ',');

      // if no comma, find the new line
      if (!pNext) pNext = strchr(pToken,'\n');

      // overwrite the delimiter with a zero terminator
      if(pNext) *pNext = 0;

      // handle the field
      Parsetoken(pToken);

      // advance the pointer past the delimiter
      pToken = pNext+1;
    } while (*pToken); // until there are no more tokens

    printf("\n");

  }
}

fclose(fIn);
```

Given an input file containing this data:

```
East,563,865.34,973,387.5,34,276
North,735,287.03,594,179,745,390.67
South,274,194,1035,638.00,837,87.93
West,389,649,,903,234.67,
```

the program would produce the following output:

```
Record: {East} [563] (865.34) [973] (387.50) [34] [276]
Record: {North} [735] (287.03) [594] [179] [745] (390.67)
Record: {South} [274] [194] [1035] (638.00) [837] (87.93)
Record: {West} [389] [649] [0] [903] (234.67) [0]
```

Notice that the missing fields in the last record are parsed as integers with a value of zero.

## Removing the Trailing Character from a String

On many occasions you will need to remove the trailing character from a string. The trailing character may be the new-line character in the string returned by the **fgets** function, it may be a separator character, or it may be the trailing slash or backslash in a directory path.

The quick way to remove this character is to overwrite it with a zero terminator, effectively truncating the string by one character. The **strlen** function will return the length of the string, and the array subscript for the terminating character is one less than this, so the code:

```
if (Buf[0]) Buf[strlen(Buf)-1] = 0;
```

will remove the trailing character. There is a chance that the string might be empty, so the test **if (Buf[0])** tests the first character of the array: if it is non-zero, the string is not empty. The test is necessary, otherwise you risk overwriting the byte before the array, if the string is empty.

## The Arguments to scanf Must Be Addresses

The **scanf** function reads values from **stdin** according to a format string and places the values in the arguments that follow, so the code:

```
int i,j;
scanf("%d %d", &i, &j);
```

will cause **scanf** to read two integers, separated by white space, and to place them in **i** and **j**.

The arguments must be addresses. This is important, because the compiler is unable to check the argument types for this function. The prototype is:

```
int scanf(const char* pFormat, ...);
```

and the ellipsis simply means "further arguments." If you write:

```
int i,j;
scanf("%d %d", i, j);  // wrong!!
```

the compiler will not complain, but your program will crash when you run it.

C++ programmers should avoid **scanf** in favor of the C++ iostream library, discussed in Chapter 12.

## TIP 335 Using Search Sets with scanf

The ANSI C standard added the ability to search for characters in a search set. This facility is rarely used by programmers used to classic C, but it is a useful feature nevertheless. The search set is similar to a UNIX regular expression, although not as complete.

The format specifier *%[search set]* searches for a string of characters such that each character in the string matches the search set. For example "%[.-]" matches either a dot or a dash and would be useful for reading Morse code. It would read "-.-."—the Morse code for C. The search set may also contain ranges. A range is a pair of characters separated by a hyphen, so "%[a-z]" matches all lower case characters. You may have several ranges in the set, so "%[a-zA-Z_-ÿ]" will match all letters in the ANSI character set, including European accented characters.

Notice that because the hyphen indicates a range, if you actually want to search for a hyphen, you must place it at the beginning or the end of the search set, like this: "%[0-9-]". This search set matches all the numbers and the hyphen.

If you place a caret ^ before the search set, **scanf** will exclude those characters from the search, so "%[^.,-]" matches all characters until either `'.'`, `','`, or `'-'` is encountered.

# The scanf Assignment Suppression Operator

If you want to scan a field, but not store it, you can use the assignment suppression operator *. The operator appears between the '%' and the field code. The format specifier "%*d" will read in an integer and discard it.

Remember that if you want to discard specific characters, you can just place them in the format string, for example:

```
scanf("%[A-Za-z] , %[A-Za-z]", Buf1, Buf2);
```

will scan two words separated by a comma. There may be optional white space before and after the comma, so the statement will parse text such as "One, Two".

Tip 331 explained how to parse comma separated lists when you are not sure how many fields there are, and what they contain.

# Recovering from scanf Errors

TIP 337

It often happens that the input does not exactly match the **scanf** or **fscanf** format string. When this happens, the function may stop scanning, or it may get out of step and scan fields into the wrong variables. It is important to be able to detect these errors and recover from them.

For most types of input, it is sufficient to recover to the end of the current line. For some types of input, such as program source code, more sophisticated error recovery would be in order, but the **scanf** function is unsuitable for this type of input in any case.

A simple way of checking lines and recovering if necessary is to read a line of input and then to scan it with **sscanf**. The **sscanf** function is similar to **scanf** except that it reads from a string or buffer in memory. All the **scanf** functions (including **scanf** and **fscanf**) return the number of fields that they have successfully parsed and stored. If this value is less than expected, then an error has occurred. Here is a program that reads records from a file, line by line:

```
// open the file
FILE* fIn = fopen("comma.txt", "r");
```

```
// until end of file
while (!feof(fIn)){
  char Buf[80];
  char F1[12];
  float F2,F3,F4,F5,F6,F7;

  // read a line, break if eof
  if (!fgets(Buf, sizeof(Buf), fIn)) break;

  // scan the line and check that 7 fields are read
  if (sscanf(Buf,
      "%[^ ,] , %f , %f , %f , %f , %f , %f ",
      F1, &F2, &F3, &F4, &F5, &F6, &F7) <7)
  {
    printf("Bad record\n");
  }

  // if the record is good process it
  else printf("%s %.2f %.2f %.2f %.2f %.2f %.2f\n",
         F1, F2, F3, F4, F5, F6, F7);
}
fclose(fIn);
```

If the file contains the text:

```
East,563,865.34,973,387.5,34,276
West,389,649,,903,234.67,
North,735,287.03,594,179,745,390.67
South,274,194,1035,638.00,837,87.93
```

the program will output:

```
East 563.00 865.34 973.00 387.50 34.00 276.00
Bad record
North 735.00 287.03 594.00 179.00 745.00 390.67
South 274.00 194.00 1035.00 638.00 837.00 87.93
```

If a file contains bad records, you might not want to use it, but it is still of benefit to the user if you can find all the bad records in one go.

# Avoid Using the scanf Function to Read Directly from The Keyboard

When the standard input stream is the keyboard, you should avoid using **scanf** to read from it directly. If you do, you run the risk of getting stuck inside **scanf** if the user's input is not quite right. In particular, a white space in the format string will absorb any number of carriage returns.

As with files, when reading from the keyboard it is better to get a line with **fgets** or **gets** and then to process the line with the **sscanf** function. Specify **stdin** as the stream argument if you use **fgets**.

# Dynamic Precision with the printf Function

It is possible to have a dynamic field width and precision in the **printf** statement: this is allows you to give the user a means of setting the field width and precision.

To set either the field width or the precision dynamically, use an asterix * in place of a value, and supply the actual value as an argument to the **printf** function:

```
 // imagine user has an option to set these values
int nWidth = 10;
int nPrecision = 2;
float aFloat = 1234.5678;

printf("%s :%*.*f \n", "A float", nWidth, nPrecision, aFloat);
```

This code will produce this output:

```
A float :   1234.57
```

It is important to place the width and precision variables in the correct place in the argument list, just before the value. You may use the * operator for other format codes that use the width and precision

operator—it is not restricted to floats. If you specify a precision for integers, it specifies the minimum field width, and the value will be padded with leading zeros if necessary. If you specify a precision for a string, it specifies the maximum field width, and the string will be truncated if it exceeds this value.

C++ programmers should use the iostream library in preference to **printf**.

## Dynamic Justification with the printf Function

The last tip showed you how to have dynamic field widths and precisions, selectable by the user. You can also make justification within a field dynamic. If the field width is positive, the item is right justified, while if it is negative, the item is left justified. If the field width is zero, the field width is the width of the item. Here is a program that illustrates different justifications:

```
int nWidth = 10;
int nPrecision = 2;
float aFloat = 1234.5678;

enum Justification{LeftJust=-1, NoJust=0, RightJust=1};

printf("%s :%*.*f: \n","A float",
      LeftJust*nWidth, nPrecision, aFloat);
printf("%s :%*.*f: \n","A float",
      NoJust*nWidth, nPrecision, aFloat);
printf("%s :%*.*f: \n","A float",
      RightJust*nWidth, nPrecision, aFloat);
```

This code will produce the output:

```
A float :1234.57   :
A float :1234.57:
A float :   1234.57:
```

This also works with strings and integers, notice that you are not obliged to use a double *.*—a single * operator for the width is legal too and is useful for strings, for example:

```
int nWidth = 10;
char* pText = "Hello";
```

```
enum Justification{LeftJust=-1, NoJust=0, RightJust=1};

printf("%s :%*s: \n","A string",LeftJust*nWidth, pText);
printf("%s :%*s: \n","A string",NoJust*nWidth, pText);
printf("%s :%*s: \n","A string",RightJust*nWidth, pText);
```

This code produces:

```
A string :Hello     :
A string :Hello:
A string :     Hello:
```

## Accessing Variable Argument Lists

C lets you declare a function with a variable number of arguments using the ellipsis "...", for example:

```
int sum(int n, ...); /* return the sum of some numbers */

/* . . . */

printf("The sum is %d\n",sum(34,-56,67,89,23,0));
```

To actually access these arguments, you need to use the **va_start**, **va_arg**, and **va_end** functions in conjunction with a **va_list** type. These functions are macros defined in **stdarg.h**. Here are their prototypes:

```
void va_start(va_list Args);
type va_arg(va_list Args, type);
void va_end(va_list Args);
```

The **va_start** macro function initializes the list, **va_arg** extracts parameters of a given type from the list, and **va_end** cleans up afterwards. Here is an example:

```
/* return the sum of a zero-terminated list of ints */
int sum(int n, ...)
{
  int Result = 0;      /* the sum */
```

```
  int Arg = n;          /* the current value */

  va_list Args;         /* the list of arguments */
  va_start(Args, n);    /* initialize list with first arg */

  while(Arg) {
    Result += Arg;
    /* get next arguments */
    Arg = va_arg(Args, int);
  };

  va_end(Args);         /* clean up afterwards */
  return Result;
}
```

Notice that the first call to **va_arg** returns the first optional argument, not the argument (here **n**) specified in the function declaration. These functions are the ANSI standard, but some UNIX systems use slightly different functions, defined in **varargs.h**.

You might care to examine the **stdarg.h** file for your compiler to see how these macros are implemented. Very often, it will be implemented with **va_list** defined as a **void*** typedef. **va_start** assigns **va_list** the address of the first argument incremented with its size, and **va_arg** dereferences **va_list** and adds the size of the argument type to it. The **va_end** macro usually does nothing.

## How to Pass a Variable Argument List to Another Function

If you have a function with a variable argument list, you may want to pass the arguments on to another function. The obvious way to do this might be simply to call the other function with the required argument:

```
int Sum(int n, ...);

void PrintSum(char* pMess, int n ...)
{
   printf("%s %d", pMess, Sum(n));   /* Wrong! */
}
```

This will work in some implementations, but generally will not. It will not work with DOS compilers. The only portable way of passing argument lists is to declare a function that takes a type **va_list** as an argument and pass that. The called function will use **va_arg** to extract the arguments, and the caller will use **va_start** and **va_end** to set up and clean up the **va_list**. Here are two functions that do just that:

```
/* return sum of list */
int Sum(va_list Args)
{
  int Result = 0;
  int Arg;
  do  {
    /* get an argument */
    Arg = va_arg(Args, int);
    Result += Arg;
  } while(Arg);
  return Result;
}

void PrintSum(char* pMess,...)
{
  /* initialize a va_list */
  va_list Args;
  va_start(Args,pMess);

  /* pass it on to Sum */
  printf("%s %d",pMess,Sum(Args));
}
```

**PrintSum** is called like this:

```
PrintSum("The sum is:",23,56,89,-34,0);
```

# Passing Variable Arguments on to printf

As the previous tip showed, if you want to pass a variable argument list on to another function, you must initialize a **va_list** type and pass that. Functions that take variable argument lists often want to

print or display the arguments, and for that there are special versions of **printf** that accept a **va_list**. Here are the functions:

```
int vprintf(const char* pformat, va_list Args);

int vsprintf(char* pBuffer,
             const char* pformat,
             va_list Args);

int vfprint(FILE* Stream,
            const char* pformat,
            va_list Args);
```

These functions are useful for building extended versions of **printf**, perhaps to display text in color on a workstation screen or on a color printer. Here is a function that displays text at a certain position on a device:

```
void xyprintf(int x, int y, char* pFormat, ...)
{
  /* initialize a va_list */
  va_list Args;
  va_start(Args, pFormat);

  /* somehow move to a position */
  MoveTo(x,y);

  /* pass the arguments on to vprintf */
  vprintf(pFormat, Args);
}
```

This function would be used in a manner similar to **printf**, but with the extra two arguments in front of the format string.

# The C++ iostream Library

# Use iostream in Preference to printf and scanf

Although input and output are not part of either the C or the C++ languages, there are standard function libraries available for C and C++ programmers. C programmers have the stdio library. This library contains a number of general purpose I/O routines, but the central functions for formatted I/O are **printf** for output and **scanf** for input.

The stdio library is available to C++ programmers, but they also have the much more powerful iostream library. Among other things, the streams library lets you define formatted input and output for your own classes. The iostream library may be powerful, but a C programmer, new to C++, may be tempted to carry on using the C stdio library. Surely the standard library, used by C programmers for years, is good enough for applications with relatively simple I/O requirements.

The main problem with the stdio routines is their lack of type checking. It is very easy to make a type error when using these routines. The compiler is completely unable to check the types of the arguments, and a type error will usually result in the program crashing. The problem is especially acute when programming for the PC, because the programmer must also take care to differentiate between near and far pointers when using these routines.

Take a look at these examples and see if you can spot any errors:

```
void func(int& aValue)
{
  int Result = 10;
  char* Msg = "The result is";
  char Buffer[30];
  printf("%s %u", Msg, aValue);
  printf("%s%d", Result);
  scanf("%d %s", Result, Buffer);
}
```

The second **printf** statement is missing a string argument, and the arguments to the **scanf** function should be pointers.

Formatted I/O using the stdio library is extremely difficult to get right. A **printf** or a **scanf** with several arguments may well have two or three errors, which means that you might find an error, rebuild the system, run it and debug it to find out why it crashed, only to find another error in the same statement.

When you use the iostream library, you have all the benefits of type checking. The compiler will convert types for you when possible, or will give you an error message if you make a mistake. If you program in C++, you should use the iostream library now, simply because it is less trouble to use than stdio. Later on, when you have more experience with the iostream library, you will be in a position to take advantage of some of its more powerful features.

## Understanding Streams

TIP 345

The C++ stream is a class for formatting text. In fact, there is a hierarchy of stream classes, so that a programmer can choose a stream suited to the actual I/O device, which may be the computer screen, the keyboard, a file, or perhaps a memory buffer. It is possible for a programmer to extend the hierarchy to do stream I/O with more specialized devices, such as a window in a graphical user interface, but most programmers find that the standard library contains enough facilities for everyday needs.

The stream classes have overloaded the shift operators << and >> to act as streaming operators. When the >> operator operates on a stream it becomes an extraction operator, for extracting values from an input stream. Similarly, the << operator becomes an insertion operator, for inserting values as text in an output stream. Normally, it would be considered bad practice to overload an arithmetic operator for a completely different purpose, but the iostream library can be considered an exception to the rule. The >> and << operators convey the impression of values flowing to and from the stream. The >> and << operators also have a lower precedence than most of the other addressing and arithmetic operators, so there is usually no need to resort to extra pairs of parentheses when streaming values.

It is important to realize that the << and >> operators only act as stream operators when the operand to the left of the operator is a stream. If the left-hand operand is anything else, an integer say, then the << and >> operators still act as shift operators.

The stream classes have overloaded the >> and << operators for all the primitive types, so that for instance, when you stream an integer to an output stream, the stream will convert the integer to a text representation of a decimal integer. Later tips will show you how to stream your own classes as text.

Compare these statements. The first of each pair does I/O using the C library, and the second using the C++ streams. Note that **cout** is the standard output stream.

```
int i = 10;
printf("A quarter of %d is %f\n",i, i/4.0);
cout << "A third of " << i << " is " << i/3.0 << '\n';
```

```
    float f;
    scanf("&d&f", &i, &f);
    cin >> i >> f;
```

Die-hard C programmers will maintain that the C library version is more natural and easier to read, but whatever your views on the matter, you will find that the streams version is easier to maintain, because you do not have to make sure that the format string and the arguments stay in agreement.

## Flush the Output Before Reading Input

A stream output statement such as:

```
cout << "The result is " << Result;
```

does not automatically generate a new line. To force a new line, you may either add a new-line character to the stream:

```
cout << "The result is " << Result << '\n';
```

or you may use the **endl** manipulator. The **endl** manipulator flushes the stream as well as adding a new line.

```
cout << "The result is " << Result << endl;
```

If you are streaming several lines one after the other, there is no need to flush the stream after each line, but if the line is a prompt for some input, you must make sure that it is flushed to the output device or the program will be waiting for input before the user has seen the prompt.

When you want the input to follow the prompt on the same line, use the **flush** manipulator to flush the prompt to the device before reading the input:

```
cout << "Enter a number: " << flush;
int nInput;
cin >> nInput;
```

Note that since there is no automatic new line, you are free to lay out the stream statements as you like, and there is nothing to prevent you from streaming one item in each statement:

```
cout << "The result is ";
cout << Result;
cout << '\n'
```

## Using Stream Manipulators

TIP 347

The last tip introduced the **endl** manipulator, which adds a new line to a stream and flushes the stream. A manipulator is a function that affects, or manipulates, the stream. Most manipulators do not output anything to the stream, but there are exceptions, such as **endl**. Typically, a manipulator sets the stream up for the following item. Here is a list of the most common manipulators:

| | |
|---|---|
| dec | outputs subsequent values in decimal |
| hex | outputs subsequent values in hexadecimal |
| oct | outputs subsequent values in octal |
| endl | outputs a new line and flushes the stream |
| ends | inserts a null byte in a string |
| flush | flushes the stream |
| setfill(int c) | sets the padding character to c |
| setw(int n) | sets the field width of numbers to n |
| setprecision(int n) | sets floating-point precision to n |
| setiosflags(long f) | sets the format flags in f |
| resetiosflags(long f) | clears the format flags in f |

The stream library that comes with different compilers may have a slightly different set of manipulators, but the set shown in the table should be available in every library.

Here is an example of using manipulators to output integers in hexadecimal:

```
int i = 134;
cout << "The value " << i << " in hex is ";
cout << hex << i << dec << endl;
```

producing the output:

```
The value 134 in hex is 86
```

Notice here that after using the **hex** manipulator you should use the **dec** manipulator to restore the default decimal mode. Notice also that you will need to include **iomanip.h** when you use any manipulator that takes an argument, such as **setw(int n)**.

## Setting the Case for Hexadecimal Numbers

You can set the case, upper or lower, for hexadecimal numbers using the **ios::uppercase** flag. In common with the other **ios** flags, once this flag is set, it remains in effect until reset.

```
unsigned i = 0xabcd;
cout << "The value " << i << " in hex is ";
cout << setiosflags(ios::uppercase);
cout << hex << i << dec << endl;
```

This produces the output:

```
The value 43981 in hex is ABCD
```

The **ios::uppercase** flag also affects the *E* character in scientific floating numbers such as 123.45E02, but it does not convert ordinary text to upper case.

TIP 349

## Specifying a Field Width

When you are preparing a report containing sets of numbers, you will usually want to arrange the numbers in columns. This is easy to do with the **setw** manipulator.

By default the output stream will output numbers without any padding at all. If you use the **setw** manipulator, the stream will pad out the next item so that it occupies the number of characters specified in the **setw** manipulator. The **setw** manipulator affects the item immediately following it in the stream, and only that item, so be careful to put the manipulator in the correct position. If you want to output several items with the same padding, you will still need to place a **setw** manipulator before each one. The following code outputs some figures in the form of a table:

```
int i=0;
int Figures [3][4] = {{45, 178, 55, 63},
                      {49, 172, 61, 59},
                      {44, 181, 52, 64}};
```

```
//  Output a heading
cout << setw(15) << "";
cout << setw(10) << "1st Qtr";
cout << setw(10) << "2nd Qtr";
cout << setw(10) << "3rd Qtr";
cout << setw(10) << "4th Qtr";

// output a 1st row
cout << endl << setw(15) << "East" ;
for (i=0; i<4; i++)
  cout << setw(10) << Figures[0][i];

// output 2nd row
cout << endl << setw(15) << "Central" ;
for (i=0; i<4; i++)
  cout << setw(10) << Figures[1][i];

// output 3rd row
cout << endl << setw(15) << "West" ;
for (i=0; i<4; i++)
  cout << setw(10) << Figures[2][i];
cout << endl;
```

This code produces this output:

```
                 1st Qtr   2nd Qtr   3rd Qtr   4th Qtr
           East       45       178        55        63
        Central       49       172        61        59
           West       44       181        52        64
```

## Aligning Left, Right, or Center

TIP 350

When you specify a field width using the **setw** manipulator, the text will be aligned to the right of the field. You can have the text aligned to the left or centered by setting one of the flags defined in the **ios** class.

Once you set an alignment flag, it remains in effect until you either clear it or set a different alignment flag. Here is some code that outputs a table with the names aligned to the left and the figures to the right:

```
cout << setiosflags(ios::left) << setw(15) << "Windleside";
cout << resetiosflags(ios::left) << setw(8) << 174 << endl;

cout << setiosflags(ios::left) << setw(15) << "Morchester";
cout << resetiosflags(ios::left) << setw(8) << 2013 << endl;

cout << setiosflags(ios::left) << setw(15) << "Orbury";
cout << resetiosflags(ios::left) << setw(8) << 10394 << endl;

cout << setiosflags(ios::left) << setw(15) << "Dorstable";
cout << resetiosflags(ios::left) << setw(8) << 63 << endl;
```

Note that the **setiosflags** manipulator sets a flag, and the **resetiosflags** manipulator clears the flag. In this case, clearing the **ios::left** flag resets the default right alignment. The output from this code is:

```
Windleside          174
Morchester         2013
Orbury            10394
Dorstable            63
```

## Showing the Base of Hexadecimal or Octal Numbers

If you set the **ios::showbase** flag using the **setiosflags** manipulator, numbers will be formatted in a form recognizable by a C++ compiler. Hexadecimal numbers will be preceded by "0x" and octal numbers will be preceded by a zero.

For a single isolated hexadecimal or octal number, you might consider adding the "0x" or "0" as text, rather than setting the flag; however, you will find that you will need to use the flag if you also set the field width using the **setw** manipulator, and of course, the flag is more convenient when you need to output several hexadecimal or octal numbers.

```
unsigned i = 0xabcd;
cout << "The value " << i << " in hex is ";
cout << setiosflags(ios::uppercase | ios::showbase);
cout << hex << i << " and in octal is " << oct << i;
cout << dec << endl;
```

This gives the output:

```
The value 43981 in hex is 0XABCD and in octal is 0125715
```

Notice how the hexadecimal prefix 0x is in uppercase when the **ios::uppercase** flag is on. Notice also how the bitwise OR operator | serves to combine multiple flags.

## Making Dot Leaders

TIP 352

When an item is smaller than its field, the empty space is normally filled with a space character, but you can change the padding character to something else, using the **setfill** manipulator. Here is how to output a table with dot leaders:

```
cout << setfill('.');  // set the fill character to a dot
cout << setiosflags(ios::left) << setw(15) << "Windleside";
cout << resetiosflags(ios::left) << setw(8) << 174 << endl;

cout << setiosflags(ios::left) << setw(15) << "Morchester";
cout << resetiosflags(ios::left) << setw(8) << 2013 << endl;

cout << setiosflags(ios::left) << setw(15) << "Orbury";
cout << resetiosflags(ios::left) << setw(8) << 10394 << endl;

cout << setiosflags(ios::left) << setw(15) << "Dorstable";
cout << resetiosflags(ios::left) << setw(8) << 63 << endl;
cout << setfill(' '); // set it back to a space
```

This code produces the output:

```
Windleside..........174
Morchester.........2013
Orbury...........10394
Dorstable...........63
```

## Padding Out Hexadecimal Numbers to Suit the Word Length

Hexadecimal (and octal) numbers usually refer to the contents of items in computer memory or a disk file. Either way, these values are easier to read if they are padded out to the natural word length of the computer. Hexadecimal values would be four digits on a 16-bit machine, and eight digits on a 32-bit machine.

You can format hexadecimal numbers in this way by specifying "0" as the padding character and then setting the field width to 4 or 8. If you also want the "0x" prefix, you should set the **ios::internal** flag. This flag indicates that the fill characters should be inserted after the base indicator, but before the value.

```
cout << setiosflags(ios::uppercase | ios::showbase | ios::internal);
cout << hex << setfill('0');
cout << setw(6) << 0x1a << " " << setw(6) << 0xabc;
cout << dec << setfill(' ') <<endl;
```

This code generates:

```
0X001A 0X0ABC
```

To have the same result but without the "0x" base indicator, leave the **ios::showbase** and the **ios::internal** flags off, and set the field width to 4 (or 8 for 32-bit values).

## Setting the Precision and Format of Floating Point Numbers

You may set the precision and the format of floating point numbers using the **setprecision** manipulator and the **setiosflags** manipulator with the **ios::fixed** and **ios::scientific** flags.

The meaning of the **setprecision** manipulator depends on the flag settings. If either the **fixed** or the **scientific** flag is set, **setprecision** specifies the number of digits after the decimal point. If neither flag

is set, **setprecision** specifies the total number of digits in the floating point value. The following example illustrates different combinations of **setprecision** and the floating point flags.

```
float f1 = 123.4567;
float f2 = 12.3;

cout << setprecision(4);
cout << setw(10) << f1 << setw(10) << f2;
cout << " no flags    - precision 4\n";

cout << setiosflags(ios::fixed) << setprecision(2);
cout << setw(10) << f1 << setw(10) << f2;
cout << " fixed      - precision 2\n";

cout << resetiosflags(ios::fixed);
cout << setiosflags(ios::scientific) << setprecision(2);
cout << setw(10) << f1 << setw(10) << f2;
cout << " scientific - precision 2\n";
```

This code generates:

```
     123.5      12.3 no flags   - precision 4
    123.46     12.30 fixed      - precision 2
 1.23e+002 1.23e+001 scientific - precision 2
```

Notice that when no flags are set, numbers are not padded out with trailing zeros to fit the precision, but when the fixed flag is set, they are. For most conventional uses of floating point numbers, you should set one of the flags and use the **setprecision** manipulator to specify the number of decimal places.

## Using the ios Class Public Member Functions

Rather than using stream manipulators, you can call the stream class public member functions directly. Each stream class has its own public member functions, but since all streams are ultimately derived from the **ios** class, the **ios** public member functions are always available.

While some of the public member functions correspond to manipulators, there are also member functions for which no corresponding manipulators exist. Many of these functions return the current state of the stream's flags or values. The following functions correspond to a manipulator:

| Member function | Manipulator |
|---|---|
| setf | setiosflags |
| unsetf | resetiosflags |
| fill | setfill |
| precision | setprecision |
| width | setw |

Other useful functions include:

| | |
|---|---|
| good | Returns 1 if no error has occurred |
| bad | Returns 1 if an error has occurred |
| eof | Returns 1 if the end of file has been reached |
| fail | Returns 1 if an error has occurred |
| rdstate | Returns the error flags |
| clear | Sets or clears the error flags |
| operator !() | Returns 0 if no error has occurred |

Here is an example of how to use the member functions directly:

```
cout.fill('0');
cout.setf(ios::hex);
cout.width(4);
cout << 0x1a << " ";
cout.width(4);
cout << 0xabc << endl;
if (!cout) { // use ! operator
  cerr << "Error occurred\n";
}
cout.unsetf(ios::hex);
cout.fill(' ');
```

There is no advantage in using **ios** member functions in place of manipulators, but the error detection member functions are important, especially when reading and writing to disk files. The **eof** function will inform a program when it has read to the end of a disk file. Notice here how the ! operator is used to check whether an error has occurred on the stream.

## Writing to a Memory Buffer

TIP 356

You may use the **ostrstream** class to create a stream on a memory buffer. This will have the same effect as using the C I/O library function **sprintf.** You may either provide your own buffer and let the **ostrstream** class write to it until it is full, or you may let the **ostrstream** class create its own internal buffer that you can extract later. The following tip explains how this is done.

Once the stream is open, you can write to it as you would to any other stream. The **ends** manipulator is useful for memory buffer streams: it writes a terminating null byte and flushes the stream. The following example prepares a message in a memory buffer and then displays the buffer using **cout** (so that you can see that something has happened):

```
const int BufSize = 80;
char Buffer[BufSize];

ostrstream Ostr(Buffer, BufSize);
Ostr << "The result is " << 0x555 << ends;
cout << Buffer;
```

## Using ostrstream with an Internal Buffer

The example in the previous tip provided its own buffer to **ostrstream**, but it is usually better to let **ostrstream** allocate the buffer itself internally. If you do that, the **ostrstream** class will expand the size of the buffer when necessary to fit the data that is being streamed to it. With the internal buffer, you do not need to worry unduly about how much text you place in the buffer, and you do not need to allocate a very large buffer "just in case."

To use an internal buffer, simply declare an instance of **ostrstream** without providing an external buffer:

```
ostrstream Ostr;
```

Once the instance is declared, you can stream data to it and the instance will begin allocating memory for the buffer. To access the buffer, use the **ostrstream str** member function that returns the address of the buffer.

When you call **str**, the **ostrstream** instance will lock the buffer and you will not be able to stream any more data to it. The reason for this is that if the **ostrstream** class needs to allocate a larger buffer, it may need to release the old buffer and allocate a larger one elsewhere in memory, and that would invalidate the address returned by **str**.

When you have finished with the buffer returned by **str**, you should unlock it with the **freeze(0)** function. The following example shows how this is done; it streams some data to an instance of **ostrstream**, and then it outputs the contents of the internal buffer:

```
ostrstream Ostr;
Ostr << "The result is " << 0x555 << ends;
cout << Ostr.str();
Ostr.rdbuf()->freeze(0);
```

The **str** function returns a pointer to the internal dynamic array, and also freezes it. The last statement retrieves the stream's internal buffer and unlocks it.

An alternative to unlocking the buffer is to leave it locked and to delete it explicitly with the **delete** operator:

```
ostrstream Ostr;
Ostr << "The result is " << 0x555 << ends;
char* pStr = Ostr.str();
// cannot stream any more data to Ostr
// since the buffer is locked

cout << pStr;
delete [] pStr;
```

The **ostrstream** destructor will not delete the buffer if it is locked.

## Using ostrstream to Write to Graphical User Interfaces

GUIs such as Microsoft Windows, the Macintosh and the UNIX X-Window system do not directly support the **cout** stream. Sometimes there is the possibility to simulate a console window and to use **cout** to write to that, but then the resulting application is no more than a character mode application running in a window.

If you have a proper GUI application, you frequently want to output formatted messages or pieces of text to a part of a window, or to a control or widget within a window. The **ostrstream** class is ideal for this. It lets you format your text in a buffer, and then to use a GUI API function to transfer the contents of the buffer to the window, control, or widget.

## Writing Your Own Manipulator

It is especially easy to write a manipulator that does not take an argument. There is no need to write your own class, or to use any macros. Here is a manipulator that outputs the current date in the form mm/dd/yy.

```
#include <time.h>

ostream& date(ostream& theStream)
{
  char Date[10];
  return theStream << _strdate(Date);
}
```

This manipulator uses the standard C library function **_strdate** to convert the current date into text. This manipulator can be used like this:

```
cout << "Today's date is "<< date << endl;
```

Although it is possible to output a date without using a manipulator, the code is messy because the **_strdate** function requires a temporary buffer. Using a manipulator hides the implementation details.

All manipulators that are used without arguments have the same form of manipulator function. The function takes a reference to the stream as argument and returns this stream after having manipulated it. Notice that the manipulator is not called directly. The stream has overloaded the << operator to accept a manipulator and to call it. The overloaded << operator for **ostream** will look something like this:

```
ostream& ostream::operator << (ostream& (*aManipulator)(ostream&))
{
  // call the manipulator with the stream as argument
  (*aManipulator)(*this);
  return *this;
}
```

This overloaded function states that if the item to the right of the << operator is a function that takes a stream reference argument, then call that function with the current stream as argument. This has the effect of calling the manipulator.

## Writing a Manipulator That Takes an int or long Argument

Manipulators that take an integer argument are almost as easy to write as manipulators without arguments, but you will need to make use of the macros defined in **iomanip.h**. You will recall that you need to include **iomanip.h** if you use any manipulator that takes an argument, even the standard, predefined manipulators. This file contains definitions for **IMANIP** and **OMANIP**, classes used to call manipulators with arguments.

To write a manipulator taking an int or long argument, first write the manipulator in this form:

```
ostream& ManipulatorName(ostream& theStream, int Arg1)
{
  // the code of the manipulator
  return theStream;
}
```

and then write a function in this form:

```
OMANIP (int) ManipulatorName(int Arg1)
{ return OMANIP(int)(ManipulatorName, Arg1);}
```

Here is an example. The manipulator **newlines(int n)** outputs a number of new-line characters.

```
ostream& newlines(ostream& theStream, int n)
{
  while (n-- >0) theStream << '\n';
  return theStream;
}

OMANIP(int) newlines(int n)
{
  return OMANIP (int) (newlines, n);
}
```

and here is an example of some code that uses the manipulator:

```
cout << "First Line" << newlines(3) << "Fourth Line" << endl;
```

## How to Write Manipulators with Non-integer Arguments

When a manipulator has an argument that is neither int nor long, you will need to declare the type using the **IOMANIPdeclare** macro before defining the manipulator itself. Apart from the declaration, the rest of the manipulator implementation is similar to a manipulator that takes an **int** argument.

The following manipulator **time** takes an argument of type **time_t** and streams it out in text format:

```
IOMANIPdeclare(time_t);

ostream& time(ostream& theStream, time_t theTime)
{
  // convert the time to a tm structure
  struct tm* ptm = localtime(&theTime);
  // convert to text
  char * pTime = asctime(ptm);
  pTime[strlen(pTime)]=0;  // remove trailing \n
  return theStream << pTime;
}

OMANIP(time_t) time (time_t theTime)
{
  return OMANIP (time_t) (time, theTime);
}
```

Here is an example of how the **time** manipulator might be used:

```
time_t theTime;
time(&theTime);

cout << "The time is " << time(theTime) << endl;
```

## How to Define a Manipulator with a Complex Type of Argument

The **IOMANIPdeclare** macro expects a type name of one identifier, and will not accept types containing the * operator, or parentheses ( ). To get around this problem, just declare a **typedef** for the complex type and use that. For example, to declare a manipulator that takes a **char*** argument, you will need to write something like this:

```
typedef char* PSTR;

IOMANIPdeclare(PSTR);

ostream& ManipulatorName(ostream& theStream, PSTR Arg1)
{
  // Manipulator code goes here
  return theStream;
}

OMANIP(PSTR) ManipulatorName (PSTR Arg1)
{  return OMANIP (PSTR) (ManipulatorName, Arg1);}
```

## How to Write Manipulators That Take More Than One Argument

It is possible to write manipulators that take two or more arguments when they are used, although in the manipulator function itself you will need to wrap the arguments up into a structure. Here is a manipulator that formats values, placing a dollar sign before them in a field of a certain width. This is awkward to do with the standard **setw** manipulator, since **setw** aligns the dollar sign, but not the value that follows:

```
struct MoneyFieldType{
  int Width;
  double Value;
};
```

```
IOMANIPdeclare(MoneyFieldType);

// The MoneyField manipulator function
ostream& MoneyField(ostream& theStream, MoneyFieldType Arg)
{
  ostrstream Buf;

  // write the dollar sign and the value to a buffer
  // in the form $XXX.XX
  Buf << setiosflags(ios::fixed) << setprecision(2);
  Buf << '$' << Arg.Value << ends;

  // write the buffer to the stream, setting the field
  // width
  theStream << setw(Arg.Width) << Buf.str();

  // unlock the buffer locked by Buf.str()
  Buf.rdbuf()->freeze(0);
  return theStream;
}

OMANIP(MoneyFieldType) MoneyField (int Width, double Value)
{
  MoneyFieldType Arg;
  Arg.Width = Width;
  Arg.Value = Value;
  return OMANIP (MoneyFieldType) (MoneyField, Arg);
}
```

Notice how this manipulator uses a memory stream **Buf** to format the value, and then sends the entire text to the main stream in one go. This allows the **MoneyField** manipulator to use **setw**. Here is an example of how **MoneyField** might be used:

```
cout << setw(20) << "Widgets " << MoneyField(10, 123.95) << endl;
cout << setw(20) << "Knick-Knacks " << MoneyField(10, 49.95) << endl;
cout << setw(20) << "Oojamaflips " << MoneyField(10, 9.95) << endl;
```

and the output:

```
            Widgets     $123.95
       Knick-Knacks      $49.95
        Oojamaflips       $9.95
```

# Overloading The << Operator to Stream a Class

When you write your own class, you can also overload the << for that class, to define how the information in the class instance should be formatted as it is streamed.

When you overload the << operator, you must do so as a global function, not a member function of your class. This is because the operand to the left of the << operator is a stream, rather than an instance of your class. It is usual to declare the operator as a friend function of your class, so that it has the same privileges in accessing your class data as a class member function would have. Here is an example << operator for a complex number class:

```
class Complex {
public:
  Complex(float r=0.0, float i=0.0):r(r),i(i){};
  // other operations
  friend ostream& operator << (ostream& theStream, const Complex& c);

private:
  float r,i;
};

ostream& operator << (ostream& theStream, const Complex& c)
{
  return theStream << '(' << c.r <<',' << c.i << ')';
}
```

This operator formats the two components between parentheses, with a comma between them. A statement such as this:

```
cout << setiosflags(ios::fixed) << setprecision(2);
cout << "Complex value: " << Complex(2.75, -1.5) << endl;
```

would produce this output:

```
Complex value: (2.75,-1.50)
```

Notice that the operator declared the second argument, the class instance, as a **const** reference. If you do not declare the argument constant, you will not be able to stream **const** instances, and if you do

not declare the item as a reference, the compiler will copy it to the << operator function, rather than passing a reference.

## Dealing with Separators While Extracting

The >> operator is overloaded for extracting values from an input stream. The standard >> operator relies on white space separating items. White space means any invisible layout character, usually spaces, tabs, and new lines. Whenever the standard extraction operators find some white space, they stop reading and return the value read. Before reading the next value, they first skip over any white space.

This is fine if the items in the input stream are separated by white space, but frequently they are separated by some other character, and in particular, it is very common to find numbers separated by commas.

A quick way to deal with these separators is to try to read a number, and if the operation fails, to try to read the separator instead. Remember to clear the fail bit using the **clear( )** function before reading the separator. The following code reads some numbers from a stream. The stream could have been **cin** or an input file, but this example uses a memory buffer stream so that you can see what the input stream contains:

```
char* Text = "49, 185, 7 , 1036";
istrstream Source(Text, strlen(Text));
while (!Source.eof()){
  int n ;
  Source >> n;         // try to read a number
  if (!Source){        // if that does not work
    Source.clear();    // clear the error
    char c;
    Source >> c;       // read the separator
    if (c == ',')        // and read the next number
      Source >> n;
  }
  cout << n << endl;
}
```

This code does not insist on the numbers being separated by commas. Numbers may be separated by commas, by white space, or by both. It reads numbers as a human reader might.

Notice that the **eof( )** function works for memory streams as well as file streams.

## Using the seekg and tellg Functions While Parsing

The **seekg** and **tellg** functions respectively set and return the current stream pointer. They work with all streams, not just file streams. This is easy to forget, since the C library contains similar functions, **seek** and **tell**, which only work with files.

The **seekg** and **tellg** functions are useful when parsing an input stream, because if you do not find what you are looking for, you can back up and try something else. This is useful when you overload the >> extraction operator for a class, because you are likely to find some sort of syntax error while extracting the values. If you do, you can back up to where you started and set the fail bit in the stream. Here is an extractor for a complex number class that does this:

```
class Complex {
public:
  Complex(float r=0.0, float i=0.0):r(r),i(i){};
  // other operations
  friend istream& operator >> (istream& theStream, Complex& c);
  friend ostream& operator << (ostream& theStream, const Complex& c);

private:
  float r,i;
};

ostream& operator <<(ostream& theStream, const Complex& c)
{ return theStream << '(' << c.r <<',' << c.i << ')';}

istream& operator >> (istream& theStream, Complex& c)
{
  long BackUp = theStream.tellg();  // save the start position
  char lParen, Comma, rParen;
  float r,i;
  // try to read the complex
  theStream >> lParen >> r >> Comma >> i >> rParen;

  // check that the items read are as expected
```

```
  // the syntax is bad if there is a stream error, or if
  // lParam, Comma or rParen do not contain appropriate items
  if (!theStream || lParen!='(' || Comma != ',' || rParen != ')'){
    // bad syntax !
    theStream.clear();
    theStream.seekg(BackUp);
    theStream.clear(ios::failbit);
  }

  else {  // OK
    c.r = r;
    c.i = i;
  }
  return theStream;
}
```

This function saves the stream position before it tries to parse the complex number. The number is supposed to have the format (**real,imaginary**), but if there is a syntax error, the function restores the stream to where it was and sets the fail bit.

Here is some code that parses a string for numbers that might be either real or complex:

```
char * Text = "(1.25,0.45), 234.23, (2#4), 12.34";
istrstream Source(Text, strlen(Text));
while (!Source.eof()){

  // is it a float?
  float f;
  Source >> f;
  if (!!Source){
    cout << "It is a float : " << f << endl;
    continue;
  }

  // is it a Complex?
  Source.clear();
  Complex aComplex;
  Source >> aComplex;
  if (!!Source){
    cout << "It is a complex : " << aComplex << endl;
    continue;
  }
```

```
    // check for the comma
    Source.clear();
    char c;
    Source >> c;
    if (c == ',') continue;

    // unexpected input
    // recover to next comma
    while (!Source.eof() && c != ',') Source >> c;
    Source.clear();
    cout << "I give up" << endl;
  }
```

This function first looks for a float. If that does not work, it looks for a complex number. If that does not work it checks for a comma and discards it. If that does not work either, it discards input until it finds a comma. Notice the double !! operator: a single ! returns TRUE if there was an error, so a double !! returns TRUE if there was no error. Here is the output from this program:

```
It is a complex : (1.25,0.45)
It is a float : 234.23
I give up
It is a float : 12.34
```

This is a cheap and cheerful way of parsing that is suitable for simple jobs like parsing a command line, but you would not want to write your C++ compiler this way.

Remember that if the input stream is actually a file, **seekg** should not cause a disk seek unless the distance moved is large. Usually **seekg** will just move a pointer within an internal buffer.

## TIP 367 Streaming on Binary Files

Many applications use binary files for storing internal data structures. Often the data in the file is just an image of the C structures used in the application. You can read and write these structures directly, using the **read** and **write** functions with a cast:

```
DataStruct theData;
in.read((char*)&theData, sizeof(theData));
```

This will work, and this is the way that a C programmer would read the structure. Unfortunately, It is all too easy to make a mistake while writing this sort of code, and because there is a cast, the compiler cannot look for type errors. In C++ it is much neater to write an extractor and an inserter to read and write the structure:

```
istream& operator >> (istream& theStream, DataStruct& ds)
{  return theStream.read((char*)&ds, sizeof(ds));}

ostream& operator << (ostream& theStream, DataStruct& ds)
{  return theStream.write((char*)&ds, sizeof(ds));}
```

This is just as tricky as before, but you only need to write them once. Thereafter, when you need to read or write the structure, you just write:

```
DataStruct theData;

// read the structure from a file
in >> theData;

// write the structure to a file
out << theData;
```

There is no need to declare the inserter and the extractor as a friend function, because data in a C structure is always public.

## Streaming Class Instances

TIP 368

You can also stream class instances to and from binary files. This will tend to be more difficult, because C++ classes are likely to be more complex than C structures. There is no special reason why a C structure should not be as complex as a C++ class, it is just that C programmers take care to simplify their structures if they think that they may have to write them to a file. In particular, they would take care to use fixed size character arrays, rather than pointers to dynamic arrays. In C++, simplifying the data in the instance is likely to lead to a more complex class, and so the C++ programmer would prefer to stream the class as it is.

To stream a class, it is usually sufficient to stream the class members one by one. If a member is itself a class, it should have its own extractor and inserter functions. Here is a class that can stream itself to and from a binary file:

```
class Example {
public:
  // constructors
  Example(){a=0;b=0;pString=NULL;}
  Example(int a, int b, char* pArg)
    :a(a),b(b){
      // copy argument into a new buffer
      pString = new char[strlen(pArg+1)];
      strcpy(pString,pArg);
    }

  // copy constructor
  Example(const Example& Right)
    {pString=NULL; *this = Right;}

  // destructor
  ~Example(){delete pString;}

  // assignment operator
  Example& operator =(const Example& Right);

  // streaming operators
  friend istream& operator >>
    (istream& theStream, Example& anExample);
  friend ostream& operator <<
    (ostream& theStream, const Example& anExample);

private:
  int a;
  int b;
  char* pString;
};
```

The **Example** class has three private data items, one of which is a pointer to a buffer. Since there is a pointer, the class has copy constructors and assignment operators to copy the buffer if necessary, and the destructor will delete the contents of the pointer. The class also declares the streaming operators as global friend functions. Here is the definition of the extractor:

```
// extractor
istream& operator >> (istream& theStream, Example& anExample)
{
  delete anExample.pString;  // delete existing string
  // read the integers
```

```
  theStream.read((char*)&anExample.a, sizeof(anExample.a));
  theStream.read((char*)&anExample.b,sizeof(anExample.b));
  int slen;  // read the string length
  theStream.read((char*)&slen,sizeof(slen));
  // create a new string
  anExample.pString = new char[slen];
  // read the data into it.
  theStream.read(anExample.pString,slen);
  return theStream;
}
```

The extractor will read the values from a stream. Before doing so, it must delete the existing buffer, otherwise this buffer will be orphaned. The data has been stored as three integers followed by a string. The third integer gives the length of the string. The extractor allocates a buffer for the string, and reads the string into it.

The inserter is more simple, because it just needs to write the three values and the string to the stream.

```
// inserter
ostream& operator << (ostream& theStream,
                      const Example& anExample)
{
  // write the integers
  theStream.write((char*)&anExample.a,sizeof(anExample.a));
  theStream.write((char*)&anExample.b,sizeof(anExample.b));

  // write the string length
  int slen = strlen(anExample.pString)+1;
  theStream.write((char*)&slen,sizeof(slen));

  // write the string
  theStream.write(anExample.pString,slen);
  return theStream;
}
```

The assignment operator has nothing to do with streaming: it just duplicates the contents of the string buffer.

```
// assignment operator
Example& Example::operator =(const Example& Right)
{
  a = Right.a;
  b = Right.b;;
```

```
    char* pTemp = new char[strlen(Right.pString)+1];
    strcpy(pTemp, Right.pString);
    delete pString;
    pString = pTemp;
    return *this;
}
```

It is possible to stream instances of this class to and from binary files:

```
ofstream out("Test.dat", ios::binary);

// stream out an instance
out << Example(13,99,"Hello");
out.close();
ifstream in("Test.dat", ios::binary);

// stream in an instance
Example anEx;
in >> anEx;
```

Although the principal is the same for all classes, you will need to decide how the class data will be represented in the stream. Do not forget that when you are streaming into a class instance, you may need to delete the contents of pointers.

## TIP 369 Look Out for an Archive Class

Using the iostream library for streaming class instances in binary is cumbersome, especially since you need to use **read** and **write** to stream the primitive types. You cannot use the >> and << operators, because these convert the type into text. In addition, if you overload the << and >> operators to stream a class in binary, you cannot use the operators to stream the same class in formatted text.

To get around these problems, many compilers supply some sort of archive class as part of their library package. An **archive** class is similar to the **ios** class in that both classes can overload the << and >> operators, but the archive class is not derived from the **ios** class. This means that a class can overload the << and >> operators both for streams, in text mode, and for the archive class in binary mode. The archive class also overloads the << and >> operators for all the primitive types in binary mode, so classes do not need to use **read** and **write** to stream their members.

Try to find the archive class in your compiler package. It might not be called an archive class, it could be called "persistent streams" or even "object-oriented database."

## The get Function for Reading to Delimiters

There are two forms of the **get** function. The first form just gets a single character from the input stream:

```
istream& get(char& c);
```

The second form is more interesting:

```
istream& get(char* pBuf, int nBufSize, char Delimiter='\n');
```

This form reads characters from the stream into the buffer until either **nBufSize** characters have been read, or the end of the file has been encountered, or the delimiter has been found. The delimiter itself is not read in. If you do not specify a delimiter, then the function reads up to the next new line.

This function is useful for reading text fields separated by commas or some other punctuation mark.

## Redefining cin and cout

TIP 371

The standard **cin** and **cout** streams are derived from the special stream classes **istream_withassign** and **ostream_withassign**. These streams have the property that they can be redefined to point to other streams or to use other **streambuf** instances. This means that it is possible to redefine **cin** and **cout** to use other streams, and in particular file streams.

To switch the standard streams back to the default device, you create an instance of **filebuf** on one of the standard files **stdout**, **stdin**, or **stderr**, and assign the stream to that.

```
ofstream OutFile("milton.txt");
cout << "Going to switch to a file now" << endl;
```

```
cout = OutFile;   // switch to file

cout << "The savoury pulp they chew, and in the rind" << endl;
cout << "Still as they thirsted scooped the brimming stream" << endl;

 // switch back to stdout
filebuf fb(fileno(stdout));
cout = &fb;
cout << "back again" << endl;
```

This example switches **cout** to a file named **milton.txt** and writes a quotation about stream input from *Paradise Lost.*

# MS-DOS Specifics

# Segmented Architecture

# Understanding the Intel Segmented Architecture

The Intel 80x86 series of processors and the Intel Pentium processor feature a segmented architecture. With this architecture, the processor accesses an address in memory via a segment register and an offset. The offset may also be the contents of a register. The segment register indicates the address of an area in memory, and the processor adds the offset to the address of this area to get the address of a particular item.

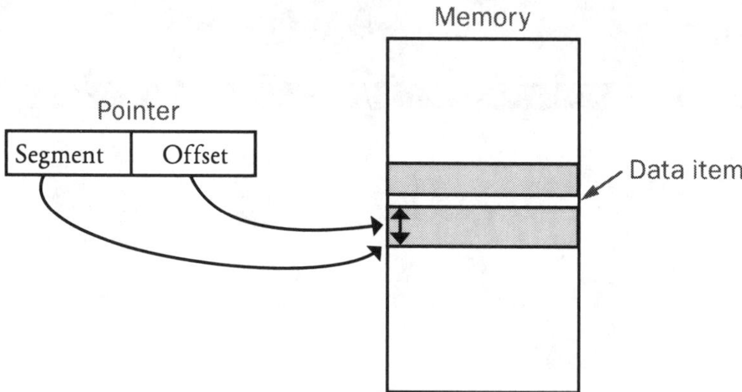


Other processors, such as the Motorola 68000, access the address directly, without going through a segment register. This is the flat address space architecture. The segmented architecture is flexible, because it gives an operating system or compiler designer a choice from a number of schemes for managing memory and processes. It even makes it possible to access memory outside the range of an offset register, so that a 32-bit Intel processor could access memory larger than 4Gb. It is possible to simulate a flat addressing model with a segmented architecture by keeping the segment registers constant and using the offset as a direct memory address.

The Intel processor has four segment registers:

| | |
|---|---|
| CS | For the code segment, containing instructions, including compiled instructions, corresponding to the statements of a C program. |
| DS | For the data segment, containing fixed data and static data in C programs. |

| | |
|---|---|
| SS | For the stack segment, containing the procedure stack and the data heap. Procedure local variables and **malloc** data will be in this segment. |
| ES | For the extra segment, used by certain instructions. |

Notice that this use of the segment registers is not just conventional, it is built into the hardware. Whenever the processor executes a stack instruction, for example, it will automatically use the SS register; and when it executes a jump or a function call instruction, it will automatically use the CS register.

## When to Use a 32-bit Compiler

TIP 373

The Intel processors from the 80386 up (including the 80386SX) are 32-bit processors with 32-bit registers. This means that on these machines a segment can be 4Gb long and an offset can access the entire segment. Because 4Gb is sufficient for most applications these days, it is feasible to use the flat memory model with these processors.

The processors prior to the 80386, including the 8086 and 80286, were 16-bit processors, and a segment on these processors is restricted to 64K. Although small applications and utilities can run in 64K, many applications need more memory, either for code or data. These large applications must be divided into a number of segments, each smaller than 64K, and the compiler must take care of loading the segment register with the address of each segment before accessing any data within that segment.

Unfortunately, since there are still a lot of these 16-bit processors in use, most software has to be designed and compiled to run on them. 16-bit software will still run on 32-bit processors, but will not take advantage of the 4Gb segments available on these processors. Even if you know that your application will only be run on machines with a 32-bit processor, you cannot run a 32-bit application under a 16-bit operating system, such as DOS, without an interface layer, or an extender between the operating system and the application.

If you are writing a large application and you expect your users to have at least a system based on the Intel 80386SX, you should consider using a 32-bit compiler in conjuction with a 32-bit operating system such as OS/2 or Windows NT. Alternatively, you could use a 32-bit compiler in conjunction with a 32-bit extender, such as the Phar-Lap extender or the Win32s extender to the 16-bit versions of Windows. A pure 32-bit application will run faster than an equivalent 16-bit application, primarily because the machine will no longer need to load the segment registers with different values during program execution.

# TIP 374 Choosing a 16-bit Memory Model

Most 16-bit compilers for the Intel architecture offer a choice of memory models for applications of different sizes. The larger the model, the larger the application that will fit into it, but the larger models are less efficient than the smaller models because they cause the compiled code to load the segment registers more frequently.

Here are the most common memory models:

| Model Name | Code Segments | Data Segments |
|---|---|---|
| Tiny | Code and data share same segment | |
| Small | One | One |
| Medium | One segment per module | One |
| Compact | One | One segment per module, but arrays must be smaller than 64K |
| Large | One segment per module | One segment per module, but arrays must be smaller than 64K |
| Huge | One segment per module | One segment per module and no restriction on array size |

If there is only one code or data segment for the application, it is limited to 64K. If the model provides for a data or code segment for each module in the application, then the total for all the modules may exceed 64K. The total amount of code for any one module may not exceed 64K, and for the Compact and Large models, arrays may not be larger than 64K.

The Tiny model allows the linker to generate a .COM file rather than the normal .EXE file, but does not offer any other advantages over the Small model. If possible, use the Small model. Applications with a lot of code but a small amount of static data may need to use the Medium model, while small applications that need a lot of data may need the Compact model. Big applications with a lot of data may need the Large model. If you are in doubt, try the Small model and link the application. If the application is too big, the linker will give you a message saying that either the code or the data segment is too small, and you can try either the Medium or the Compact model.

Notice that all of these models are relevant for 32-bit compilers, but because the Small 32-bit model supports 4Gb of data and code, there is rarely any need for the larger 32-bit memory models, and few compilers support them.

## Use a Macro for the Near, Far, and Huge Address Modifiers

Compilers that support 16-bit memory models also support additional address modifiers that allow you to mix memory models within an application. Unfortunately, the actual names of these modifiers differ between compilers. The modifiers may be **near**, **far**, and **huge**, **_near**, **_far**, and **_huge**, or **__near**, **__far**, and **__huge**. Some compilers accept two or more of these forms.

The ANSI standard for C requires that implementation-specific keywords should begin with an underscore, so the form without an underscore is obsolete, although many compilers still support it.

If you need these modifiers, you should define a macro for them, using upper case, for example:

```
#define NEAR _near
#define FAR _far
#define HUGE _huge
```

There are two advantages to using these macros. First, you can easily change the macros to support a compiler that only supports the old form of the names, without an underscore. Second, and more importantly, you can port the application to a 32-bit environment by redefining these macros to be null strings.

```
#define NEAR
#define FAR
#define HUGE
```

If you are writing applications for the Windows operating system, you will find that these macros are already defined in the WINDOWS.H include file.

## Try Promoting Your Application to a Smaller Model After Optimization

You would normally develop an application with many of the compiler optimization features turned off. If the application is somewhat too large for a particular model, it may fit the model when compiled with optimizations on.

When you are nearly ready to release the application, take a look at its size, and unless the application is obviously far too big, try rebuilding for the smaller model with space optimization on and see if it fits. The linker can produce a map file showing the sizes of the application's segments.

It is important to recompile for the smaller model, because if you recompile for the larger model, the code will be inflated by all the extra segment operations.

## When Using the Medium and Large Models, Declare Local Functions as static Near

In the Medium and Large models there is a code segment for each module in the application, and all functions are far functions by default. Calling a far function is more costly than calling a near function, because the compiler must load the CS segment register with the segment of the function to be called, and reload the old value of the CS segment register when the function returns.

Many modules have a number of local "helper" functions which are only used within that module, and are not intended to be used by other modules. The compiler will use far calls for these functions as well, even though they are always called from within the same segment.

You can optimize calls to these local functions by declaring them as **static** near, for example:

```
#define NEAR _near

/* . . . */

static NEAR void func();
```

Declaring the function as near lets the compiler generate the more efficient near call, which does not reload the CS segment register. You must also declare the function as **static** to be sure that you do not accidently call the function from another module with a different code segment.

Note that it is important to use function prototypes when you do this. If you call the function before declaring it as near, the compiler will still generate a far call to the near function.

## Remain Within a Model by Declaring Certain Items as Far

When an application is just too big for a memory model, because there is either too much code or too much data, rather than moving the whole application up to a larger memory model, you can remain within the smaller model and declare certain items as far.

If there is too much data for the Small or Medium model, you can declare perhaps one or two large arrays as far and place them in a different segment, so that the remaining data fits in the model. Accessing these far arrays will be slower than if they were near, but this is better than making all the data in the application far.

Exactly how you place the data in a separate segment will depend on the compiler. One method that works with most compilers is to place the data in a module that is compiled with the Large or Compact model.

You can also declare a large function as far, but then you need to be careful that the function does not call other functions, or they will need to be declared far as well. You are likely to have more chance of remaining in a model by declaring a large piece of data as far, rather than trying to make the function far.

Remember that if you have pointers to the far data, these pointers will also need to be declared as far, for example:

```
extern FAR char LargeBuf[];


void func()
{
  char FAR* pBuf = LargeBuf;
  /* . . . */
}
```

## Using Huge Pointers

Although **malloc** takes an integer argument, there are ways of creating arrays larger than 64K using a 16-bit compiler. The compiler library may contain a routine, such as **halloc**, for allocating arrays greater than 64K. If you are programming for Windows, you can use the **GlobalAlloc** function to allocate a large buffer.

If you use either a near or a far pointer to such an array, the pointer will wrap around at the 64K boundary and reference the beginning of the array. You cannot set these pointers to reference the data beyond 64K. It is understandable that a near pointer should do this: a near pointer is only 16 bits wide and cannot reference further than 64K from the beginning of the segment; but it may be difficult to understand why a far pointer should do the same. A far pointer is actually two 16-bit values—a segment and an offset. For efficiency, the compiler only does arithmetic on the offset, and so the offset cannot reference further than 64K from the start of the segment.

If you declare the pointer as huge, the compiler will do proper 32-bit arithmetic on both the segment and the offset, and so a huge pointer can reference arrays larger than 64K. You should realize that 32-bit pointer arithmetic with a 16-bit compiler is much slower than 16-bit pointer arithmetic, meaning that you should use huge pointers only when it is really necessary.

If you really need arrays larger than 64K, and many scientific and engineering applications need large amounts of data in memory, you should consider moving to a 32-bit programming environment.

## Moving V-tables to the Code Segment to Stay in the Medium Model

If you have a C++ application and you are running out of space in the data segment, you can consider moving the virtual function tables (v-tables) to the code segment. Many compilers have a compilation switch or option to do this.

If you have many classes with virtual functions, moving the v-tables can free up quite a lot of space in the data segment. The drawback is that the compiler converts the v–tables to 32-bit pointers, so the code segment will expand by about twice as much as the data segment shrinks. Calling the virtual functions will also be fractionally slower when they are moved to the code segment. In spite of this,

moving the v-tables to the code segment is still preferable to moving the complete application to the Large model, and does not require any changes to the source code.

Remember that if you use a class in several modules, the compiler will normally generate a v-table for each module. Some compilers have switches or options to flag v-tables in the object file so that the linker can discard all but one of the duplicate v-tables. This can save a lot of space, but because the object files are no longer standard, you cannot link them using a linker from another company.

## Matching Libraries with the Memory Model

A 16-bit DOS compiler will supply a version of the run-time library for each memory model. A letter within the library name will identify the model. For example, the libraries may be called **CS.LIB**, **CM.LIB**, and **CL.LIB** for the Small, Medium, and Large models.

It is important to link the correct library for the model, so if you have compiled everything using the Medium model, you must link with the medium model library. If you do not, your program will crash. The same rule applies to other libraries, for example, there may be floating point mathematics libraries called **MATHS.LIB**, **MATHM.LIB**, and so on.

If you have a mixed model application, you have to choose one of the libraries and only call it from within the same model. If you have an application that is mostly Large, but which includes a module compiled with the Small model, then functions in that module cannot directly call a library routine, because they would make a near call to a far routine, and would pass near pointers when the library routines expect far pointers.

## Creating a Library That Can Be Linked with Any Model

If you do not wish to create separate libraries for each model, or if you are creating a library to be used in mixed-model applications, you can create a single model library.

In a single model library, you must declare each function to be far, and all pointer arguments and return values must be far. For example:

```
char FAR* FAR TranslateToDanish(const char FAR* pEnglishText);
```

It goes without saying that you must provide a header file with the function prototype. It does not matter very much in which model you build the library itself: you could use the Small model, provided that you maintain far pointers as far. If the function above were built with the Small model, it would have to declare a far pointer if it made a copy of the far argument. The compiler will give an error if you accidentally assign a far pointer to a near pointer.

Although such a library can be linked with applications of any model, there is the small overhead of converting between near and far pointers if the application model is smaller than Large. This technique is used in Microsoft Windows to create Dynamic Link Libraries. Because the library is model independent, a single copy can be linked dynamically with many applications, compiled using different models.

## Linking to Standard Libraries from Mixed Model Applications

Although you cannot directly call a library of one memory model from a module compiled with another memory model, there is a way of calling the standard library functions from a mixed model application.

You need to link with the Large version of the library, and include a copy of the library header file that you have edited to declare functions and pointers as far. This is not so difficult to do. The function definitions in a typical library header file might look like this:

```
/* . . . */
int __cdecl printf(const char *, ...);
int __cdecl putc(int, FILE *);
/* . . . */
```

With your editor, you can change all occurrences of **__cdecl** to a macro, say **LIBFUNC**. Similarly you could change all occurrences of * (except for the * in comments), to **LIBPTR** *. The functions will now look like this:

```
/* . . . */
```

```
int LIBFUNC printf(const char LIBPTR *, ...);
int LIBFUNC putc(int, FILE LIBPTR *);
/* . . . */
```

At the head of the file you can insert something like this:

```
#if defined (MIXEDLIB)
  #define LIBFUNC _far __cdecl
  #define LIBPTR _far
#else
  #define LIBFUNC __cdecl
  #define LIBPTR
#end
```

Now if you compile the application with the **MIXEDLIB** macro defined, all the library functions and pointers will be declared as far, and any module will be able to call them, regardless of the model. If you do not define the **MIXEDLIB** macro, the functions will be called according to the ambient model, and you will have to be sure to link to the correct version of the library.

Some compilers provide header files with this mechanism built in. The macro will probably not be called **MIXEDLIB**, of course, but if you look at the header files for your compiler you will see whether it uses a macro and what the macro name is.

## If You Need to Specify Far Pointers, You Must Do The Same for References

Many compiler manuals do not make this clear, but if you are calling functions across memory models, and the functions have C++ reference arguments, you may need to declare those references as far. If the function has been compiled with the Compact or Large model and is called from a module compiled with the Small or Medium model, you must declare both pointers and references, whether arguments or return values as far, for example:

```
istream FAR & _cdecl operator>> (unsigned long FAR &);
```

You may also declare near references. Near references and pointers are not so common, but can be used for local functions using data from the local data segment in the Large model.

## Group Similar Functions in Segments to Optimize Memory Management

When a large application has been compiled with the Medium or Large model, each module in the application has its own code segment. There are DOS overlay managers that can swap these segments in and out of extended or expanded memory as they are used. The Microsoft Windows system can discard code segments that are not in use if the system needs memory for some other purpose.

These memory management schemes will work better if you can group functions so that a segment contains functions that are likely to be needed at more or less the same time. For example, if you group all the application initialization routines into one segment, the system can discard that segment after the application has been initialized. If, however, you place a screen formatting routine in the same segment as the initialization routines, the system will be obliged to keep the whole segment available whenever the screen is being updated.

Similarly, if you have a collection of general purpose routines, it is worth separating routines that are called rarely and routines that are called frequently into different segments.

# Directory Services

# TIP 386 Displaying the Files in a DOS Directory

The library functions **_dos_findfirst** and **_dos_findnext** will together provide details of files in a directory. Here are the prototypes:

```
unsigned _dos_findfirst(char* pFileSpec, unsigned attribute,
                        struct find_t* pFileInfo);
unsigned _dos_findnext(struct find_t* pFileInfo);
```

The **_dos_findfirst** routine sets up the search and provides details about the first file found. The **_dos_findnext** routine provides details about each successive file. If the routine returns a non-zero value, there are no more files. The **pFileSpec** argument is a file path, which may include a directory specification, and the file name may contain wild card characters. The wild card characters are *and *?*. The *character matches any text, and the *?* character matches any single character. The directory part of the specification may not contain wild characters. Here are some sample specifications:

| | |
|---|---|
| *.* | All files in the current directory |
| C:\MYAPP*.EXE | Executable files in C:\MYAPP |
| SUBDIR*.? | All files in the subdirectory SUBDIR of the correct directory with a one character subscript (such as ABC.5) |

The attribute argument specifies the attribute that the files must have. Check your compiler manual for a list of these, since they may vary between compilers. The attribute for normal files will be something like **_A_NORMAL**. The structure **find_t** is defined in the **DOS.H** file for your compiler. The structure contains the name and size of the file, the time it was last modified, and its attributes.

The functions are not difficult to use, but a common mistake is to forget the case when there are no files that match the specification. The thing to do is to check the code returned by **_dos_findfirst**, and if it is non-zero there are no matching files. If there is at least one file, you can then use a **do** loop to find the others. The **do** loop is not used very often in C programming, but here is one occasion when it is useful:

```
struct find_t theFile;

/* looking for executable files in current dir */

if (_dos_findfirst("*.exe", _A_NORMAL, &theFile))
  printf("No files found\n");
else do {
```

```
    printf("%12s %li\n", theFile.name, theFile.size);
  } while (!_dos_findnext(&theFile));
```

This example will print the name and size of each executable file in the current directory, if there are any.

## Directory Listings with the Date and Time

The previous tip showed how to use the **_dos_findfirst** and **_dos_findnext** library functions to get a list of the files in a directory that match a specification. The **_find_t** structure that these routines use contains the date and time of the last modification packed into two integers, **wr_time** and **wr_date**:

```
struct find_t {
  char reserved[21];
  char attrib;
  unsigned wr_time;
  unsigned wr_date;
  long size;
  char name[13];
};
```

The first five bits of **wr_date** contain the day of the month, the next four bits the month, and the last seven bits the number of years since 1980.

These values are not easy to extract, so one way of alleviating this is to declare a structure using bit fields, and to have a union map this onto the **find_t** structure:

```
struct FileDirStruct {
  char reserved[21];
  char attrib;
  unsigned secs:5; /* in two sec units */
  unsigned mins:6; /* 0-59 */
  unsigned hours:5;/* 0-23*/
  unsigned day:5;   /* 1-31 */
  unsigned month:4;/* 1-12 */
  unsigned year:7; /* since 1980 */
  long size;
  char name[13];
};
```

```
union FileDirInfo {
 struct find_t dos;
 struct FileDirStruct fd;
};
```

The bit fields map onto the **wr_time** and **wr_date** fields in the **find_t** structure. File times on the PC have a resolution of two seconds, so **secs** gives the number of seconds divided by two. The next example uses this structure to print the time and date of the last modification of the executable files in a directory:

```
  static char* Months[13]=
    {"","Jan","Feb","Mar","Apr","May","Jun",
     "Jul","Aug","Sep","Oct","Nov","Dec"};

  FileDirInfo theFile;
  if (_dos_findfirst("*.exe", _A_NORMAL, &theFile.dos))
    printf("No files found\n");
  else do {
    printf("%12s %7li %2d:%02d:%02d %2d-%s-%d\n",
     theFile.fd.name, theFile.fd.size,
     theFile.fd.hours, theFile.fd.mins, theFile.fd.secs*2,
     theFile.fd.day,
     Months[theFile.fd.month],
     theFile.fd.year+80);
  } while (!_dos_findnext(&theFile.dos));
```

Notice how the code uses the **.dos** component to call the library routines and the **.fd** component to print the results.

## Finding Special Files and Subdirectories in a Directory

The **_dos_findfirst** and **_dos_findnext** functions, described in the previous tip, can find files having certain attributes. These attributes are:

| | |
|---|---|
| _A_ARCH | Files which have changed since last backup |
| _A_HIDDEN | Files which do not appear in directory listings |
| _A_RDONLY | Read only files |
| _A_SUBDIR | Subdirectories |

| | |
|---|---|
| _A_SYSTEM | System files |
| _A_VOLID | The volume id in the root directory |

If you specify any of these attributes, the functions will return details of these files as well as normal files. This is fine if you want to see, for example, all normal files, whether read-only or not, but it can be a nuisance when you only want a list of say, subdirectories.

To filter out normal files, compare the **attrib** field in the **find_t** structure with the attribute and reject any files returned by the functions that do not match. For example, if you only want the subdirectories, call **_dos_findfirst** with the **_A_SUBDIR** attribute and discard any files that do not have the **_A_SUBDIR** attribute. For example:

```
FileDirInfo theFile;
/* look for subdirectories and normal files */
if (_dos_findfirst("*.*", _A_SUBDIR, &theFile.dos))
  printf("No directories found\n");
else do {
  /* only consider files with the _A_SUBDIR attribute */
  if (theFile.fd.attrib & _A_SUBDIR)
   printf("%12s\n", theFile.fd.name);
} while (!_dos_findnext(&theFile.dos));
```

This example uses the structures described in the preceding tips. The same applies to other types of files, so if you are interested in hidden read-only files, you could write this:

```
FileDirInfo theFile;
if (_dos_findfirst("*.*", _A_HIDDEN | _A_RDONLY, &theFile.dos))
  printf("No files found\n");
else do {
  if (theFile.fd.attrib & (_A_HIDDEN | _A_RDONLY))
   printf("%12s\n", theFile.fd.name);
} while (!_dos_findnext(&theFile.dos));
```

## Making Sorted Directory Listings

TIP 389

The directory functions described in the previous tips do not sort the files into any order: they just return files as they are found in the file system. If you have sorted the file system with a special utility, or if you have installed some software onto an empty disk, then the files may be sorted alphabetically, but once you start creating and deleting files, they are soon out of order.

If your program is going to present the directory listing to the user, it is obviously useful for the files to be sorted. The **qsort** routine, described in Tip 316, can sort the list in any way you wish: by name, modification time or size, forward or reverse.

The **qsort** routine sorts an array, but the problem is that the program does not know how many files there are until it has scanned the directory. This means that it cannot allocate an array of **find_t** structures. The program could scan the directory once to find out how many files there are and then scan it again when it has allocated the array, but scanning the directory can be slow, particularly on diskettes or CD-ROM drives.

Allocating a large array would be an answer, but the **find_t** structure is 44 bytes long, and the array would consume a lot of memory. An alternative is to allocate a large array of pointers to a **find_t** structure, and to allocate the structure itself when the **_dos_findnext** function returns a file. The **qsort** function can sort arrays of pointers as well as arrays of structures.

An additional point is that the **_dos_findfirst** and the **_dos_findnext** functions must use the same **find_t** structure, if you pass **_dos_findnext** the next item in an array of **find_t** structures it will not work. Instead, use a working **find_t** structure and after calling **_dos_findnext**, copy the working structure into the array.

Here is an example that sorts a directory listing in alphabetical order. It uses the sort function:

```
typedef int(*CompFunc)(const void*, const void*);

int SortDir(const FileDirInfo** A, const FileDirInfo** B)
{
  return strcmp((*A)->fd.name, (*B)->fd.name);
}
```

The function needs a double indirection, because the example uses an array of pointers.

```
const int nDirSize = 1000;  /* size of the array */
 int i;

 /* allocate the array of pointers */
 FileDirInfo** Info =
    (FileDirInfo**)calloc(nDirSize, sizeof(FileDirInfo*));
 if (!Info) /* error! */;
 unsigned nItemsRead = 0;

 /* find first file */
 FileDirInfo theFile;
 if (!_dos_findfirst("*.exe", _A_NORMAL, &theFile.dos))
```

```
do {
   /* copy struct into array
  if ((Info[nItemsRead]  (FileDirInfo*)malloc(sizeof(FileDirInfo))))
     *Info[nItemsRead] = theFile;
  } while (Info[nItemsRead++] &&
    !_dos_findnext(&theFile.dos) &&
    nItemsRead < nDirSize);

/* sort the items */
qsort(Info, nItemsRead, sizeof(FileDirInfo*), (CompFunc)SortDir);

/* display the files and free the memory */
for (i=0; i<nItemsRead; i++){
   printf("%s\n", Info[i]->fd.name);
   free(Info[i]);
}
printf("%i files in all\n", nItemsRead);
free(Info);
```

The main **do** loop reads files, until there is no more memory, or there are no files, or the pointer array is full.

## Remember That the chdir Function Does Not Change the DOS Drive

The **chdir** function will change the current directory on UNIX systems. It will do this on DOS systems too, but DOS also has the concept of a disk drive, A:, B:, C:, and so on. It is very common for a user to have more than one logical disk drive, especially when the PC is connected to a network.

The **chdir** function will change the directory on the specified drive, but it will not change to that drive. To change drives you should use the **_chdrive** function. The argument to **_chdrive** is an integer that specifies the drive. An argument of 1 changes to drive A:, an argument of 2 to drive B: and so on. If you want to change to a certain directory on a certain drive, you must call both routines. Here is a function that calls both and returns –1 if there is an error:

```
int chdrivedir(char* pDirectory)
{
  /* change to directory on the drive */
```

```
   if (chdir(pDirectory)) return -1;

   if (pDirectory[0] && pDirectory[1]==':'){
      char Drive = *pDirectory;
      /* switch to the drive specified */
      return _chdrive(toupper(Drive) -'A'-1);
   }
   return 0;
}
```

This function changes the drive only if the second character of the path is :. Here is an example of a call to **chdrivedir**:

```
/* change to a directory on drive E */
chdrivedir("E:\\CPP\\LIB");
```

Note the double backslashes in the string. A single backslash indicates an escape sequence.

## TIP 391 Searching Environment Path Strings

Among the DOS environment strings, there are some that specify a sequence of directory specifications. Applications may search these directories in order to locate certain files. The **PATH** environment variable that specifies the locations of executable files is the most well-known, but there may be others. Compilers often use a **LIB** or **INCLUDE** variable to locate libraries and header files. Some other applications also use path environment variables to locate data files. The variables are invariably defined in the **AUTOEXEC.BAT** file. For example:

```
PATH e:\viewer;c:\dos;c\utils;c:\windows;c:\windev
Set LIB=e:\c700\lib
Set INCLUDE=e:\c700\include
Set HELPFILES=c:\c700\help\*.hlp
```

There is a library function **_searchenv** that searches these paths for you. You only need to provide the environment variable name and the name of the file you are looking for and the function will search

the directories for it. If the file is present in one of the directories, the function will return its full file specification, including the directory. Here is the prototype for this function:

```
void _searchenv(char* pFileName, char* pVariable, char* pPathSpec);
```

The function will search for the file first in the current directory and then in each directory in turn, as specified in the environment variable, for example:

```
char FileSpec[120];
_searchenv("edit.com","PATH",FileSpec);
```

With the path set as specified above, the function will search for **EDIT.COM** first in the current directory, then in **E:\VIEWER**, and then in **C:\DOS**. If this is the standard DOS directory, the function will find the DOS editor and store **C:\DOS\EDIT.COM** in the buffer.

If the function cannot find the file, it will store a null string (first byte zero) in the buffer.

Remember that even though a user may use an application, the path might not appear in the **PATH** variable. This is especially likely when users have Windows installed, because they may prefer launching an application directly from the Program Manager rather than by entering a DOS command. The Windows Program Manager can store the complete path of an application, and does not need to search the **PATH** variable (although it will do so if it does not find the file in the current directory).

## Remember That Directory Names Can Have a Suffix

A DOS directory name can have a suffix, making it 12 characters long. Of course, many DOS users do not use suffixes for directories, and many do not even know that it is possible; but DOS users who have used other systems, such as UNIX, that allow long file names are quite likely to create directories with long names, for example:

```
C:\SALES\SWITZERL.AND\QUARTER.1ST\JANUARY
```

In this file specification, only **JANUARY** is a file, **SWITZERL.AND** and **QUARTER.1ST** are directories. Bear this in mind when writing code that parses or scans file path specifications. Do not assume that any string containing a dot is a file, and any string not containing a dot is a directory.

## Use 120 Characters for File Specification Buffers

Tip 391 used a buffer when calling a routine **_searchenv** that returned a file specification. For DOS applications, a file path specification can be up to 119 characters long, but there is a zero terminating byte, so the buffer containing the string must be 120 characters long.

As the previous tip showed, a directory name can be 12 characters long. DOS allows up to eight levels of subdirectories, and each subdirectory in the path is separated by a backslash. The name of the file can also be 12 characters long, and the drive specification is three characters long (C:\). The total is 3 + 8*(12 + 1) + 12 = 119.

Of course, it is very rare that a file path specification will be 119 characters long, but it is not unusual for the path to exceed 80 characters. It depends on the user. Some users like shallow directory structures with many names, while others like deeply nested structures.

Many compilers define a macro **MAX_PATH** in **stdlib.h**, but set it to 70 or 80. If you use this macro, change the **stdlib.h** file to define the macro as 120. In fact, it is possible to create directory structures deeper than eight using file utilities, or even the Windows 3.1 File Manager. You are still safe with 120 characters however, simply because file paths longer than that will crash most other applications as well as your own.

## If You Need to Keep File Path Specifications, Use Memory Allocated from the Heap

As the previous tip showed, a file path specification may be up to 119 characters long, so you should use a buffer 120 bytes long to handle it. Even so, path specifications are usually much shorter than this: many users rarely use specifications longer than 20 or 30 characters. If your application stores many file path specifications, it is wasteful to use 120 bytes for each.

The solution is to use a 120 byte buffer to collect or process the file specification, and then to allocate a buffer of the correct length from the heap, and to store the specification there, for example:

```
char* GetEditSpec()
{
  char FileSpec[120];
  char* pEditSpec;
  _searchenv("edit.com","PATH",FileSpec);
  pEditSpec = (char*)malloc(strlen(FileSpec)+1);
  strcpy(pEditSpec, FileSpec);
  return pEditSpec;
}
```

This function retrieves a file specification to a 120 byte buffer, but then uses **malloc** to allocate a buffer of the correct length. (Do not forget to add 1 to the length for the terminating byte.) The memory will be freed when the application terminates, but if the application has no further need of the string before it terminates, it should release the allocated memory with the **free** function.

If you program in C++ and your compiler package includes a **String** class, you can store the file name in an instance of **String** and return that.

# CHAPTER 15

# Debugging

TIP 395

## Examining Unassigned Return Values

It is common in C programming to call a function that returns a value, but not to assign the return value to anything. The program calls the function for its side effects. The following function call, for example, reads a record from a file:

```
fread(RecordBuffer, sizeof(RecordBuffer), 1, DataStream);
```

The **fread** function returns the number of items read. You could say that the program should check that the value returned is 1, or at least **assert** that it is 1, as in:

```
assert(fread(RecordBuffer, sizeof(RecordBuffer),
             1, DataStream) == 1);
```

However, regardless of how disciplined you are, you will find yourself debugging code where the return values are not checked or assigned; and because the program is not working for some reason, you would like to know what these values are.

On most machines function values are returned in certain machine registers: for the Intel series the registers are ax and dx. Functions will return 16-bit values in ax alone, and 32-bit values in the two registers, with the high-order part in dx.

Even if you do not know assembly language, you can look at these registers with your debugger to see the values returned by functions. If the ax register contained 0x000 after calling the **fread** function above, you would know that the function returned zero and did not read anything.

## Examining Complex Function Arguments

If a program calls a function with simple arguments like this:

```
MyFunc(aVariable, 5, pBuffer);
```

you can set a breakpoint on the source line and inspect the contents of the variables before the program calls the function. Often, however, one or more of the arguments are more complex expressions, for example:

```
MyFunc(CurrentValue(), x*y/3, &Buffer[Index]);
```

Sometimes you can try to calculate the result of the argument yourself, but then you may miss a problem. For example, if **x** is 100 and **y** is 600 you might assume that the program is passing the value 20000 to the function, whereas in reality the expression **x*y** overflows and the result is a negative number.

If the function you are calling is your own, you can compile it with the debugging option and step into it to see the actual values of the arguments, but this is more difficult when the function is a library function and the symbolic debugging information is not available.

The simplest way to see the value of the arguments is to view the source in assembler mode when you reach the breakpoint. The compiler will calculate the value of each argument in the ax register and then execute a **PUSH ax** instruction to copy the value to the function stack. If you examine ax just before this push, you will see the value of the argument.

The compiler evaluates the arguments of C functions from right to left, so it will first push the value of the last argument. If the function is a class member function, the compiler will push an extra argument after the others. This extra argument is the address of the class instance.

Long values and far pointers will be calculated in ax and dx. The dx register will contain the high-order part of the value, or the pointer segment and the compiler will first push dx and then ax. The compiler will evaluate floating point values on the floating point stack. It cannot push the floating point value directly, so it generates something like the following assembler instructions:

```
; evaluate floating argument
sub sp,OFFSET 8    ; allocate space on stack
mov bx,sp
fstp               QWORD PTR ss:[bx] ; copy float to space allocated
```

If there are mixed simple and complex arguments, the compiler will push the value of the simple arguments directly, without first evaluating them in ax.

## Use the Debugger to Test Individual Routines

If you are writing an application that will be released to other users, you will want it to be reliable, and one way of making a product more reliable is to test each component as well as the complete product. The classic way of testing a function is to write a test bed that calls the function with different arguments and checks that the result is correct. The advantages of a test bed are that it generates documentary evidence of testing, and that it can be re-run if ever the function needs a modification. A test-bed will probably be mandatory for military and aerospace applications.

For commercial applications the advantages of a test-bed are often outweighed by the time and cost of preparing it. In these situations, however, you would still like to test the functions, and the easiest way is to step through the function once or twice with the debugger, even though it appears to be working correctly. By stepping through and watching the values of the local variables, you can see whether the function is working as expected or whether it is working by chance. Look at the following function:

```
int aFunc(int arg1, int arg2 )
{
  BOOL bArgsValid;

  /* . . . */

  if (bArgsValid){
    int nResult;

    /* . . . */

    return nResult;
  }
  return ERR_VAL;
}
```

This function does not initialize **bArgsValid** before testing it, however, the function will usually work because the arbitrary contents of **bArgsValid** will usually be non-zero, and because the arguments always happen to be valid. One day, the function will fail because the uninitialized **bArgsValid** variable will contain zero. If you step through this function with the debugger, you will see immediately that **bArgsValid** contains an arbitrary value instead of the expected value of 1.

If the function appears correct when you step through it with normal arguments, you can set a breakpoint on the first statement and change the arguments to the maximum allowed by the application, then see if it still works. You can also set the arguments to invalid values to check that the function detects them correctly.

## Arguments to Windows Functions Are Pushed Left to Right

When you are debugging Windows applications, remember that Windows 3.1 functions are declared as **PASCAL** in the **windows.h** header file. The functions are not written in PASCAL, but they use the PASCAL calling convention, in which arguments are passed left to right and the called function has

the responsibility of removing the arguments from the stack. In a normal C program, the code calling the function removes the arguments from the stack.

Removing arguments from the stack is only one instruction. The code only needs to reset the stack pointer back to the position just before the space where the arguments are stored. Even so, the designers of Windows reasoned that it was better to have this instruction just once in the called function rather than wherever a Windows function was called. Windows NT abandons the PASCAL convention and uses normal C function calls. These days many applications call Windows functions through a class library of some other layer and the benefits of using the PASCAL convention are not as great as they were.

## Develop Your Application Under a Protected Operating System Where Possible

If you run an application under a protected operating system such as Windows 3.1 or OS/2 (Windows 3.0 in real mode was not protected), the operating system will stop the application immediately if it tries to access memory that it has not allocated. If the application is running under a debugger, the debugger will catch the exception and show you the line or instruction that caused it.

This is an invaluable debugging aid, since it catches problems where they are caused, rather than letting the application continue with invalid data or a corrupt execution space until it fails some time later. In C and C++ programs, these protection violations are usually the result of dereferencing an invalid or uninitialized pointer. With the debugger, you can look at the source line that caused the exception and see which pointer was being dereferenced. These problems are usually easy to fix.

Remember that Windows and OS/2 do not protect applications running in a DOS window. The system will allocate the DOS window some real mode memory which it can read, write, access, or corrupt as much as it wants.

## Develop Under Windows Without Learning Windows Programming

The last tip showed how protected mode operating systems such as Windows help with debugging by detecting bugs when they occur.

While it will be worthwhile learning Windows programming if you are writing applications with a user interface or a graphic output, many applications have neither. You might want to write scientific filters that read a data file, process the data, and write it to another file. You might be writing mathematical functions for other users, or you may be learning or experimenting with C or C++.

In any of these cases, you can use a special Windows library that many compiler vendors supply. The Borland system is called EasyWin, and the Microsoft Visual C++ system is called QuickWin. With these libraries, you write your application as a standard C or C++ program, with a **main** function. You then compile and link the application with a special switch. The Microsoft switch is **/Mq**, and the Borland switch is **–W**. The linker will then add a library that displays a simple window and calls the program's **main** function. The program can use **stdin**, **stdout**, and **stderr**, or **cin**, **cout**, and **cerr** to read and write to this window.

The application can use most of the standard library routines, with the exception of some system functions that are not compatible with Windows. All the examples in this book will run under either EasyWin or QuickWin.

When your program or function is fully developed and tested, you can recompile it as a DOS program or library and release it to the users.

## TIP 401 Interrupting a Windows Program

Another good reason for running your application under Windows is that you can interrupt it and call the debugger using the CTRL-ALT-SYSRQ key. You will need at least an Intel 80386 processor to do this, and you may need to install a driver, delivered with the compiler or debugger.

To interrupt the application, run the debugger on the application and get it going. When you press CTRL-ALT-SYSRQ, the debugger will stop the application and show you exactly where it was stopped. This trick is invaluable for debugging programs that have got caught in a loop, or when you have forgotten to set a breakpoint in the correct place before starting the application.

When the debugger has caught control, you can examine the application and set breakpoints as usual, and then let the application continue.

# Do Not Single Step Through System Code After an Interrupt

When you interrupt an application with the CTRL-ALT-SYSRQ key, you might interrupt it while it is calling a system routine. The debugger will display the assembler instructions that the routine is executing, and you will not be able to examine the program stack.

If you are in a system routine, you should not try to single step back to your application, because doing so is likely to cause a complete system crash. If you think you know where the application might be looping, you should set a breakpoint in the loop and let the application run to it. If you have just modified the application, for example, it is likely that the application is looping in the vicinity of the modification.

If you have no idea at all where the application might be looping, you can risk crashing the system and try single stepping anyway. It is possible that the application has not stopped in a system routine, but in a library function, and you may be able to step back into a recognizable part of your application. You should be prepared for a system crash even so, and be sure that you have no other Windows applications open with unsaved data. In particular, make sure that you have saved all the modified files in your program editor.

# Finding the Calling Point When an Exception Occurs in a Library Routine

When you are running under a protected operating system such as Windows, if a program crashes in a library routine with an exception, the debugger will stop and show the assembler instructions of the library routine. Usually, the error is caused by your own program passing invalid arguments to the library routine, so you would like to see the C code that called the routine, and the values of the arguments.

Most debuggers have a facility to display the function call stack in symbolic form, and allow you to go to the source of any function call on the stack. Unfortunately, when the debugger halts in a library

routine it is often unable to display the function call stack. Library routines are often written in assembler and do not need to obey standard C conventions for register and stack usage, so the debugger loses its way in the data on the stack.

When this happens, try moving the instruction pointer past the code that causes the error and then single step a number of times. Use the "jump over" step instead of the "jump into" step. If you do this you will often find that the function returns back into the C code, and you can then see what caused the error.

To move the instruction pointer, just put the new value in the ip register. Look at the instructions displayed and choose the address of an instruction after the break.

## What Happens if You Delete an Instance Twice

A frequent C++ programming error is to delete a pointer when it has already been freed elsewhere. As Tip 150 points out, you can usually avoid this problem by setting the pointer to null after deleting its contents. Deleting a null pointer is legal, and has no effect.

When the program tries to delete the pointer a second time, there will usually not be a protection fault. The **new** routine will usually claim large blocks of memory from the operating system and then return a pointer to some data within this block whenever the application needs a small block of memory. When the large block is exhausted, **new** will claim another block from the system, and when **delete** has freed all the small allocations within the block, it will return the block to the operating system.

In general then, the invalid pointer will point to a valid block of memory, but memory which is marked as free, or which **new** has reallocated to satisfy a request from elsewhere in the program. When the **delete** routine tries to walk through the heap, it will either get stuck in a loop or it will display an error message saying that the heap is corrupt. If the program loops, and you are running the debugger on a Intel 80386 machine or better, you can interrupt it.

If the debugger stack displays a destructor or a **delete** statement when you interrupt the program, then it is almost certain that this instance has already been deleted elsewhere.

# Do Not Shoot the Compiler Writer

TIP 405

If you find an obscure problem in your program that you just cannot solve, it is very easy to convince yourself that your compiler has a bug. Compiler bugs are not unknown of course, but they are not very common, especially when the compiler is distributed widely. The problem is much more likely to lie in your program or in your understanding of the C/C++ language.

Many of the "compiler bugs" reported to compiler technical service groups turn out to be programming misconceptions on the part of the submitter. Very often, the submitter has written one of the ten bugs outlined in the first chapter of this book.

If you have an insoluble problem, try showing the code to a colleague. Very often, the problem will be obvious to someone else. If you do not have a suitably knowledgeable colleague, try submitting your problem to a public forum, such as those on CompuServe or the Internet. If you submit code to a public forum, you should reduce the problem to around a dozen lines of code, stripping out all unnecessary detail. There is every likelihood that someone will look at your example and spot the problem.

# Index



*All references are to tip numbers.*

## B



## C

## D

## G



## H



## I



***All references are to tip numbers.***

## J



## K



## L



## M

## N



## O



## P

## Q



## R



## S

## T



## U



## V